STICKS
AND STONES

STICKS AND STONES

and

Other

Student

Essays

TENTH EDITION

EDITED BY

RISE B. AXELROD
UNIVERSITY OF CALIFORNIA,
RIVERSIDE

CHARLES R. COOPER
UNIVERSITY OF CALIFORNIA,
SAN DIEGO

bedford/st.martin's
Macmillan Learning

Boston | New York

For Bedford/St. Martin's

Vice President, Editorial, Macmillan Learning Humanities: Edwin Hill
Executive Program Director for English: Leasa Burton
Senior Program Manager: Laura Arcari
Marketing Manager: Vivian Garcia
Director of Content Development: Jane Knetzger
Executive Development Editor: Jane Carter
Advanced Development Editor: Sherry Mooney
Editorial Assistant: William Hwang
Senior Content Project Manager: Peter Jacoby
Senior Workflow Project Supervisor: Susan Wein
Production Supervisor: Lawrence Guerra
Senior Media Project Manager: Allison Hart
Assistant Media Editor: Daniel Johnson
Editorial Services: Lumina Datamatics, Inc.
Composition: Lumina Datamatics, Inc.
Text Permissions Manager: Kalina Ingham
Photo Permissions Editor: Angela Boehler
Director of Design, Content Management: Diana Blume
Cover Design: William Boardman
Printing and Binding: LSC Communications

Manufactured in the United States of América.

1 2 3 4 5 6   23 22 21 20 19 18

For information, write: Bedford/St. Martin's, 75 Arlington Street, Boston, MA 02116   (617-399-4000)

ISBN 978-1-319-21848-5

Preface for Instructors

Sticks and Stones and Other Student Essays is a reader designed to accompany *The St. Martin's Guide to Writing*. Now in its tenth edition, *Sticks and Stones* continues the tradition of its predecessors: to celebrate student writing.

Enduring features of *Sticks and Stones* include the following:

- *Forty student essays* written in each of the *Guide's* ten genres, from "Literacy Narratives" to "Analyzing Stories."

- *Chapter introductions* that motivate students to want to write in each genre. In each chapter introduction, we aim to increase students' interest and investment by explaining in simple terms the distinctive features and purpose of each genre, how the genre relates to and builds on the others, and what students will gain academically and personally by working in it.

- *A list of the basic features in each genre* that helps students spot the conventions writers employ to achieve specific rhetorical goals.

- *Headnotes for each essay* that invite students to become attentive readers of each genre. Headnotes help students approach the essays as models for their own writing by spotlighting how the writers' essays were effective and inviting further reflection on the genre and their own writing.

- *Two final sections, "A Note on the Copyediting" and "Sample Copyediting,"* that explain the role of editing in published writing and let students see the editing process in black and white.

- *An essay submission form* designed to encourage students to submit their own essays. As an instructor, you should feel free to provide extra encouragement to a student who writes an outstanding essay.

Few students have ever thought their assigned essays could be published for a national audience to read. You might work with a student on further revision and assist with filling out the submission form.

New to the Tenth Edition

Important new features enhance this edition:

- **New student essays.** Joining the most popular essays from the ninth edition, seven new essays offer students helpful and reliable examples of effective writing. These essays focus on topics that are sure to excite students' curiosity, such as animal rights, super-volcanoes, and online piracy.

- **A new chapter on literacy narratives** offers two fantastic models of this key writing genre, along with a Peer Review Guide to provide a useful framework for student analysis.

Suggestions for Using *Sticks and Stones*

Sticks and Stones is an ancillary that can be used alongside *The St. Martin's Guide to Writing.* You could have students read a chapter in *Sticks and Stones,* select a favorite essay, and analyze how it exemplifies the genre as outlined in the relevant *Guide* chapter's Basic Features section. Because the essays in every chapter of *Sticks and Stones* vary so much in subject and approach, you and your students could explore essays that model the many different ways writers organize ideas, structure sentences, use vocabulary and tone, address an audience, and center themselves in a genre.

You might want to walk students through a few paragraphs of the copyedited essay at the end of the book. The editing displaces, replaces, adds, and subtracts in order to focus and speed the reading and make the relationships among ideas clearer. Students could learn from speculating about reasons for some of the edits, not all of which are immediately obvious or intuitive (as you will readily recognize).

To inspire thoughtful revision and editing, you could have your students submit essays that were based on assignments in the

Guide—or even inspired by essays in *Sticks and Stones* itself—to be considered for publication in the campus newspaper or the next editions of the *Guide* and *Sticks and Stones*. You will find a submission form at the end of this book.

These suggestions address but a few of the numerous possible uses of *Sticks and Stones*. We would be delighted to learn how you use this book, as well as what you would like to see in the next edition. Please feel free to send comments and suggestions to us by visiting **macmillanhighered.com/contactus**.

ACKNOWLEDGMENTS

We are grateful to many people who made this edition of *Sticks and Stones* a reality. Most of all, we would like to thank the hundreds of students who have conceived, drafted, written, revised, and polished the essays we have received over the years. Although we cannot include every essay submitted to us, we have read each one with interest and care.

We also thank the instructors who encouraged their students to submit their work for this collection or who submitted their students' work themselves. *Sticks and Stones* would not exist without the generous efforts of these instructors.

Many thanks go to the instructors whose students' work is published in this edition: Sandra Baringer, University of California, Riverside; Sebastian Beauclair, Grand Rapids Community College; Dave Beglin, University of California, Riverside; Kristin Brunnemer, Pierce College; Wallace Cleaves, University of California, Riverside; Sean Connelly, Chaffey College; Rob d'Annibale, University of California, Riverside; Kerry Dickenson, Texas Woman's University; Michelle Dowd, Chaffey College; Cheri Edwards, Texas Woman's University; Shelley Garcia, University of California, Riverside; Sean Henry, Mt. San Jacinto College; Lesa Hildebrand, Triton College; Chandra Howard, University of California, Riverside; Karen Maple, Murray State College; Eva Mutschler, Oakland Community College, Orchard Ridge; Gray Scott, Texas Woman's University; Megan Stein, University of California, Riverside; Shannon Tarango, University of California, Riverside; Hannah Tenpas, University of California, Riverside; Ruthe Thompson, Southwest Minnesota State University; and Janice Zerfas, Lake Michigan College.

We would also like to extend our sincere appreciation to Ruthe Thompson, Elizabeth Rankin, Paul Sladky, and Lawrence Barkley, whose fine work on previous editions of this book set the standard for everything that followed.

Rise B. Axelrod
Charles R. Cooper

To the Student

The essays in *Sticks and Stones* weren't selected based on subject matter (though many diverse and fascinating topics are covered), nor because they were flawlessly written, but rather because each of these essays offers you a great example of organized, carefully researched, and diligently edited student writing. These essays were written by students just like you in writing classes just like yours across the country. If you think that you're not like the students whose essays appear in this book, that you could never write this well—let alone get your work published—take heart! The truth is, the essays in this book didn't always look like they do now. They began as just a few sentences: notes taken from a research source, an idea written on the back of an old receipt, a tentative paragraph in a first draft.

And as you may have found with your own writing, even when the essays began to take shape, it was a rough shape. Some essays shifted from one rough shape to the next for a long time. But the writers persisted. They tested the advice of their peers and instructors. They gathered more material to support their arguments, whether that meant interrogating their memories, returning to a profile place, consulting more books and electronic databases, or watching a film a second time. They pushed themselves to think of new ways to say what they wanted to say. And they took the time to edit and revise and rewrite so that their arguments would be clear and persuasive to their intended audiences.

There's no question that writing something good enough for publication is hard work. But there's also no question that doing so is possible for every student reading this book. As you read through these essays, the Peer Review Guides that follow each chapter introduction will help you spot some of the techniques each student used to craft his or her essay.

Here's an easy way for you to increase your chances of getting published: As you write, ask yourself, What can I do to help the readers of *Sticks and Stones*—other students like me—understand what I am trying to say in this essay? A metamorphosis will begin. You will no longer think of yourself as someone who is merely completing an assignment for your writing class; you will begin to think of yourself as a writer in conversation with your readers.

You will notice that the writers whose work is collected here are determined to seize their readers and provoke a response. The tone of their writing is not "Hey, would you mind reading my work?" nor is it that of a class assignment written for an audience of one—the instructor. Instead, these essays clearly belong to writers who have something to say, who are writing for an audience they know exists beyond themselves and those grading their work.

What are you passionate about? What are you curious about? We can't wait to hear what *you* have to say.

Contents

Literacy Narratives 1

In an academic context, literacy has traditionally been measured by one's ability to read and write. In today's ever-evolving world of language, media, and genre, however, literacy is more widely understood as the ways we make and derive meaning through the application of a multitude of skills, not just reading and writing.

Literacy narratives span a variety of formats and approaches, built on the common strategies of naming, detailing, and comparing. The goal of composing a literacy narrative is to help authors navigate their personal experiences in ways that extend meaning to readers. Authors who use the strategies of naming, detailing, and comparing to reflect on past experiences have the opportunity to teach readers what they learned about their own acquisition of a new skill.

As you read the literacy narratives presented in this chapter, consider the common emphasis on learning. Although each author was working toward a different goal, the underlying sequence of observing and mimicking successful models helped them practice more confidently and increase their literacy. Authors reflect on their personal experiences to teach readers that attempting an unpracticed task (like coaching or speaking a foreign language) may seem intimidating at first but can be overcome with careful observation and practice. As you read, try to pinpoint the strategies of naming, detailing, and comparing, and ask yourself how these strategies strengthen authors' descriptions of characters, places, and their relationships to them.

Use the guidelines in the Critical Reading Guide that follows to practice peer review using the essays in this chapter.

A CRITICAL READING GUIDE

A WELL-TOLD STORY

How effectively does the writer tell the story?

Summarize: Highlight the initial conflict or problem that sets off the action.

Praise: Cite a passage where the storytelling is especially effective—for example, a place where the story seems to flow smoothly and maintain the reader's interest.

Critique: Tell the writer where the storytelling could be improved—for example, where the story lacks tension or conflict, or the chronology is confusing.

VIVID DESCRIPTION OF PEOPLE AND PLACES

Do the descriptions help you imagine what happened?

Summarize: Choose a passage, and analyze how and how well it describes a significant person or place.

Praise: Identify a description that is particularly vivid—for example, a graphic sensory description or an apt comparison that makes a person or place come alive.

Critique: Tell the writer where the description could be improved—for example, where objects are not described with enough specific detail (colors, sounds, smells, textures) or where the description is sparse. Note any words or phrases that undermine the dominant impression.

AUTOBIOGRAPHICAL SIGNIFICANCE

Is it clear why the event was important to the author's literacy development or practices?

Summarize: Briefly describe what you think the author learned (or failed to learn) about how to communicate, and tell the writer why you think the event was significant.

Praise: Give an example where the significance of the literacy event comes across effectively—for example, where remembered feelings are expressed poignantly, where the present perspective seems insightful, or where the description creates a dominant impression that clarifies the event's significance.

Critique: Tell the writer where the significance could be strengthened — for example, if the conflict is too easily resolved, if a moral seems tacked on at the end, or if more interesting meanings could be drawn out of the experience.

Lost in Translation

Jonathan Escobar

University of California, Riverside
Riverside, California

Many of the most vivid descriptions seem to come from negative events, as with Jonathan Escobar's recalling of the bullying he experienced as a child in El Salvador. Escobar carefully combines key background information about his family with important details about the emotional impact of the changes he was experiencing. It is in recounting the bullying he experienced in his new school, however, where his descriptions truly come alive. Notice how Escobar uses sensory details such as sounds and shapes alongside figurative language to fully paint the picture of his first few months in his new school.

Children are mean. While growing up I faced a number of bullies who joked about everything about me: my height, my weight, and my accent to mention just a few. However, it is my very first bullies whom I shall never forget. 1

At the age of ten, my world was turned upside down. My grandfather, just about the best paternal figure I could ever have, was abruptly deported. Having lived with him basically since birth, it was decided that my family would move to the impoverished country of El Salvador in order to stay together. As a kid, I never truly understood what was going on around me or how to feel about this complicated situation. All I knew was that I missed the man who had filled the role of my dad, and I needed him so that I could feel at peace again. And thus my journey began. 2

It wasn't until my first day of school that I truly realized the challenge waiting for me. Salvador Martinez Figueroa, named after some relevant historical figure, was a small but cozy cluster of buildings that would become both a battleground and a haven for me. I arrived my first day of fifth grade and noticed two things: first, that 3

4

I was an outsider already, and second, that I didn't even know how to present myself to my classmates. My Spanish didn't really pass the usual "Hello, my name is . . ." I tried to contain them, but soon my face was flooded by tears. I felt lost in a crowd of unknown faces, unable to yell for help. Three hours I cried that day, and looking back, I believe my sobs stemmed from my inability to communicate as much as from my yearning to return to how things were before.

A large clattering began in the classroom, and I felt even worse 4 upon realizing I couldn't distinguish half of what was being said. It merely sounded like the buzzing of a hive. Maria, a beautiful and kindhearted girl in my class, approached me and asked, "Are you okay? Why are you crying?" To this day, I still ask myself why I responded as I did. I looked at her harshly and answered, with what little knowledge of the language I had, "What you care?" And so she, who would eventually become my savior and first friend in a time when I desperately needed help, turned around and left me to wallow in my despair.

A boy then came to my desk. He was short and dark skinned, 5 but his face resembled that of a lion ready to pounce. When I finally presented myself to the class, he took every opportunity to mock me and point out my mistakes. You might say one bully isn't a big deal, but the problem was that most of the class rallied behind him. Thus began a time of teasing and mocking, and I could do nothing but sit back and listen.

I still recall the different nicknames they had for me, such as my 6 favorite, "Hippopota-piggy." An overweight ten-year-old who could barely say "shut up" without sounding foolish . . . I guess it became easy for my classmates to find new ways to frustrate me. I tried to fight back, however, tried to learn new words daily so that I could respond. I never felt prouder than when I was finally able to confront my tormentors. One day as I innocently arrived to school, I could see the thoughtful looks on the faces of the children as they pondered which new insult they could throw at me. But something different happened that cloudy but warm day — a preemptive strike. I still don't know how I did it, but I was able to warn them, without a single error: "Not one word, or there will be problems." It goes without saying that I was anything but menacing. Nonetheless, the accuracy with which I was able to express myself left my peers bewildered; they could not believe that I had finally been able to defend myself without sounding like a cheap online translator. I had at last done it, and they respected me for it. Where I started off saying "Quiet be you," I learned to say "Stop bothering me if you have nothing better to do." The pressure to defend myself fueled my passion for learning.

Being able to reply "Doo-doo head" or "Dumb Kid" to my then enthusiastic bully instructors was enthralling, but the best moment of my development belongs to another event. That humid, beautifully sunny day will forever play in my mind. I walked up to my angelic Maria and said, "I'm fine. Please tell me how you are." Seemingly insignificant, this moment marked my literary accomplishment but, more importantly, a new chapter in my life. 7

Looking back on this experience today, I realize how my inability to communicate led me to drive people away and made me a target. I'm friends with most of my childhood bullies now, and to some extent I'm thankful to them for giving me a reason to push myself to learn to master the Spanish language in order to actually thrive in the new environment, which I would grow to call home. 8

The Game
Gabriel Zamora
University of California, Riverside
Riverside, California

Gabriel Zamora begins by creating the scene—evoking the smell of freshly cut grass and the sound of shouting—before locating the reader within it. This vivid description sets the backdrop for the literacy narrative to follow, one in which Zamora explores his development not just as a learner but as a teacher. It is clear that the early failure he describes was a key element in his growth as a baseball coach and, as is often the case with literacy narratives, as a person. Pay attention to the way that Zamora weaves in memories of his early baseball practices and his love of the sport. Early in the piece, these memories make a sharp contrast to the experiences of his young team. Later in the piece, they become the pivotal element that unites Zamora with his students.

Early on a Sunday morning, the sounds of kids shouting and baseballs being crushed filled the air. I smiled as I stepped onto the freshly cut grass; the ballfield was a familiar and comforting place to me. I had played on this field hundreds of times. However, as I walked between the foul lines, I knew this time would be different. This would be my first time on this field not as a player but as a coach. 1

I felt nervous yet excited to teach others within my community how to play the game I loved. As a player with fourteen years of experience, I thought, How hard could it be? To my dismay, I would find that coaching is just as hard as hitting a curveball. 2

The players trickled onto the field, and I watched their expressions as they prepared for practice. I could see a hopeful and excited look in their eyes. Once they had all arrived, I invited them onto the field to play catch. They swarmed out of the dugout as if it had caught fire. A beautiful symphony of baseballs thudding against 3 gloves filled the ballfield. This symphony, however, would be frequently interrupted by the rattling of a chain-link fence. This sound would occur when a ball targeted for a player's glove would miss its mark and soar over the player's head, crashing against the fence behind him. This sound, though annoying, was to be expected from a group of seven-year-old ballplayers. I attempted to explain to them how to properly throw a baseball and what their mechanics should look like. After I explained, I gauged the team to see if they understood. I found that half the team was snickering as they played with each other's hats. The other half seemed to be mesmerized by the infield dirt, drawing shapes and smiley faces with their cleats. Growing a bit impatient, I suggested we move on to base running.

The kids ran to home plate, and I got them into a single-file 4 line. I explained to them that they were to run across all four bases. Jonah, one of the most popular kids on the team, volunteered to go first. I pointed out that he should touch the corner of each bag as he rounded them. A slight grin emerged on his face as he nodded.

"Go!" I exclaimed. 5

He took off. 6

A cloud of dust kicked up behind him as he flew down the base- 7 path. A feeling of joy filled me as he hit the corner of the bag, just as I had instructed. This feeling suddenly disappeared as Jonah, with a grin on his face, completely skipped second and ran straight to third. The other kids laughed in approval. My face turned red with embarrassment and anger as the kids continued to not take my practice seriously. Jonah knew that second base was to be touched after first base, but he skipped it anyway. I was disappointed not only in Jonah but also in my own performance as a coach. I decided it was time to act.

"That's it!" I yelled, angry and fed up. 8

I ordered the entire team to run to the outfield fence and back as 9 punishment. As they ran, I thought about how I would scold them upon their return.

As all the players returned to the infield, however, I found myself 10 once more studying their expressions. Sweat glistened across their brows as they tried to catch their breath.

I was just about to speak when Dillon, one of the more timid 11 kids on the team, said, "This isn't very fun, Coach Gabe."

My heart ached as I thought about what he had just said, and I 12 could feel all their eyes on me. I found myself not able to speak as I noticed that their once excited expressions had disappeared. I could only ponder what he had said to me. I thought to myself, Baseball is supposed to be fun. Why don't they love this game as much as I do? That is when I realized my mistake. Baseball is just a game, so why not teach it that way?

"Who wants to play a game?" I asked. 13

"Me!" they shouted in unison. I split them into two teams and 14 introduced them to a game called Pickle. This game involved proper base running and catch. I promised the winning team Big League Chew, the chewing gum of choice among most ballplayers. The game was full of laughs, shouts, and competitiveness. I was impressed as I saw them execute several perfect throws and run as fast as they could. An alarm on my watch signaled to me that our scheduled practice time was over.

"Time to pack up," I stated. 15

Jonah raised his hand and asked, "Coach, can we please stay and 16 practice a little bit longer?" A smile grew on my face as I nodded. The kids cheered.

I often look back to this day, when I learned to effectively com- 17 municate with these kids. It reminds me that everyone has a different perspective. Everyone looks at life through a different lens. Everyone has different paradigms. Perhaps, most importantly, everyone deserves to be understood.

2 Remembering an Event

Narratives like the ones you'll find in this chapter are some of the most common essays we read. They connect us to other people and teach us about ourselves. In fact, your sense of who you are—your personal identity—depends on narratives: the stories told and retold in your family and among your longtime friends, the stories you tell and retell yourself in moments of reflection. These stories may calm and center you, or they may alarm and agitate you, but together they define who you are and provide the foundation for your future.

Listening to gossip, watching a movie, or reading a short story can be enjoyable. But to be on the shaping end of a story—to tell or write a story about your own life—is even more rewarding. Telling about an event might allow you to discover its particular significance in your life. For example, by writing about her first construction job, Julia Barojas discovered new respect for her hardworking brother. Or it might help you see more clearly how a past event made you feel: Stephanie Legge's story about a tragic car accident can be seen as a case study in how to describe a vivid event and its impact on our emotions.

Essays that relate a remembered event take on a variety of topics but always include several basic features. Most important, a remembered-event essay is well told, features vivid descriptions of people and places, and holds autobiographical significance for the writer. To tell a story is to re-form an event in your mind and examine it from your current perspective—through the greater knowledge you have gained from more education and a larger life experience. As you write and revise your remembered-event essay, take advantage of this perspective: Take time to see your story anew, to read each draft as if you didn't already know its details. That way you can look for con-tradictions and inconsistencies in your thinking, and examine and

10

reconsider any rapid conclusions you may have initially drawn about the experience. Sharing drafts with classmates and your instructor will give you even more perspective on the event and your response to it, and will refine and deepen your insight into the event's meaning.

Whatever you do, as you cull your memory for details of a remembered event, keep an open mind. Reseeing events can lead to self-judgment and judgment of others: "I wish I had done this" or "If only she hadn't said that!" But these seemingly useless reflections can be important, allowing you to notice unresolved tensions below the surface of your memory and teaching you to reserve judgment as you struggle to understand the event.

Although language is slippery and imperfect, writing about your past is a powerful tool, allowing you to revisit remembered events, bring together your scattered thinking about them, and achieve significant insights. Your revised essay will document this voyage toward understanding.

Use the guidelines in the Peer Review Guide that follows to practice peer review using the essays in this chapter.

A PEER REVIEW GUIDE

A WELL-TOLD STORY

How effectively does the writer tell the story?

Summarize: Circle or highlight the inciting incident and the climax of the story.

Praise: Cite a passage where the storytelling is especially effective — for example, a place where the story seems to flow smoothly and maintain the reader's interest, or where the narrative action is compelling or exciting.

Critique: Tell the writer where the storytelling could be improved — for example, where the suspense slackens, the story lacks tension or conflict, or the chronology is confusing.

VIVID DESCRIPTION OF PEOPLE AND PLACES

Do the descriptions help you imagine what happened?

Summarize: Choose a passage or description, and analyze how and how well it uses the describing strategies of naming, detailing, and comparing.

Praise: Identify a description that is particularly vivid—for example, a graphic sensory description or an apt comparison that makes a person or place come alive.

Critique: Tell where the description could be improved—for example, where objects in the scene are not named or described with enough specific detail (colors, sounds, smells, textures) or where the description is sparse. Note any description that contradicts the dominant impression; it may suggest how the significance can be made more complex and interesting.

AUTOBIOGRAPHICAL SIGNIFICANCE

Is it clear why the event was important to the author?

Summarize: Briefly describe the story's dominant impression, and tell the writer why you think the event was significant.

Praise: Give an example where the significance comes across effectively—for example, where feelings are expressed poignantly, where the present perspective seems insightful, or where the description creates a strong dominant impression that clarifies the significance.

Critique: Tell the writer where the significance could be strengthened—for example, if the conflict is too easily resolved, if a moral seems tacked on at the end, or if more interesting meanings could be drawn out of the experience.

Sticks and Stones

Nicole Ball

Niagara University
Niagara, New York

Nicole Ball tells a remembered moment from her childhood that many may relate to. The title alludes to a familiar childhood saying: "Sticks and stones may break my bones, but words will never hurt me." Ball's purpose, however, appears to be much deeper than a tale of classic schoolyard bullying. Her essay confronts the power of words to hurt, as well as the failure of words in response. The narrator's attempts to ignore the bully's harsh taunts are futile, school authorities refuse to help, and parental words of advice prove useless. As you read, notice how Ball offers small details to suggest familial solidarity. She denies her readers a happy ending, but in so doing she paints a memorably realistic coming-of-age story.

James Nichols was short and scrawny, the smallest kid in the entire eighth-grade class. But he had a foul mouth and a belligerent attitude to make up for it. And he was a bully. 1

James sat in the front seat of the school bus, relegated there by the bus driver after some infraction or other. The driver, a balding, heavyset man who paid little or no attention to the charges he shuttled back and forth, rarely spoke and, except for that act of discipline, seemed disinclined to do anything else. The punishment, however, didn't seem to faze James; in fact, he reveled in it. Sitting in the front put him at the head of all the action and surrounded him with easy victims: those too timid or meek to trespass into the "tough" zone at the back of the bus. 2

I was a year older than James and, though not very tall myself, was at least a foot taller than he was. But by my last year in junior high school, I had a terrible complexion, a mouthful of braces, and a crippling shyness. I sat in the second seat on the school bus, only because I couldn't get any closer to the front. 3

13

My brother, Greg, who was a year younger, generally sat with   4
me because while he was a bit shorter, and much more confident,
he had no more desire to mix with the cigarette-toting crowd in the
back of the bus than I did. And although we didn't always get along
well at home, we both felt that it was nice to have someone to sit
with on the bus, even if we didn't talk much.

In our junior high, as in all junior highs, skill at socializing out-   5
ranked skill in classes. And since Greg and I were both social out-
casts, we endured our share of teasing and taunts. But James Nichols
set out to top them all.

At first, of course, his words were easy to ignore, mostly because   6
they were nothing new. But as his taunts grew louder and nastier, he
developed the habit of kneeling on his seat and leaning over the back
to shout his unrelenting epithets down upon us. The kids in the back
of the bus relished every moment of our humiliation, often cheering
him on. James puffed up with pride over his cruelty. The bus driver
never said a word, though he could not have helped but hear the
barrage of insults. Inside, I seethed.

"Ignore him," my parents insisted. "He'll eventually stop when   7
he realizes that you're not going to react." Their words were well
meant but didn't help. The taunts continued and even intensified
when we got to school. Upon arrival, the buses lined up in front of
the school building, waiting until exactly 8:10 to release their passen-
gers. Those long moments sitting in the parking lot, staring at the
red plastic seat in front of me, praying for the bell to ring so I could
escape James, were pure torture.

Each morning, Greg and I would flee from the bus. "I can't take   8
this much more," I would rage under my breath. Oh how I longed
to tear James to pieces. And although I knew I would never physically attack James, I felt better imagining myself doing so. Greg,
though, would never respond to my frustrated exclamations, which
only added to my wrath. After all, didn't he hate James too? But
more often than not, I was just too furious to care what Greg might
have been thinking.

The showdown, I suppose, was inevitable.   9

One morning as we sat in the school parking lot, James took   10
his taunting too far. I don't remember what he said, but I remember what he did. He pulled a long, slender, wooden drumstick from
his pocket. He started to tap Greg on the top of the head, each hit
emphasizing every syllable of his hateful words. My brother stared

straight ahead. James laughed. The kids in the back of the bus laughed. The bus driver ignored everything.

My anger boiled over. "Don't you touch him!" I shrieked, strik- 11 ing out and knocking the drumstick from James's hand. At that moment, I didn't care that my parents had advised us to ignore James. I didn't care that everyone turned to gape at me. I didn't care that even the bus driver glanced up from his stony reverie. I only wanted James to leave my brother alone. As the stick clattered to the floor, audible in the sudden silence, I bit my lip, uncertain of what I had done and afraid of what might result.

My mistake, of course, was thinking my screams would end the 12 taunts. The crowd at the back of the bus waited to see James's reaction. With his authority threatened, James turned on me like a viper. "Shut up, bitch!" he hissed. Coming from a home where "shut up" was considered strong language, James's swear word seemed the worst of all evils.

My eyes wide, I shuddered but didn't respond. Words were 13 words, and if I had done nothing else, at least I had caused the bully to revert to words instead of actions. I turned my face to the window, determined to ignore his insults for the few remaining minutes before school. But a movement from Greg caught my eye, and I looked back.

In one swift movement, Greg reached into the front seat, 14 grabbed James by the coat, yanked him out into the aisle, pulled him down, and delivered two quick, fierce jabs to James's face. Then he released him without a word and settled back into his seat. James, for once in his life, was speechless. His cheek flaming red from where the blows had struck, he stared at my brother without moving until the bus driver clicked open the doors a moment later, indicating we could go into school.

My parents heard about the incident, of course, and called the 15 assistant principal about the entire matter. When the vice principal questioned my brother, Greg's explanation was simple: "He called Nicole a swear word, and no one calls my sister that." Greg had never said anything more touching.

I have heard it said that violence never solves anything, and it 16 didn't. The bus driver was advised to keep an eye on James, but no admonition would have spurred the driver to interfere in anything. The teasing went on, cruel as ever, until James threatened to slit our throats with a knife he swore he had hidden in his locker at school.

After that, even though a locker search turned up nothing, my parents drove us to school every morning, and my mother talked to us about what to do if James ever pulled a knife on us at school.

But for me, an imagined weapon paled when compared with the vivid memory of the complete silence on the bus, the blazing red mark on James's face, the calm little smile that tugged at the edges of my brother's mouth, and the click of the bus doors as they opened to free us.

17

In a Ditch

Stephanie Legge

University of California, Riverside
Riverside, California

In this essay, Stephanie Legge relates a moment that holds particular significance in her life: the freedom of obtaining a new driver's license soon followed by a terrifying car crash. Legge engages
readers by using dialogue throughout, allowing them to feel as
though the event is happening at this very moment. Note the way
she begins her story with a measured pace and then slowly builds
urgency. Was she successful in creating suspense? You might not
have a near-death experience to write about, but Legge's essay can
still teach you a lot about how to use vivid descriptions and drama-
tization to enhance a remembered event.

"You're going to get us lost again," Nathan muttered from the pas-   1
senger seat. "I told you we should have waited for Dad."

"Shut up!" I growled back. "It was your fault we got lost last   2
time anyway!"

"Yeah, sure, Stephanie," said Nathan. "You're the one driving.   3
Can't you even figure out where you're going?" He leaned forward
so he could peer through the window at the houses flowing by.
"Where are we?"

The truth was I had no idea. We (or rather I) must have turned   4
too early from the main street into a different neighborhood. We
had been driving for an hour on our way to our dad's friend Marty's
house, where Marty was holding a barbecue, and along the way, we
had lost sight of our father on his motorcycle between the mass of
cars moving steadily along the freeway. I trusted my instincts to find
the way to our destination, but it seems my instincts were slightly
askew. My brother's head and mine turned left and right as we
scanned our surroundings for any familiar sign. I didn't tell Nathan,

but a nervousness was creeping its way through my stomach; I'd had my license for only two weeks, and if I made a mistake while looking for the right path out of that neighborhood, I'd be in trouble with the DMV for driving my younger brother before I was eighteen. That nervousness on top of being lost was beginning to show as I gripped the steering wheel harder.

"There!" I pointed through the windshield. "Jurupa Road! We   5
can follow that to Van Buren and just follow it to Marty's house."
The nervousness drained out of me like cool water. I turned to
Nathan with a cocky smile. "See? I can find my way around."

"Yeah, right!" said Nathan, picking the calluses off his fingers.   6
"After following every road in Riverside, you'll eventually find your
way to the right place."

"One slight detour and you think I can't find my way any-   7
where!" I sighed. I scrubbed a fingerprint off my dashboard with my
sleeve; I hated it when my car got dirty. "Anyways, at least we know
where we are. Daddy's probably already at Marty's house by now. I'll
tell him it was your fault."

"My fault!" Nathan slapped his hands down onto his thighs and   8
glared at me. "My fault! Who's driving here? You can't even find
your way to a place we've seen Dad drive us to a hundred times and
you think I should be the one watching where you're going?"

"Why not?" I replied, looking over my left shoulder to change   9
lanes. "You obviously seem to know a lot more than I do about
everything. Maybe if you'd been paying attention more, we'd be
there by now."

"Maybe if you weren't such a loser, we wouldn't get lost so   10
mu—Steph!"

I didn't have time to look at Nathan. I didn't even have time to   11
complete my lane change. I snapped my head to the front and saw a
flash of white in front of me so close—too close. A white truck was
slamming its brakes, and I was still driving at sixty miles per hour. We
were flying right at it. Nathan braced himself in his seat, and I frantically swung to the left knowing it was useless; I waited for the crash
to sound. Yet amazingly enough, I missed the truck by centimeters
and felt a rush of relief so great it made my body prickly with goose
bumps.

Then the screeching started. Not from me or Nathan but from   12
beneath us. The world started rotating and suddenly we were sliding sideways at the same frightening speed. Trees flashed by so

fast it was sickening. I raced the steering wheel the other way and then we were facing the opposite direction, watching a rock wall become a blur. Left and right—left and right—fishtailing round and round—Nathan next to me shrieking, "Steph! Steph!"—things were bouncing around inside the car and hitting us painfully—now we were spinning uncontrollably and everything became obscured in one big twirl of color—BAM—CRUNCH.

The radio was still playing and the engine was still running, but after the screech of the tires and the pounding of whatever damage was being done, it seemed utterly silent. I was frozen in my seat, not entirely sure of what I was seeing; the sky was blue through the windshield, partially blocked by the twisted branches of a thrashed tree that was on its side. My car had spun around to face the opposite direction we had been traveling in so that I could see the path of the ditch my car was in winding away into the distance, and I could see the white truck parked on the side of the road. After picking up the mangled table that had fallen out of the back of his truck, the driver climbed back in and started down the road toward us. He slowed as he came close, and I looked back at him, not sure of what to do or even of what had really happened. He looked at me curiously, then without another glance, picked up speed and drove away. 13

Nathan and I were alone. My father had no idea where we were, and we had no way of reaching him. Suddenly, the weight of the situation fell on me like a sack of bricks, and I felt the sickness of grief well up in my throat. Nathan was the first to react. He pushed at the door but found it wouldn't open. I didn't watch him as he climbed over the seat and got out through the back, but I saw his face clearly as he went around to the front and looked at my car with wide eyes and a dropped jaw. 14

"Oh my God, Steph," he whispered. I knew then I couldn't look at my car. 15

"Nathan," I gasped. "Oh my God . . ." I stared ahead and, feeling the engine start to shudder, a flicker of panic jump-started my heart. "Nathan, I've got to move my car!" 16

We were stranded with no communication, no help, so moving my car seemed like the logical thing to do. I clumsily put my hands on the steering wheel and revved up the motor, but beneath me I could hear the wheels spinning in place. The engine shuddered so violently that in another spurt of panic, I imagined the car catching fire. I let off the accelerator, shut off the engine, and the silence 17 set in so dramatically it was frightening. Images flashed before me again of sliding down the road, and the white truck driving away, and the blue sky with the broken tree. It was so hard to believe that we weren't still driving to Marty's house for a fun day at the pool. It felt so much like a dream.

After a few minutes of sitting there frozen in my seat, I heard the clapping of someone hurrying toward us. A man and a woman appeared from behind the tree, and their faces were filled with fear. 18

"Are you okay?" stammered the woman. "We saw everything from the street!" 19

I found it hard to speak and could only stare. 20

"We're okay," said Nathan. "Someone stopped ahead of us, and we barely missed him." He paced back and forth in front of my car, surveying every inch of damage. At that same moment, someone called to us. 21

"Hey! Are you guys all right?" A man was stepping from a white convertible. "It looks like you need some help." 22

I could hear the man talking to the couple and my brother, but I wasn't quite sure what they were saying. Then the man approached me in my car. He was fairly young, with black hair and eyes hidden behind a pair of shades. "Do you have a cell phone?" 23

"No," I croaked. 24

"Have the police come by yet?" 25

"No," I answered and swallowed hard. It was becoming easier to talk. "We need to find my dad." 26

"Here," said the man, and he handed me a black cell phone. "Call who you need to call so they know what's happened." 27

I didn't know Marty's phone number and I knew no one would be at my house, so I called my friend Jim who'd helped me get my car a year before. When I heard his voice on the other end, I could feel mine grow hoarse. 28

"Hi. Jim?" I murmured. 29

"Yello there, Stephanie!" Jim chuckled. He was eighty-two years old and always cheerful. "What's goin' on?" 30

"Jim . . . I'm, um, in a ditch on the side of the road," I replied, glancing again at the mutilated tree. 31

"You're what?" 32

At that moment, a shiny black-and-white police car pulled up. The officer, a tall man, stepped out and walked over to us as if this were a normal part of his day. The man in shades spoke to him first. 33

I was grateful for this because I wanted to let my friend know where I was.

"Jim, I'm in the center divider on Van Buren, just past Jurupa Road. Can you find us?" I said hurriedly. 34

"Well, sure I can find ya, but—are you okay?" he replied with a note of worry in his voice. 35

"We're fine," I said. "We're just really shook up." 36

I could see Nathan talking to the policeman, and the policeman was expressionless. Then with a sickening jolt, I remembered I was in more trouble than I had anticipated; I had been driving Nathan and that was illegal since I wasn't eighteen yet. I made sure Jim knew exactly where we were and after I handed the cell phone back to the man in shades, the policeman marched through the debris from the tree and stood at the open car door to peer inside at me. 37

"Hello," he said calmly, as if I were parked outside a grocery store. "Everyone okay here? No one hurt?" 38

"No, nobody's hurt," I said. I found it hard to look into his eyes and instead stared at my shoes. 39

"Well, I need you and your younger brother to stay inside the vehicle so we can stop the traffic and get you out of here," said the police officer, "and I'm going to need your license and registration." Nathan was already climbing into the backseat as I rummaged through my purse and handed the policeman my license, then I realized as I opened my glove compartment that I had taken my registration out of my car when I signed up for insurance. It was unhelpfully at home. 40

Well, everything else that day had been going horribly. One more screwup wouldn't be too inconvenient. I told the policeman I didn't have the registration, and the look he gave me was enough to make the lump in my throat even sorer. He marked something on his clipboard and then asked me for a detailed account of the accident. 41

Ten minutes later, the man in the sunglasses had left and Jim had pulled up alongside us over the ditch. He greeted us with the sentence that we would hear a thousand times that day. "Thank goodness you aren't hurt!" he said as he shuffled over to us. He waited with us for twenty minutes until the tow truck chugged its way up the street. Finally, I was forced to leave my car and look at the scene from the outside. I could hardly keep my emotions under control. 42

The passenger's side looked like a piece of crumpled paper. All along the door and the fender, the impact of the tree had caused the 43 whole side to dent inward. Three tires were flat, and the wheel that had hit the curb was bent the wrong way. Even the side of the car that hadn't hit the tree was dented in places; the hood was bent and the headlight hung miserably from its socket by a wire. The tree was in the street, cut clean off at the roots. A track of winding skid marks led to the wreck. To top it off, everything was covered in a thick layer of dirt.

I watched as the truck driver hitched up my car and dragged it   44
up onto the bed. I couldn't believe how wrong everything had gone. Jim and Nathan stood next to me, talking about how fortunate we had been, but I couldn't see any of it. Sure, nobody had been hurt, but I had broken the law, been unable to present registration, and been left at the scene when the white truck had left us there. Also, my insurance rates were going to rise, and worst of all, my car was most likely totaled. The best thing I had been looking forward to for two years was dashed in a matter of seconds; I wouldn't be able to drive again for a very long time.

We prepared to move out, taking the crumpled car with us, and   45
I told the driver that I wanted the car to be taken to my house. He dumped the car on my driveway as pitifully as it had been dragged up, and finally we knew we had to find our dad. Jim offered us a ride to Marty's house, and along the way, I couldn't imagine how I would ever be able to tell my dad what had happened. We parked in front of Marty's house and noticed that Dad's motorcycle was missing.

"He must be looking for us," said Nathan as he climbed out of   46
Jim's car.

"Now listen," said Jim. "Make sure Marty's there and see if he   47
knows where yer dad is. If he's not there, yer welcome to stay at my house 'til someone shows up, 'kay?"

"Thanks a bunch, Jim," I said and followed Nathan up the steps   48
to the front door. As expected, the living room was empty except for the movies, chips, and sodas still stacked up for the party that had never started because the company had never shown up. We walked to Marty's room, where he was sleeping lightly. He woke when he heard Nathan say his name and blinked in surprise.

"Your dad's looking for you," he said, chastising. Nathan and I   49
looked at each other. I didn't feel right telling Marty the story before telling Dad.

"When did he leave?" I asked instead.   50

"He called from his house about ten minutes ago, and he's   51
on his way back here," said Marty. He sat up and rubbed his eyes.

"He's been looking all over Riverside and San Bernardino for you. Where've you been?"

I knew then I couldn't keep it from him before Dad got back. 52 "Marty . . . we crashed."

He froze. I could see he hadn't been expecting that kind of 53 explanation. Marty put his hands down and raised his eyebrows. "Really?" I nodded, and he chuckled with a sad note. "Your dad's going to be really upset. How'd you crash?"

I gave Marty a brief description of the crash, but I wanted my 54 dad to know the whole story first. When I had finished, I heard the deep rumble of a motorcycle approach. Nathan looked up at me with a look of anticipation. We knew it had to be Dad.

My brother and I left the room at the same time and headed to 55 the front door almost dreamlike. How was I going to start? Would he be angry? What would he say when he found out what had really happened? Nathan stopped in the doorway as I walked ahead of him onto the porch. I didn't want to have to confront him alone, but then everything had been my fault. I could hear the thud of boots and my dad rounded the corner, and we froze, staring. There was silence deeper than when all the thrashing had stopped at the accident. Then my dad removed his sunglasses and looked at me with an expression I had never seen him give me. It was unreadable.

"I saw the car," he said. 56

The lump in my throat rose again. Not having to tell him the 57 reason for us being gone was worse than having to. My dad moved toward me quickly and I shrank, not knowing what he would do. Then his arms fell around me and he hugged me so tightly it shocked me. I could feel him shaking all over, and I realized I was shaking too. For the first time since the crash, tears poured down my cheeks, and I buried my face into my dad's shoulder. Everyone kept saying we were lucky not to have been hurt, but I didn't believe how fortunate we were until my dad proved the gravity to us. Nothing else had mattered until that point, when all emotions were let loose.

We later learned that the steering mechanisms had broken when 58 the car hit the curb at sixty miles per hour. It would be three months and a thousand dollars later before I could drive it again. Our insurance placed me at fault for "driving down a highway, losing control of the vehicle, and hitting a tree." Visiting the site again, we learned how vital the tree had actually been in the accident; at that speed, had the tree not been there, the car would have flipped over and rolled onto the railroad tracks. Far from being an object of destruction, the tree had ironically brought relief. I drive by that scene often, observing how the skid marks flow left and right, swirl, then end at a blank spot between the line of trees.

Today, the car remains dirty and dented, and the door can only be closed if the passenger slams all his weight into it. Of course I'm restoring it piece by piece, but I understand now that it's not as important as it was before. Suddenly everything seems so different, as if the world changed. My car is no longer my flashy pet but my clumsy, mechanical legs. Likewise, roadsides, deep rivers, and the tops of mountains are tangible in a way that's not defined simply by peering through a window at them. I'd seen that ditch in the roadside hundreds of times, but being in it gave me a whole new perspective of the landscape around me. I felt vulnerable and small, like how a baby bird must feel when it falls from its nest. I don't know if this was a good or a bad experience for me, but the experience changed me from a bouncy teenager to a conscious adult. 59

Starving for Control
Samantha Wright
University of California, Riverside
Riverside, California

A remembered event might happen in a single moment or it might span several days, weeks, or months. In this essay, Samantha Wright recalls both: a single event that dramatically changed the next few months of her life and that still affects her today. The mature reflection on the decisions of her younger self help the reader feel the frustrated helplessness of the child while appreciating the full implications this event had on Samantha's life. As you read, notice how Wright describes concrete details that stand out in her memory—details that help make the story come alive for readers.

Like a lot of American girls, I developed an eating disorder when I was thirteen years old. To be honest, I'm surprised it took that long. My body had always confused me; I mean, I started getting my period before I'd mastered long division. I had pointy little tits and no bras, which led to an embarrassing yearbook photo every single year. My hair grew fast, but not on my head. To sum it up neatly, I was a wreck and fully aware of it. But somehow, I didn't really care. Yes, I knew what beauty was, and yes, I knew that I didn't fit the mold, like, at all, but don't remember taking the stupid construct to heart. I was free little me. Well, whatever fueled my carefree outlook was killed by the unstoppable force of adolescent insecurity. 1

During my first year at Laguna Middle School, my P.E. class transitioned into its healthy fitness unit. The unit was treacherous and insulting; we'd done it all before. The trunk lifts, crunches, pacer test, mile run—each one of the gimmicky exercises had the same lame familiarly. Well, with the exception of the BMI test. 2

As everyone knows, the BMI rubric is determined by height and weight. No running, no stretching, no activity was required for this 3 fitness test. It's funny looking back; the least demanding activity in the unit would become one of the most internalized instances in my life to that point. Six years later, I can remember standing in that school's little gym with my ugly uniform on. The walls were green, the room was cramped, and well over capacity. A single sheet hung in the middle of the room, separating the girls from the boys.

When the teacher saw the numbers on the scale, she would say them out loud to her student aid, who'd promptly scribble them down. As the line shortened and I grew closer and closer, it was obvious that there wasn't much of a range. 4

"98, 84, 108, 112." The numbers seemed so fluid, so congruent. There was a uniform beauty to it. They were lofty ballerinas side-by-side, none more distinct than the other. 5

"104, 94, 110." 6

Approaching. 7

"96, 100, 118." 8

I stepped on the scale. 9

"135." 10

I felt an immediate isolating force. 11

I dismounted the scale with a blank expression and left the building to find my friends. Whatever conversation we had following my weigh-in was irrelevant. I felt funny. I thought about what I ate that day. I abused myself a little. I walked over to my friend Kendall, who weighed eighty-four pounds. 12

"Hey, Kendall, who do you think is the fattest girl in the class?" I was noticeably anxious. She furrowed her brows and thought for a minute, and after looking between me and our peers told me that the fattest girl was Summer Stanley, a loner with a solid build, who I would find out weighed four pounds less than me. I checked out and went through the motions of the day with a vacant headspace. Well, vacant besides the inadequacy, self-doubt, and need for validation molesting my mind. When it came time to head home, I felt this urgency to address what was making me feel so ironically empty. I got online. 13

The first diet plan that attracted me was the military diet. It lasted three days and allowed for the consumption of hot dogs and vanilla ice cream, both of which I loved. I quickly reminded myself that this wasn't a good thing, though, and that it was necessary to avoid anything I was already eating. The game plan was this: renovate everything I thought was right. It wasn't up to me at that 14 point, and I had an urge for someone, something, to push me in the right direction, whatever that was. Then I found it. After skimming through Adkins, the Master Cleanse, and Raw Till 4, I found just what I needed. For the next two weeks, I would follow the almighty guide of the grapefruit diet.

The grapefruit diet required absolute self-control and a complete   15
diet change. I'd have to eat two hard-boiled eggs and half a grapefruit for breakfast, an undressed salad with deli ham and a grapefruit
for lunch, and another mixed green salad with deli ham for dinner, of
course paired with grapefruit.

Even though the plan suggested avoiding snacks, I decided   16
it would be fine to allow myself an apple or a couple of carrots in
between lunch and dinner. My parents had no concerns with my
plan. They were actually thrilled about my new mentality. I remember them saying repeatedly that anything healthy can't be a bad
thing. So, with the plan set in motion, the following week would be
dictated by the guidelines I had taped to my wall just in view of my
bed. Remarkably, I stayed on track.

Looking back on the whole ordeal, it really shouldn't have gone   17
the way it did. There was nothing I had done before that point that
would've suggested I had the willpower to cut out one of my only
comfort sources. At the time, I was a mostly social kid who looked
forward to cheap cookies, candy, junk food, and television. I'd never
given any activity all of my energy and was content with the situa-
tional outcomes that I'd receive. It was hard for me to finish projects
before jumping aboard new ones, but when it came to my diet, I
used all of my strength, energy, and will to reach my goal, which,
looking back, was dangerously unclear. Even though I hated the taste
of grapefruit and my stomach would constantly growl, I didn't give
in to my cravings. Strangely, it wasn't that hard to do. It felt like
there was something inside of me. Something strong, something
that could take control and tell me what to do and what not to do.
I liked this new feeling, even though it told me not to trust anything
I organically did, said, or thought.

The following Sunday, I got on my bathroom scale to measure   18
my progress. I don't know what I was expecting, but I was stunned
to learn that I weighed in at 127 pounds, eight pounds lost in a single week. I was thrilled yet incredulous with this outcome, to the
point where I literally got off the scale and mounted it again, thinking that the number was just a delusion. It wasn't. The satisfactory

high didn't last long, though. I instantly craved more. Lost weight equated to personal gain. That's when I became an addict, hungry for the rush of losing and horrified at the possibility of gaining—a truly twisted logic.

My motives weren't clear after my first instance of weight loss.   19 Eventually I'd start exercising compulsively, then I'd skip lunch. I'd strive to burn more calories than I'd take in, then I'd start making myself throw up. I'd start taking laxatives, then started impulsively counting. Among the anorexia, bulimia, and body dysmorphia, I developed full-fledged OCD. I'd favor the right side of my body, and threaten myself with morbid punishments if I did so much as exit a flight of stairs on my left foot. I'd only chew with the right side of my mouth. I'd count on my pinky, middle, and thumb fingers, one two three, constantly and compulsively. The right was my balance, and though I've since developed methods of controlling this obsession, to this day I can't shake the nonsensical ritual while performing routine tasks. It doesn't go away.

I received an intervention three months in from when I'd began.   20 By this point I was urinating blood but stopped getting my period. I was so terrified of gaining weight that I stopped drinking water and swallowing my spit. My diet consisted of mostly ice. I'd spend most of my time in the bathroom completely naked: chewing gum (on the right side of my mouth), spitting in the toilet, and weighing myself repeatedly for hours on end. I couldn't understand the emotions of my family, and when they told me that they thought I would die, I told them I didn't care. I wasn't myself anymore. Just a cold shell vaguely resembling who I once was, possessed by a demonic combination of self-repulsion and misery. I was forced into group therapy with other anorexics and bulimics, where we'd journal, receive individual treatment, and discuss our anxieties over the meals we were basically force-fed. After I "graduated" from the program, I was no longer 100 pounds. To my disgust, eating a normal diet made me gain back twenty pounds in no time, and before I knew it, I was back to 135. It's a shame I couldn't see the humor of the situation back then, all that work and permanent mental damage just to get right back to where I started. But I guess that's what happens when you dedicate yourself to a goal with no endgame; you just end up playing yourself.

Though today I can look back at how I was in horror, I can't   21 disregard what brought me to those extremes. There was the sense of purpose and control I got from losing weight, something my strict and anxious upbringing didn't allow me to have. There was also the glamorous aspect of starvation: at one point I wanted to be as thin as the girls on *America's Next Top Model*—a ridiculous concept considering I'm 5'4" with a curvy build. Somehow, I saw what I was doing as a good thing. I thought I was motivating myself, when in actuality, I grew more and more detached with every pound I lost. My friends and family couldn't stand my new personality, so I was left alone. Being alone, that's really what all my troubles amounted to. I drew an invisible line separating myself from reality, and nobody dared cross into my territory. No friends, no father, no sister, no mother. Just me. Alone. Empty. It's a feeling you can't just forget about.

Almost Quitting

Julia Barojas

University of California, Riverside
Riverside, California

Julia Barojas's essay is about perseverance. Barojas vividly describes the physical experience of suffering through a difficult first day as a construction worker—the hot sun, the blisters on her hands, the overpowering smells, and the pain in her back. Just as she is about to quit because the work is too hard, a comment by her supervisor makes her change her mind. You won't be surprised at this turn of events—the essay is called "*Almost* Quitting," after all. Barojas is not trying to create suspense about whether she will quit, though; she is writing about an event that ultimately filled her with confidence in her own abilities.

I awoke to the loud drone of my alarm as it rang directly next to my head. My eyes opened instantly, but it took me quite some time to understand what was going on. Then it finally clicked: It was 4:00 a.m., and I needed to get ready for my first day of work as an apprentice carpenter for a concrete company called Shaw & Sons. Somehow I found the strength in my feeble arm to turn off the alarm. The ringing echoed in my ears for a few seconds. 1

I sat up in bed and was surrounded by a piercing silence. The room was pitch-black and I staggered out of bed, waving my hands in front of me as I frantically searched for the light switch. After what seemed like hours, I found the switch and flipped it; my eyes slammed shut instantaneously. It took me some time to grow accustomed to the brightness, but little by little I regained my sight. 2

I began to get ready for work. As I laced up my black work boots and put on a bright green shirt with the company name "Shaw & Sons" written on the front in bold black letters, I heard the loud rumble of my brother's truck and realized it was nearly time to go. 3

I made my way through the dark hallway, out the front door, and into the truck.

My brother and I talked the entire way to work.   4

"Are you excited?" he asked.   5

"Of course I am! I'm going to be making my own money," I   6
responded.

"Well, you know it's not going to be easy, right?"   7

"What are you talking about? Of course it's going to be easy! Any-   8
thing you can do, I can do better. If you can manage, then so can I."

I felt very confident in myself and expected work to be a piece of   9
cake. In my mind, I would simply show up, do some simple work, go
home, and then get a paycheck at the end of the week.

The drive went quickly and before I knew it we had arrived at   10
the work site, located on the Pacific Coast Highway in the city of
Huntington Beach. We parked, and as I opened the truck door an
aroma of salt and fish filled my nostrils.

My brother and I walked for a few minutes and passed dozens of   11
boutiques and restaurants. Soon the massive foundations of hollow,
unfinished buildings came into sight. I followed my brother as we
made our way to our work location. There, he introduced me to the
other workers and my new boss, Gilbert Gomez. Gilbert gave me a
quick tour and went over some basic rules and expectations. Then he
led me to the orientation room, located in what would soon become
an underground parking structure. There I was given my hard hat
and safety glasses, and strict instructions to wear them at all times.

After the orientation I made my way back to the work site but got   12
lost in the maze of pilasters that sustained the heavy foundation above.
I eventually found an exit, and it led me straight to our location.

I was put to work right away. It was almost 9:00 a.m., and the   13
heat of the sun was warm and comforting. My first task was to glue
half-inch-thick strips of foam all along the base of the buildings. At
first the task seemed simple, but after a while the strong smell of the
glue spray started to get to me. My legs began to quiver from squat-
ting and standing repeatedly. My back began to ache tremendously.
My knees felt as though they would break soon from all the pressure
I was placing on them. A small red blister formed on the tip of my
index finger from spraying adhesive onto the foam and the building.
I checked the time on my cell phone and the clock read 9:47 a.m. — I
had been working for less than an hour.

After I finished gluing the foam, my next task was to nail plastic 14
devices called Speed Dowels onto the wooden framework. One by
one I nailed the Speed Dowels. After I had nailed about twenty of
them, the hammer began to feel heavier and heavier. I picked up the
third-to-the-last dowel and placed it against the wood, I put the nail
in its proper position and swung the hammer with a mighty force. As
I hit the nail, my finger slipped and the hammer smashed down on
my middle finger. The hammer dropped to the ground as I shook my
hand in a desperate attempt to alleviate the pain.

As the day dragged on, the heat coming from the sun grew more 15
intense. The initial comfort I had felt that morning was long gone.
My forehead was soaked with sweat, and my head was throbbing
viciously.

I stood up from my workplace and decided it was time for a 16
break. Without realizing it, I took a step back and stumbled over a
broomstick that had been left on the floor. I landed heavily on my
right hip and elbow.

That was the last straw! This job was more than I could handle. I 17
was sweaty and tired. Both my hip and elbow ached. Despite the fall,
the hammer remained in my hand. I threw it and it hit the ground
with a loud thud. I stood up and marched over to Gilbert, preparing a
long speech about why I would not be returning to work the next day.

As I neared my destination, I looked to my right and caught a 18
glimpse of my brother. I stopped dead in my tracks and just stared
at him. He was on his knees, his face smeared with black streaks of
concrete and blotches of white powder all along his shirt and pants.
He had been working at this job for nearly two years, and I could not
remember ever hearing him complain about how difficult work was.

As I stood there, transfixed in admiration, I was startled by a 19
loud voice that came from behind me.

"He's a hard worker, isn't he?" 20

I nodded my head in agreement. I turned around and saw that it 21
was Gilbert.

"Hey, Gilbert, you're just the person I was looking for," I said. 22
"So . . . um . . . I . . . I . . ."

I wanted to tell him that I quit, that I was hot and hungry and 23
frustrated, but somehow the words just wouldn't come out.

After an awkward moment of silence I suddenly blurted out, "I 24
want to thank you for hiring me . . . and I want you to know that I
truly appreciate it."

"It's my pleasure," he responded.

We exchanged smiles and I made my way back to my workplace. The hammer I had thrown to the ground was still there, waiting for my return. I picked it up and resumed my duties. My index finger still had a painful blister on the tip; I was still hot. My middle finger continued to throb. I was sweating profusely. However, things didn't look as bad as they had just a few minutes ago. This wasn't the most exciting job in the world, or the easiest, but it could be worse.

I began to work intensely, and before I knew it, my phone read 3:00 p.m.; the day had finally ended. As my brother and I made our way back to the truck, I removed my safety glasses and hard hat. With the back of my dirty hand I wiped away the ring of sweat that had formed on my forehead. I looked at my brother's dirty clothes and then looked down at my own. The layers of dirt that had accumulated throughout the day would have repulsed me a few days ago, but today I felt a sense of accomplishment; I hadn't given up. I simply smiled and climbed into the truck, and away we went.

Worse Than a Lump of Coal

James Ziech

University of Wisconsin, Baraboo/Sauk County
Baraboo, Wisconsin

In this humorous essay, James Ziech's idea of the perfect Christmas Eve is ruined by something "worse than a lump of coal": a trip to the emergency room. His memories of pleasurable anticipation of celebrating Christmas with his family are suddenly replaced by his memories of the fiercest stomach pain he'd ever known. Ziech builds the story around his increasingly painful symptoms and uses time markers to let the reader see the progression of symptoms over several days. Ziech's figurative language makes the reader feel his pain; fortunately, his good humor makes the essay fun to read, rather than actually painful.

——————

1 I was only fifteen, but I was about to stare fate right in the face. It was just a week before Christmas Eve, the time of the year I anticipated the most. As I came home from school that Friday, I kept thinking about the events of Christmas Eve: People would carol in the streets while the snow collected on the trees; our family would gather around to eat in front of a tree that sparkled like a thousand gold and silver goblets. It was going to be the perfect Christmas Eve.

2 That evening, however, my stomach began to growl and ache. Maybe it was gnawing on itself in anticipation of Christmas. Whatever the feeling was, it did not stop. Thinking it wasn't serious, I brushed it off and tried to get some sleep. That night I tossed and turned enough times to turn my sheets into a straitjacket. I decided to tough the stomach pain and insomnia out, hoping that it would pass and sleep would come. It never did.

3 After spending I'm not sure how long inventing a new kind of yoga, I hurried to the toilet before the stomach pain could squeeze me like an overstuffed tube of toothpaste. I threw up. I flushed,

wiping the half-digested lasagna from my chin. Even after a thorough clean, I still tasted the residue on the back of my tongue. I even felt the smell lighting a match to my nostrils. I still told myself it wasn't serious and went back to bed.

The morning came, sooner than I wished. I went to lie on my mom's bed, under a dozen or so blankets. My arms were frosty and pale, while my legs lay still like dead weights.   4

"Does this hurt?" my mom asked me, feeling the area between my belly button and my waist. I couldn't feel any difference in the pain when she poked me. Since I didn't answer, she guessed I had a bug that was going around her workplace, or something that I caught at school. Stomach flu, maybe.   5

"Here, eat some soup," she said, sitting next to me on the bed.   6

"You want me to throw up?"   7

"We need to get some liquid down."   8

"Yeah, down on that floor. . . ."   9

Every once in a while she would feed me. Even though I knew it was a bad idea, I tried to eat. I still could not keep food down, but by mid-afternoon I was on the road to recovery—or so I thought.   10

On Sunday, even though the good snowy weather was on its way, the fever I had had since Friday night was getting worse. Eventually I was able to sleep again. When seven o'clock came around, every pain I had was gone, my temperature stabilized, and, best of all, I could eat without any nasty side effects.   11

Mom intervened when I hurried off to the door with my book bag.   12

"Where are you going?" she asked.   13

"To school. It's seven, and I'll be late for the bus!" I said, about to brush her aside.   14

"You're not going anywhere. It's seven p.m.—on Sunday."   15

I couldn't believe I had gotten so confused. I was actually relieved because I didn't finish any of my homework for the weekend. I got some of it done and went to sleep. The bug was gone now and I accepted Monday morning as it came. Despite it being a normal school day, I was colder than usual, and that night the vicious cycle of squeeze and squirm started again. I even considered sleeping in the bathroom to avoid climbing a flight of stairs in between the trips. I couldn't handle the pain any longer. I had to get help.   16

"Mom, something's terribly wrong with me. . . ."   17

"When did you get that idea?" Mom asked.   18

"Midnight," I said. 19

"Why did you wait so long to tell?" she exclaimed, fumbling 20 around in her bedroom for some slippers or tennis shoes. She knew that if I complained about being sick, I was serious about it. She dialed the hospital right away.

Lying down on the couch, I thought about Christmas Eve. The 21 caroling, the snow, the food, the family traditions . . . everything was going down the drain, and I couldn't stop it.

We left for the hospital in the dead of night. As soon as we 22 entered the emergency room, several nurses sprang into action. They moved me to a wheelchair, wheeled me to an examination room, and started to do a few oral tests.

"Does this hurt?" asked the nurse, pushing on my abdomen. "I 23 want you to rate it on a scale from one to ten."

I don't remember what number I said, but it was in the double 24 digits.

After she was done, she gave me a chalky vanilla substance to 25 drink and a small dish tub if I needed to throw up. Since I had no other option, I drank almost half of it before I needed the tub.

The nurse wheeled me into a room with a CAT scan machine in 26 it, and I climbed onto the slab. The machine made several passes and the technician looked at all the images that spat up onto the computer screen. He poked the region between my belly button and my waist — right where my mother had poked me days before. . . .

The next thing I knew doctors were wheeling me down a bright 27 hallway.

"What's happening to me?" I asked. 28

The doctors continued their jargon-filled conversation until one 29 of them answered me.

"Your appendix ruptured. I want you to be strong for me, can 30 you do that?"

I nodded. 31

"We're going to give you some anesthesia," one of the voices 32 said. "Could you count backwards from ten?" Someone slung a mask around my nose. I looked to my left and my right. My mom was disappearing from sight. Door signs and figures became mirages. Ten, nine, eight. . . .

Some time later, I woke up from the anesthesia. I was lying in a 33 hospital bed bound by tubes and cords. My stomach was red and stapled shut from the belly button to the waist, and I had a temperature of 106 degrees. The doctor was there, waiting with my mom and grandparents. I felt lucky to be alive.

Lying in my hospital bed, I thought about the Christmas Eve I had hoped for. Instead of playing in the snow, I saw it from a three-story window. Instead of eating a traditional dinner and drinking eggnog, I ate tasteless Jell-O and drank lukewarm water. Instead of excitement and glee, I got something worse than a lump of coal. I spent all of Christmas confined to my hospital room, and by the time I was out, only a few days remained of my winter break. Maybe next year I'll pick a less scary time of year to look forward to—like Halloween.

34

3 *Writing Profiles*

The essay you write for this chapter will almost certainly be the one you least expected to write in this class. It will not draw you back into memory, as the remembered-event essay did (Chapter 2), nor will it lead you to the library, as the other kinds of essays in this book are likely to. Instead, it will take you off-campus to see someone else's environment and—stranger still—require you to ask that person about it and capture what he or she says as a primary source for your essay.

It may seem daring or even reckless to walk into an unfamiliar place and ask strangers about their activities. Countless students given this assignment have nevertheless done so, gaining self-confidence and satisfying their curiosity about some unfamiliar corner of the everyday world—such as the police station, printing press workshop, drive-in movie theater, and record store visited by the student essayists in this chapter. The biggest surprise for many profilers is how willing strangers are to talk about their work and other interests.

As you read through the profiles that follow, note some of their basic features: specific information about the subject, a clear and logical organization, the writer's role as either a participant or a detached observer, and the writer's unique perspective on the subject.

You may find your expectations about the people or place confirmed, but more likely you will be surprised or even astounded by what you learn—so surprised you may need to make a second visit to gather more information and to figure out how it all fits together. What you need in this special situation of observing and writing is an open mind—or better, a curious mind. Cultivating a curious mind will help you to think productively in any writing situation you encounter in college and, later, in your career. Anticipate that you will be surprised at what you see and hear in your visit and interviews. Embrace that surprise, use it in your essay, and continue to cultivate the curiosity that inspired it.

Use the guidelines in the Peer Review Guide that follows to practice peer review using the essays in this chapter.

A Peer Review Guide

SPECIFIC INFORMATION ABOUT THE SUBJECT

Does the writer portray the subject in enough well-chosen detail to show us why it's interesting?

> **Summarize:** Tell the writer one thing you learned about the subject from reading the essay.

> **Praise:** Point out one passage where the description seems especially vivid, a quotation stands out, or another writing strategy works particularly well to present information.

> **Critique:** Point out one passage where description could be added or where the description could be made more vivid, where a quotation that falls flat could be paraphrased or summarized, or where another writing strategy could be used.

A CLEAR, LOGICAL ORGANIZATION

Is the profile easy to follow?

> **Summarize:** Identify the kind of organization—narrative, topical, or a blend of the two—that the writer uses.

> **Praise:** Comment on the cues the writer gives that make the profile easy to follow. For example, point to a place where one topic leads logically to the next or where transitions help you follow the tour or narrative. Also, indicate what in the opening paragraphs grabs your attention or why you think the ending works well.

> **Critique:** Point to information that seems out of place or instances where the chronology is confusing. If you think the opening or ending could be improved, suggest an alternative passage in the essay that could work as an opening or an ending.

THE WRITER'S ROLE

Is the author's role, whether spectator, participant-observer, or both, clear?

Summarize: Identify the role the writer adopts.

Praise: Point to a passage where the spectator or participant-observer role enables you to identify with the writer, enhancing the essay's immediacy or interest.

Critique: Point out any problems with the role — for example, if the participant-observer role becomes distracting, or if the spectator role seems too distant.

A PERSPECTIVE ON THE SUBJECT

Does the author have a clear point of view on the subject?

Summarize: State briefly what you believe to be the writer's perspective on the subject and the dominant impression you get from the essay.

Praise: Give an example where you have a strong sense of the writer's perspective through a comment, description, quotation, or bit of information.

Critique: Tell the writer if the essay does not have a clear perspective or does not convey a dominant impression. To help him or her find one, explain what interests you about the subject and what you think is important. If you see contradictions in the draft that could be developed to make the profile more complex and illuminating, briefly explain.

To Protect and Serve

Isaiah Williams

University of California, Riverside
Riverside, California

Discovering surprising or even conflicting information about the person you interview can lead to a particularly compelling narrative. Isaiah Williams made this discovery when he entered a police station with one set of expectations and left after his interview with a new perspective on a person — and a role — he thought he already understood. As you read, notice how the mundane and specific details help to ground and reassure the reader and how Williams presents his change of heart as a gradual process.

A chilling breeze whipped across my face as I stood before the brown-bricked building with the word "Police" spelled out above the main entrance. I was ironically skittish as I traversed up the steps of the building that housed the several sworn police officers who were dedicated to protecting the students on the UC Riverside campus. My rather irrational fear stemmed from the recent hysteria and harsh images that have been surrounding police officers in America. Like many, I hadn't personally experienced any instance of injustice, but the various images and videos circulating on the Internet were enough to tempt me to buy into the delirium. However, I resolutely cleared my mind as I approached the building's main entrance.

I timidly pulled the glass door open and walked across the appropriately colored blue and gold doormat. I was instantly greeted with "Isaiah?" I peered up, expecting to see a decked-out police officer in full uniform, but what I saw was quite unexpected. I saw a well-dressed man standing behind the bulletproof window in front of the receptionist's desk looking directly at me. He appeared as if he were going to church, with his gray striped collared shirt, black slacks that read "Izod," and matte-black dress shoes. He was an all-around normal-looking person, from his light blond hair that was combed over to one side, to the natural scruff that encroached on various places on his face. He called out directions in a friendly voice from the other side of the glass window, telling me to meet him at the massive wooden door that stood to the left of the receptionist's desk. He had to go through two other doors before getting to the one where I was standing. I watched as the tall, muscular man clumsily fumbled his keys at the first door, trying a few different ones in the keyhole before actually getting to the correct key. He eventually got through both doors, opened the one directly in front of me, and greeted me with a smile. "Detective Dombrowski," he said with an extended hand. With a sturdy handshake he welcomed me into the back office area.

To my surprise, the facility was much bigger than it initially   3 looked from the outside. It housed everything that you would find in a standard police facility: an armory, an evidence room, a large meeting room, and the report writing–lockup room. Dombrowski's voice harbored a distinct tone of irritation as he described the tiring number of hours spent tediously writing reports in this place. He went on a small rant about this seemingly monotonous task as I surveyed the lockup portion of the room. It was separated by another glass window and merely contained a shiny metal bench with one pair of handcuffs secured to the railing above it. It resembled every cop film I had ever seen.

Our next destination was the squad car parking lot in the back of   4 the facility, which had a surprisingly small number of police cars: six to be exact. Compared to the sheer impressiveness of the rest of the facility, the parking lot was slightly underwhelming, but it highlighted a more significant and perhaps more serious issue. For such a large campus, which held a total of roughly 28,000 combined students and staff as of 2017 (*UC Riverside Ranks and Facts*), an on-campus police force of thirty-two seemed rather small (*UC Riverside Enterprise Directory*). "We get the job done," Detective Dombrowski assured me as we headed back inside the facility. It seemed as if he felt obligated to explain how well equipped his department was and how safe the campus was in their hands. He went on to commend his whole team and had nothing but positive things to say about each of them. The soothing sense of confidence radiated from his voice as he spoke about the quality of teamwork that existed in his department.

The facility housed its very own dispatch room, which proved   5
highly impressive. The room was filled with a multitude of monitors
with brightly lit screens that served as the only source of light for the
entire room. Detective Dombrowski pointed to a small blond-haired
woman sitting behind the monitor screens, typing a mile a minute.
"I'm sure you can imagine all the crazies that we get calling here. Well,
Wendy is lucky enough to be the first person to speak with them."
She finished typing and looked over, smiling more with her eyes than
with her mouth, and introduced herself. Wendy had one of the most
stressful jobs in the whole department, as she served as the first line
of response for any emergency that was called into the station. "The
hardest part of the job is getting information out of callers," Wendy
stated in her naturally mellow voice. For having such a stressful job,
she was a surprisingly tranquil person, who could instill a sense of calm
into any person she spoke to simply through her voice, which one
could imagine was a rather useful skill to have in her position.

Our last destination was the officers' personal office areas, which   6
peculiarly resembled any other cubicle-style office in America. "This
is where all the fun happens," Dombrowski sarcastically proclaimed.
The walls of his cubicle were cluttered with pictures of his family,
and his desk was equally cluttered with loose paper that he attempted
to clear as we sat down across from each other. As we conversed,
Detective Dombrowski informed me that he had been an officer off-
campus as part of the Riverside Police Department in the early stages
of his career. Pure curiosity pushed me to ask how different the experiences of serving on-and off-campus were for him. He looked back
at the picture of his three daughters that hung above his computer
and said that the hardest part of working off-campus is going to
domestic abuse scenes where the kids are involved. With his eyes still
glued to the picture of his daughters, he swallowed roughly and said,
"You're not a father yet so you may not understand, but as a father
I can only think of my girls when I am on those cases." The emotion flew from his lips and filled the room as he told me this. The
amount of reported crime in 2017 that was classified as "offenses
against the family/children" only came out to 2 percent of all crime
in Riverside as of August 2017 (Riverside Police Department). However, it is clearly one of the toughest types of crime to handle and is a
hard distinction between serving on-and off-campus, as pointed out
by Detective Dombrowski. Conversely, he told me the best part of

his job was being able to work with the UC Riverside community. Despite a twenty-two-year low in American confidence in our police officers (Jones), Detective Dombrowski feels a great sense of support from the surrounding community and praises the UC Riverside campus for contributing to that. Dombrowski is aware of the hysteria that has shaped the public's perceptions of America's police force but says, "By speaking to me I hope that people can see that I am a normal person rather than the monster that the media portrays officers like me to be." While his words begged for acceptance, I noticed that the timidness I had initially felt entering the building had been completely relinquished. I was speaking with someone I considered once as foe but now looked upon as a friend.

WORKS CITED

Jones, Jeffrey M. "In U.S., Confidence in Police Lowest in 22 Years." *Gallup*, 19 June 2015, news.gallup.com/poll/183704/confidence-police-lowest-years.aspx.

Riverside Police Department. "Historical Crime Statistics." *City of Riverside*, 2017, www.riversideca.gov/rpd/crstats/2017_Past/AUG%2017/CITY_Part%20II.pdf.

UC Riverside Enterprise Directory. Regents of the University of California, enterprisedirectory.ucr.edu/phone/tel_search.show. Accessed 3 Dec. 2017.

UC Riverside Ranks and Facts. Regents of the University of California, www.ucr.edu/about/ranks-and-facts. Accessed 3 Dec. 2017.

Bringing Ingenuity Back

Linda Fine

University of California, Riverside
Riverside, California

When you interview someone who is passionate about something, you may discover—as Linda Fine did—that a commonplace process can turn into a memorable story. Using a straightforward interview style, with quotations and paraphrases, Fine allows the librarian featured in this essay to detail the arduous steps involved in using old-fashioned hand presses. As you read, notice how Fine's perspective changes throughout the course of her essay and how her concluding analogy leads the reader to join her in a new appreciation for the dedication and personal touch involved in this unique craft.

As I made my way to a set of elevators in the rear of our sleek new campus library, I passed students and librarians working at monitors wired into the university's online system. I also passed students sitting at tables with their laptops open and books piled nearby. A few students were using the photocopiers to scan pages onto their jump drives, and two printers on a corner table spewed paper as students stood nearby, chatting. I was on my way into the past to see hand-printing presses dating from the Civil War. The antique presses were donated to the university by Dr. Edward Petko because he favored the hand-press method over modern laser printing, and he hoped that the university would help keep the traditional process alive.

Entering an unmarked room in the basement, I saw numerous weathered wooden cases stacked twice my height and, beyond them, old iron machines in various shapes and sizes. I stepped into the room clueless but eager to learn about this nearly forgotten printing process. Sara Stilley, a thin, dark-haired woman in her late twenties, works in this room five days a week. After welcoming me, she showed me some samples of artwork she has printed. One of her most recent works was a greeting card she made for another staff member. The finished product looked very professional, but then Sara proceeded to explain to me the frustration behind this masterpiece.

The preparation work takes hours, and in some cases, days. Sara's   3 difficult task is to carefully align each individual letter by hand. The letters are made up of very thin rectangular prisms, which make them difficult to handle. Not only does Sara need manual dexterity, she also needs skilled eyes to be able to tell the letters apart. If a wrong letter, font, or size has been used, she has to go back and tediously correct the frame and setup by hand. Familiarity with what the letters will look like is essential for the setup of hand printing because the letters can be confusing. The leaded letters in the printing process work like a stamp. Instead of arranging them the way they are read, the operator must position the letters upside down and backward, like a mirror image. It takes time and effort to train the eye to recognize letters this way. Letters such as *n* and *u* are easily mixed up, as are *p* and *q*, and *b* and *d*. Formatting the letters correctly is a critical step in the printing process because any careless error in the setup leaves a noticeable flaw in the printed document.

In addition to the letter conflict, Sara said, "Many times after   4 centering the text, I would find out that I made a mistake in the formation. Instead of making it perfectly centered, I was supposed to align it to the left." I could imagine that going back and correcting the spacing would be a wearisome task.

This old-fashioned printing process has other problems and diffi-   5 culties too. For example, humid weather causes the ink to spread out, leaving the text appearing smudgy and smeared. There may also be too much or too little ink used in a working press. Sometimes Sara will run out of a specific letter for a page. The only solution to this problem is to break apart her work into two printing processes and print half the page at a time.

Sara explained that back in the 1800s, printers did not number   6 their pages when printing a book. In order to keep the pages orderly, they had to use the same word twice. For example, if a page ended with the word "boy," then the following page would have to begin with the word "boy." Not numbering the pages can easily cause them to fall out of order.

At this point in the interview, I had to ask her, "If using   7 hand-printing presses can cause so many problems, why would anyone still prefer using them over laser-printing presses?"

Sara answered, "I feel better with what I produce. For example,   8
personally baking a cake for someone is better and much more appreciated than simply buying one."

After she said that, I got the point. If I were to send out Christ-   9
mas cards, each individual card would mean so much more if I had
personally hand-printed it myself rather than buying a box of pre-
printed cards at Walmart. Craftsmanship adds value and meaning
that you can't find in industrialized commodities that you just buy.

I walked around the room and explored the shapes and sizes   10
of the various printing presses. I saw that each machine had its own
unique maneuvers. Some levers had to be pulled clockwise and
pushed down. Others simply needed to be rolled across the printing
bed and back. The cases and crates stacked around the presses contained lead-filled letters and hundreds of neatly stored rectangular
pieces. There were keys, metal washers, wooden blocks called "furniture" to keep the letters in place, ink, and galleys—all of which, I
learned, were required for the printing process.

At the very end of my interview, Sara demonstrated one of the   11
many printing presses to me, the Asbern. First she carefully arranged
the lead-filled text blocks on the printing bed and used a key to
tighten the furniture securing the letters. As she switched the power
button on, the ink rollers began to spin. A low, soft mumbling sound
stirred and filled the room. Sara slipped a piece of plain white paper
into the slot and steered the machine from left to right. Steering the
wheel seemed like a very tough job because she was jerking her entire
body to create enough torque to rotate the wheel. Soon she turned
off the machine and took the paper out. After a careful examination,
she announced that it wasn't perfect. Sara handed the page to me
expecting me to see what she saw, but as I looked at it, I found nothing wrong with the printing.

Squinting, she told me, "The text is not perfectly centered on the   12
paper. It's a bit crooked because I slipped in the paper at a slight angle."

Whoever would have thought that small errors, like slipping in   13
the paper slanted, would make such a big difference? This is one of
the many things that make hand printing more difficult than using a
modern printing press.

Had Sara not pointed out to me the imperfection in her work,   14
however, I never would have caught it. It is amazing how she can
spot a flaw in her work as quickly as a professional chess player can
call a checkmate. Sara's keen expertise in the area of hand-printing

presses impresses me. I never thought such an old-fashioned job would provide deep insight into the beauty and value of works made by hand.

As I left the room filled with irreplaceable treasures, I thought of 15 the time when my sister, Irene, knitted a scarf for her friend on duty in Iraq. Irene was very worried about making the scarf "perfect." She was so concerned about making a mistake—or not having enough time to finish the scarf—that I wondered why she didn't simply buy a scarf at Macy's. After interviewing Sara Stilley and learning more about the ingenuity of her work, I now understood why Irene chose to make the scarf by hand. The scarf she knitted for her friend had more meaning in it than a typical scarf purchased at a department store. She expressed her loving care and support through the gift she made because it took time and effort, and not just money. There are a few holes and gaps in that scarf, but I'm sure her friend, like me, didn't see the imperfections and thought the gift was simply perfect.

Modernizing a Remnant of the Mid-Twentieth Century

Bonnie Lapwood

Mt. San Jacinto College, Menifee Valley
Menifee, California

Bonnie Lapwood profiles an institution in transition: a drive-in movie theater that is modernizing to meet the needs of the twenty-first century. Lapwood begins the essay by describing the theater from a moviegoer's point of view, but she also interviews the theater manager to find out more about the theater's history and upcoming renovations. Using both of these strategies provided Lapwood with enough detailed information to profile the theater effectively for her readers. As you read, ask yourself whether Lapwood takes a spectator role, a participant role, or both in her profile.

A giant, neon-pink Stater Bros. sign looms out of the darkness as we approach Mission Blvd. The glowing letters spill out across the unseen background in a streamlined, atomic-age font. The same sign probably greeted those headed to the drive-in fifty years ago. After turning right on Mission, the sign for the Rubidoux Drive-In appears. The Rubidoux is the oldest operating drive-in theater in Southern California, and still attracts a large following. Roy C. Hunt opened the Rubidoux Theater in 1948. The miniature railroad and petting zoo that once surrounded it have now disappeared, but every night, the screen still leans gracefully over an increasing number of cars filled with expectant viewers.

At night, the large slab of screen one is visible only as a black monolith behind illuminated palm trees. Red-vested teenagers stand joking and laughing when the entrance is empty but snap to attention when prospective moviegoers approach the stone ticket huts. Our attendant is a fresh-faced young man who jovially asks us which

49

movie we are seeing, and tells us the radio frequency of the audio track for our screen. Radio-broadcast movie soundtracks are a relatively recent innovation, replacing communal speakers and individual speakers. Of course, this means that the quality of the movie audio is only as good as the quality of the car stereo, but the broadcast is clear and static-free. The parking lot is uneven, with raised rows allowing the viewers a form of tiered seating. Once parked, viewers can leave their cars to visit the brightly lit snack bar and restrooms, housed in a pink stucco building with teal trim that sits in the middle of all three screens.

Before the movie begins, people arrange themselves to enjoy it   3
comfortably. People with SUVs generally park with the back of their car facing the screen and sit on the ledge with the hatch open and the radio blasting, using blankets for warmth. Most people with sedans simply park facing the screen and sit in the car as they would if they were driving. Others eschew their car entirely, sitting on lawn chairs close to their sedans or pickups, so they can hear the sound. Some people occupying lawn chairs have neon glow sticks, which they either wear around their wrists or wave in the air. Children run around their parents' cars until chided to sit down and behave. The parking lot is almost full by the time the previews begin, and the constant stream of people moving between their cars and the snack bar has slowed to a halt. The massive screen and lack of distractions make it much easier to get absorbed in the movie than in a regular theater. Sitting in a car, it feels like the movie is being projected just for you.

Although drive-in theaters have become less popular since the   4
1960s, this drive-in theater has grown in popularity over the last six years.

"The drive-in appeals to families because it's a bargain, and   5
there's no worry over parking, or being late," says Frank Huttinger, a vice president at De Anza Land & Leisure, which owns the Rubidoux, as well as five other drive-in theaters. Frank decides which movies are appropriate for drive-in audiences, negotiates their purchase with the studios, and groups them together by screen. Family-friendly movies are always included, as are large horror and action releases (Frank says that he personally prefers to see action movies at the drive-in, and light comedies and dramas at a traditional theater). De Anza Land & Leisure itself is a family-owned company, as are most drive-in companies, and has been operating drive-in theaters in California, Utah, and Georgia since the 1960s.

With twenty-five screens spread over six theaters, it is the second largest drive-in corporation in America. Frank is a member of the family, having seen his first drive-in movie—H. G. Wells's *The Time Machine*—at ten years old. Yet he worked in new media—CDs and the Internet—for over twenty years before joining the company.

"I've been in movies for about six years. It's a fun market," 6 he says. Frank's experience in media has influenced the rebranding of the De Anza theaters, which has been taking place over the last five or six years. "We've completely moved away from newspapers, and now all our advertising is on the Internet," he states proudly. Money has also been put into revising snack-bar menus and improving technology at the theaters. Frank sees the drive-in business in a very practical, realistic light. He buys movies for their mass appeal, and despite the success of a recent series of old films shown through a partnership with Turner Classic Movies, he recognizes that audiences desire twenty-first-century entertainment. "You can't rely on nostalgia—you have to keep up and be current," he affirms. This seems to be somewhat of a personal mantra of his. The Rubidoux, with its retro coral-pink and sky-blue color scheme, is due for a "serious" remodeling in the next year or two.

Frank also acknowledges the nonmovie side of the business. "We 7 wouldn't be able to keep up without the swap meets," he reveals. Swap meets take place at the Rubidoux from 6 a.m. to 2 p.m. on Wednesday, Friday, Saturday, and Sunday. They form the daylight side of the drive-in business, and make use of the giant parking lot when sunlight prohibits movies from being projected. They have been held since the 1960s, and are an integral part of the drive-in industry—which in part explains why so few drive-ins have been refurbished or newly built. Along with the difficulty involved in buying the large amounts of land and equipment required to run a drive-in, Frank notes that it takes about five years to build up swap meets to the point of being profitable.

The drive-in experience appeals to many, as it offers low admis- 8 sion fees, the freedom to either bring your own food or buy concessions at lower prices than at traditional movie theaters, and an opportunity to relax in the privacy and comfort of your own car. The potential discomforts of a traditional theater—overzealous air-conditioning, babies crying, popcorn on the floor, taller people blocking the view, teenagers carrying out public displays of affection, having to sit apart from companions because of a lack of seats—are eliminated at the drive-in, where the air conditioner is adjustable, the seats are comfortable, and the other viewers cannot interrupt.

I was originally attracted to the drive-in theater out of sentimen-   9 tality for the design and technological innovations of the American mid-twentieth century. However, as Frank told me, nostalgia is not enough to sustain a business. I found the Rubidoux Drive-In to be a worthy rival to the modern movie theater, since it has the charm of an older drive-in with the convenience and technologies of today. This drive-in theater's resurgence in popularity may inspire more innovations in the way the American public watches movies, which may lead to more alternatives to traditional movie theaters.

Mad World Records

Natasha Farhoodi

Texas Woman's University
Denton, Texas

Natasha Farhoodi offers readers a look into a local record store in Denton, Texas, and introduces us to Dave Koen, a record collector and employee at Mad World Records. Although local music stores—and vinyl records in particular—may be considered by some to be a relic of the past, Farhoodi's essay highlights the unique and valuable experience a local shop like Mad World Records can offer for music fans. A detached observer, Farhoodi vividly describes the inside of the store and her interaction with Koen. As you read, notice the various writing strategies and descriptive language Farhoodi employs. Her evaluation of the store and her colorful observations help keep readers engaged and assist in showing a complete and nuanced picture of the store and its future prospects.

---

1   The icy wind blowing against my face, I'm a bundle of nerves as I walk down West Hickory Street toward Mad World Records. I'm about to interview an employee for a college paper—this paper—and interviewing a stranger is widely out of my comfort zone.

2   Two years ago I discovered the wonderful world of vinyl records. Admittedly, the phrase "wonderful world of vinyl records" may bring to mind the word "hipster" for more than a few people, but despite what many people may think, collecting records is becoming an increasingly popular hobby—and with good reason. The atmosphere and selection in a good local record store offers hipster and nonhipster music lovers alike the same experience a used-book store gives to a book lover. It's a chance to meet like-minded people, browse a fellow fan's unique collection, learn more about music, and discover unknown artists you may otherwise never encounter on popular streaming services like Pandora or Spotify.

Before I have a chance to step through the door and conduct   3
my interview, I stop and can't help but stare. In a window at the
front of the store, a life-sized figure of Frankenstein stares back at
me unblinkingly, discarded records scattered around his feet. This
eye-catching scene is just a small taste of the fittingly "mad" deco-
rations inside. As I walk in past Frankenstein and look around the
shop, my nerves soften. I can't help but get a warm, pleasant feeling
as I gaze around the store. The walls are painted a light pear green
and are adorned with quirky posters, an eclectic mix of images of
musicians and bands from the 1950s to the 2000s side-by-side with
classic movie posters from *King Kong*, *The Warriors*, and *Psycho*.

The records are on the left wall, with the top shelves covered   4
in toys and action figures, including characters from *South Park*,
X-Men, and *The Simpsons*. Down the back of the store, littered
among more CDs and random knick-knacks, is a rack of T-shirts and
an old Atari game system, one of the first video game consoles from
the 1980s. In the corner there is another life-size statue. This time
it's Mayor McCheese, an old advertising mascot used in McDonald's
commercials from the 1970s and 1980s. Why Mayor McCheese? I
don't know if there is a reason. But like all the other oddities in the
store, it's a colorful reminder of the forgotten corners in American
culture, a strange remnant of past trends and zany cultural figures
that fits right in here.

The center of the store is lined with racks of CDs, which, despite   5
becoming a remnant of the past themselves, are surprisingly the main
product of Mad World "Records." There's even a special listening
station where customers can listen to local Texas bands. Besides me,
only one customer is there, idly browsing.

When I first meet Dave Koen, a local photographer and record   6
collector who works at the store, I can't help but be reminded of a
young Kevin Smith, the director and well-documented comic-book
fan best known for playing Silent Bob in the 1990s films *Clerks*,
Dogma, and *Jay and Silent Bob Strike Back*. Dave is wearing a bright-
red jacket, jeans, and Converse sneakers, and his incredibly laid-back
demeanor and soft-spoken voice are very calming, in stark contrast to
all the colorful sights and sounds in the store. Through his thin black
glasses, Dave has smiley brown eyes that twinkle when he laughs, and
he sports a slight beard and dark brown hair that comes down to his
shoulders.

Gentle folk music plays softly in the background as we sit down   7
on the edge of the window display and begin the interview. By the
time I begin speaking with Dave, the butterflies in my stomach virtually disappear. I notice he fidgets a lot, cracking his knuckles and
shifting his eyes toward the wall behind me. The fact that he seems
nervous too makes me feel much better.

Dave has been working at Mad World Records for two years. He   8
tells me music has always been a big part of his life. He played in
bands as a teenager and bought his first record player when he was
fourteen. He quickly fell in love with listening to records and has
been collecting them ever since. Chuckling, he says, "I have basically
a shelf in my house that's just full of records; drawers full of 7 inches."

I ask what he most enjoys about working here. Dave ponders for   9
a moment and replies, "Probably the thing I enjoy most is just seeing
the interesting things that come into the store. Sometimes people
bring in records from bands that were never put onto CD, so you get
to see things you'll never find anywhere else."

I ask Dave what the typical customer is like, to which he   10
responds, "For the most part—well, we get all kinds of customers.
We get a lot of college-age students that come in who've, you know,
just bought their first record player, and are looking for something
to add to their collection. We have a lot of people who grew up listening to records and are trying to find things they got rid of twenty
years ago or just trying to find something new to listen to."

Has he noticed more people buying records in recent years or   11
seen more young people show interest in it?

"Yes," he says, adding that this rise in demand has made life for   12
record collectors such as him much easier. "When I started buying
records, the only place to buy them was either directly from the band
that was selling them or had released it, or used-record stores, so it's
nice to see. I guess I would include myself in the younger-person
shopping category, but it's nice that there are places where you can
go and buy new records, and it's nice to have a place where there are
people who are knowledgeable about the music, so you can—you
don't have to just guess. You can just ask whoever's working what
they recommend, so that's nice."

Curious, I ask Dave if he believes this recent rise in popularity   13
can last. He hopes so, but he's skeptical. "It's not going to happen
unless they create more pressing plants to make vinyl," he explains.

"The problem is, the machinery to make records hasn't been made in forty or fifty years, and pressing plants are, you know, few and far between. The ones that are in existence—they work really hard, but it's not cheap to make records, so if they can figure out how to make them cheaper, I think that the future looks really bright. If it stays the way it is, it's going to be tough because even we have a hard time getting in everything people want to buy."

This leads me to ask about his thoughts on the benefits of digital music and how it compares to vinyl. "I'd be a hypocrite if I said I didn't like digital because right now we're listening to an iPod," he admits, "and I have a lot of my records on my computer, so I can listen to them wherever, but I also enjoy the fidelity of records. I think they sound really good in comparison to digital. I think that they kind of go hand in hand basically. Like, I don't think that records would be around without digital downloads and things like that because people expect to be able to listen to their music whenever they want, wherever they want, and with records you can't do that, but with them both you can kind of make it work." 14

I ask Dave what he likes most about the experience of going to a record store and why he believes it's important for small record stores to stay in business. Looking wistful and with obvious affection in his voice, he says, "The thing that I like most about going to a record store is just, you never know what you're going to find. Different stores carry different things, and so going to a store you might find some limited edition record that isn't going to be anywhere else. The other thing I really like is finding good local bands. I'm from Ohio, and so whenever I go home, I always try to find good local stuff that I know I'm not going to be able to get in Texas. It's important for small record stores to stick around because for years if you needed music you went to Best Buy or Target, and the problem with that is—is that they have big music buyers that buy for everyone, so you don't get kind of the, you know—basically you have the Top 40—is all you can get there, and so in smaller record stores we can kind of order different things from people, and we can cater to a local crowd instead of catering to the national crowd, so I think that's why it's important for them to stick around." 15

After browsing through Mad World Records, it's hard to disagree. Small record stores like this offer a valuable resource to their local community and provide a funky atmosphere that you can't get at major retail stores or online. While the digital movement and major retailers still threaten to wipe out local record stores, I hope they stay around for a long time. 16

Explaining a Concept 4

Explaining a concept might seem like a broad or daunting task at first. After all, as the student writers in this chapter show us, a "concept" can refer to anything from body language to stop-motion animation. A concept is an issue, a phenomenon, or a process: Participatory culture, academic failure among college athletes, the dowry system in India, jihad, secular humanism, postcolonialism, bankruptcy, and machismo are all concepts. Nevertheless, you explain concepts much more frequently than you might realize. When you describe the latest technological feature on your smartphone to someone who has never seen it before or list the reasons one might vote for a particular political candidate (perhaps citing authoritative sources or offering evidence), you are explaining a concept.

The concept essays in this chapter share the same basic features: a focused explanation (the main thesis), a clear and logical organization, appropriate explanatory strategies (such as definition, classification, and comparison/contrast), and smooth integration of sources.

Once you have identified an issue you are familiar with or would be interested in knowing more about, your next step is to gain a quick orientation to it. Let's say you've heard about participatory culture and would like to know more. A bit of Web browsing reveals that the term "participatory culture" refers to the universe of file-sharing networks, blogs, wikis, and other platforms that enable ideas and content to flow among peers; the shared values of these participants; and the participants themselves. Voilà: This is a concept you could learn more about and write about!

Writing that explains a concept is not so personal as narrating a remembered event (Chapter 2) or profiling a place or an activity you have observed (Chapter 3). It need not be so accommodating to readers' expected resistance as arguing to support your position on an issue (Chapter 6) or proposing to solve a problem (Chapter 7). But it does invite you to attune yourself to your readers, precisely measuring what they will already know about the concept: You don't want to bore them or burden them but rather enable them to learn about your concept without too strenuous an effort. And showing off is not allowed—of course you know more than your readers do about this subject, but to win their ear, you must remain tactful throughout, authoritative yet never talking down.

Every academic discipline, profession, career, sport, governmental or political organization, local community, and religion has its concepts. Through concepts, we define, understand, and manage our world. We can't live without them. These are not just big words—they are required words. As a college student, you'll add vastly to your concept hoard. In doing so, you'll gain a wider understanding of the myriad aspects of your life and times, and you'll have the precise words—the concept names—to help you organize and deploy your new knowledge.

Use the guidelines in the Peer Review Guide that follows to practice peer review using the essays in this chapter.

A Peer Review Guide

A FOCUSED EXPLANATION

Is the explanation focused?

> **Summarize:** Tell the writer, in one sentence, what you understand the concept to mean and why it is important or useful.
>
> **Praise:** Give an example of something in the draft that you think will especially interest the intended readers.
>
> **Critique:** Tell the writer about any confusion or uncertainty you have about the concept's meaning, importance, or usefulness. Indicate places where the focus could be clearer or more appropriate for the intended readers or where the explanation could have a more interesting focus.

A CLEAR, LOGICAL ORGANIZATION

Is the concept explanation clear and easy to follow?

> **Summarize:** Look at the way the essay is organized by making a scratch outline.

Praise: Give an example of where the essay succeeds in being readable—for instance, in its overall organization, forecast of topics, or use of transitions.

Critique: Identify places where readability could be improved—for example, the beginning made more appealing, a topic sentence made clearer, or transitions or headings added.

APPROPRIATE EXPLANATORY STRATEGIES

Are writing strategies used effectively to analyze and explain the concept?

Summarize: Note which explanatory strategies the writer uses, such as definition, comparison, example, cause and effect, classification, or process analysis.

Praise: Point to an explanatory strategy that is especially effective, and highlight research that is particularly helpful in explaining the concept.

Critique: Point to any places where a definition is needed, where more (or better) examples might help, or where another explanatory strategy could be improved or added. Note where a visual (such as a flowchart or graph) would make the explanation clearer.

SMOOTH INTEGRATION OF SOURCES

Are the sources incorporated into the essay effectively?

Summarize: Note each source mentioned in the text, and check to make sure it appears in the list of works cited, if there is one. Highlight signal phrases and in-text citations, and identify appositives used to provide experts' credentials.

Praise: Give an example of the effective use of sources—a particularly well-integrated quotation, paraphrase, or summary that supports and illustrates the point. Note any especially descriptive verbs used to introduce information.

Critique: Point out where experts' credentials are needed. Indicate quotations, paraphrases, or summaries that could be more smoothly integrated or more fully interpreted or explained. Suggest verbs in signal phrases that may be more appropriate.

The Forgotten Personality
Katie Angeles
University of California, Riverside
Riverside, California

In order to explain a specialized term, Katie Angeles began with a discussion of a more widely understood subject: personality types. Aware that her audience might not be familiar with the topic, she briefly explains the history and concept of personality types. From this starting point, Angeles is able to contrast characteristics her audience may be more familiar with to those traits unique to the "forgotten" personality type—the "phlegmatic." Note how Angeles uses the illustration of the way different people behave at a party to offer readers an example they can identify with throughout the essay. Is Angeles successful at seamlessly integrating sources throughout her sentences?

———————————

The next time you're at a party or any other type of social gathering, look around. Some people are telling stories and making everyone laugh, others are making sure everything is running smoothly and perfectly, and a few individuals are the bold ones who liven things up and "get the party started." These are the obvious personalities—the "life of the party," the "busy bee," and the "leader." Personality experts call these personalities sanguine (the popular one), melancholic (the perfect one), and choleric (the powerful one). However, there's one personality that's not so easy to spot and therefore is usually forgotten—the peaceful phlegmatic.

What makes people the way they are? Why do some people command the spotlight, while others are experts at fading into the background? Personality types were first identified around 400 BC, when the Greek physician Hippocrates noticed that people not only looked different but also acted differently. He believed that each person's personality type was related to a particular body fluid they had in excess: yellow bile, black bile, blood, or phlegm. These were classified as the "four humors" (Funder 203). Around AD 149, a Greek physiologist named Galen built on Hippocrates's theory, stating that sanguines had an excess amount of yellow bile, melancholics had extra black bile, cholerics had more blood than others, and phlegmatics had an extraordinary amount of phlegm (Littauer 16). In later years, more theories evolved—American scientist William Sheldon believed that personality was related to body type, while people in India said that metabolic body type contributed to the way people behave (Funder 373). Ultimately, these theories were proven incorrect, but we still recognize different personality types. Today, what do we think determines personality?

As *Time* magazine reported on January 15, 1996, D4DR, a   3
gene that regulates dopamine, is usually found in people who are risk takers (Toufexis par. 2). However, researchers suspected that the gene itself wasn't the only cause of risk-taking and that other genes, as well as upbringing, contributed to this phenomenon (Toufexis par. 3). At the time the report appeared, people were worried that parents would use prenatal testing to weed out certain genes that invoked undesirable personality traits (Toufexis par. 6). Since all personalities have their good and bad sides, this would have been a controversial development. Thankfully, parents are not yet able to test for their child's future personality.

Moreover, we know that even though people may be born with   4
a certain personality, the way they are brought up can also contribute to how they relate to others later in life. For example, birth order has been shown to affect personality type (Franco par. 1). Firstborn children tend to be choleric since they have the job of leading their siblings; middle children are usually phlegmatic since they're in a prime negotiating spot; and the youngest are generally sanguine because they're used to being spoiled (Franco pars. 2–4). Parents can also influence the way a child's personality turns out.

Each personality type has its strength, but a strength taken to an   5
extreme can become a weakness. While sanguines love to talk, sometimes they may talk too much. Although cholerics are born leaders, they may use their influence in negative ways. Melancholics are perfectionists, but they may prefer being right to being happy, and phlegmatics tend to be easygoing and agreeable, but they may be too passive and have a fear of conflict. Their laid-back attitude can be very frustrating to the most fast-paced personalities, such as cholerics and melancholics.

Phlegmatic people can be hard to notice because they're usually   6
not doing anything to call attention to themselves. While the sanguines are talking and loving life, the cholerics are getting things
done, and the melancholics are taking care of the little details, the
phlegmatics distinguish themselves by simply being laid-back and
easygoing. Even though phlegmatic people tend to fly under the
radar, it's very noticeable when they're not around, because they
are the peacemakers of the world and the glue that holds everyone together. They are low-maintenance, adaptable, even-keeled,
calm, cool, and collected individuals. They are usually reserved, yet
they love being around people, and they have a knack for saying
the right thing at the right time. Phlegmatics also work well under
pressure. However, they hate change, they avoid taking risks, they
are extremely stubborn, and it's very hard to get them motivated
or excited, which can translate into laziness (Littauer 21). Aside
from these traits, the phlegmatic's characteristics are hard to define,
because phlegmatics tend to adopt the traits of either the sanguine
personality or the melancholy personality.

Most people are a combination of personalities—they have a   7
dominant and a secondary personality that combine the traits of
the personalities. For example, some phlegmatics are phlegmatic-
sanguine, making them more talkative, while others are phlegmatic-
melancholy, causing them to be more introverted. It's not possible to
be phlegmatic-choleric, since phlegmatics avoid conflict and cholerics
are fueled by it (Littauer 24, 25). People who try to resist their natural personality type can wind up unhappy, since they are trying to be
someone they are not.

All personalities have emotional needs. The sanguine needs   8
attention, affection, approval, and activity; the melancholic needs
space, support, silence, and stability; the choleric needs action, appreciation, leadership, and control; and the phlegmatic needs peace,
self-worth, and significance (Littauer 22). If people don't have their
emotional needs met, their worst sides tend to emerge. For example,
if a phlegmatic, easygoing, type B personality is in a family of all cholerics, or "go-getter," type A personalities, the phlegmatics may find
themselves masking their true personality in order to survive. This
can be very draining for phlegmatics, and sooner or later, their negative side will emerge.

Phlegmatics are very adaptable—they get along with every-   9
one because they are able to meet the emotional needs of all the

individual personalities. They listen to the sanguine, they follow the choleric, and they support the melancholic. In return, the sanguine entertains them, the choleric motivates them, and the melancholic listens to them. However, if phlegmatics feel as if they're being taken for granted, they will become resentful. Since they have an innate need for peace, they won't say anything, and people won't know that there's a problem (Littauer 125).

Even though phlegmatics are often overlooked, they have a lot to contribute, with their ability to work under pressure, their diplomatic skill, and their contagious contentment. So the next time you're checking out personalities at a party, try looking for the phlegmatic first. The forgotten personality might just be the most interesting person in the room.

WORKS CITED

Franco, Virginia. "Siblings Birth Order and Personality Types." *Essortment*. Pagewise, 2002, il.essortment.com/birthordersibl_rbay.htm.

Funder, D. C. *The Personality Puzzle.* 2nd ed., W. W. Norton, 2001.

Littauer, Florence. *Personality Plus for Couples: Understanding Yourself and the One You Love.* Baker Publishing Group, 2001.

Toufexis, Anastasia. "What Makes Them Do It." *Time,* 15 Jan. 1996, content .time.com/time/magazine/article/0,9171,983955,00.html. Accessed 3 Mar. 2018.

Proxemics: A Study of Space and Relationships

Sheila McClain

Western Wyoming Community College
Rock Springs, Wyoming

Essays that explain a concept are often recognizable as research papers. The writer will use (and cite) sources to validate his or her perspective on the subject. Sheila McClain was interested in researching body language, but when she found the subject too broad for a focused essay, McClain narrowed her topic to a little-known term she knew readers could relate to. As you read, notice how McClain moves between the two concepts, allowing the larger, more familiar subject (body language, or "nonverbal communication") to lead her into an explanation of the smaller, less familiar one ("proxemics"). McClain does a good job of using sources to frame her discussion (with clarification of technical terms and difficult concepts) while allowing her own voice to direct the essay.

Every day we interact and communicate, sometimes without even saying a word. Body language, more formally known as "nonverbal communication," speaks volumes about who we are and how we relate to others. As Lester Sielski, an associate professor at the University of West Florida, writes, "Words are beautiful, exciting, important, but we have overestimated them badly—since they are not all or even half the message." He also asserts that "beyond words lies the bedrock on which human relationships are built—nonverbal communication" (Sielski 238). A group of psychology students at the University of Texas recently demonstrated just how profound an effect nonverbal communication can have on people. The students conducted an experiment to test the unspoken rules of behavior on elevators. Boarding a crowded elevator, the students stood facing and grinning at the other people on board. Understandably, the people became uncomfortable;

1

one person even suggested that someone call 911 (Axtell 5–6). Why all the fuss? Unspoken elevator etiquette dictates that one should turn and face the door in a crowded elevator, being careful not to touch anyone else and honoring the sacred personal space of each individual by staring at the floor indicator instead of looking at anyone else. Although they are not written down, strict rules govern our behavior in public situations. This is especially true when space is limited, as on elevators, buses, or subway trains (Axtell 5–6).

Patricia Buhler, an expert in business management and associate professor at Goldey-Beacon College, confirms the large role nonverbal communication plays. She asserts that as little as 8 percent of the message we communicate is made up of words. We communicate the rest of our message, a disproportionately large 92 percent, with body language and other nonverbal forms of communication. While researchers have long known that nonverbal cues play a large role in communication, for many years they made no effort to learn more about them (Sielski). Amid rising public interest, several scientists pioneered new research in the field of nonverbal communication in the 1950s. Among these experts was anthropologist Edward T. Hall. He focused on a specific type of nonverbal communication called *proxemics*. Proxemics is the study of how people use space to communicate nonverbally. Whether we are conscious of it or not, our use of space plays a major role in our everyday interactions with others.

A review of some of Hall's main terms will help us better understand proxemics and appreciate just how much our use of space affects our relationships. For example, according to Hall, in our everyday interactions, we choose to position ourselves to create either "sociopetal" or "sociofugal" space. Sociopetal space invites communication; sociofugal space is the opposite—it separates people and discourages interaction (Jordan). A student in a school lunchroom may sit alone at an empty table in a corner, away from the other students (creating sociofugal space), or directly across from a person he would like to befriend (creating sociopetal space).

Hall identifies three kinds of general spaces within which we can create either sociofugal or sociopetal space. These are "fixed-feature space," "semi-fixed feature space," and "informal space" (Jordan). Fixed-feature spaces are hard, if not impossible, for us to control or change. For example, because my college English class is too small for the number of students attending, we have a hard time positioning ourselves so that we can all see the overhead projections. We cannot make the walls of the classroom bigger or the ceiling higher, and the overhead screen is likewise "fixed" in place. We must work within the constraints of the space. A semi-fixed feature space is usually defined by mobile objects such as furniture. The couches and chairs in a living room, for example, may face only the television, thus discouraging conversation and relationship building. But we are able to reposition the furniture to create a more social environment. Informal space is by far the easiest to manipulate. We each control our personal "bubble," and we can set distances between ourselves and others that reflect our relationships with them. Take, for example, the way that people approach their bosses. A man who is afraid of or dislikes his boss may communicate with her from as far away as possible. He might stand in her doorway to relay a message. Conversely, a woman who has known her boss for many years and is good friends with him might come right in to his office and casually sit down in close proximity to him. Individually, we have a great deal of control over our informal space, and how we use this space can speak volumes about our relationships with others.

After observing many interactions, Hall broke down informal 5
space further, identifying four distances commonly used by people in their interactions with others: "intimate distance," zero to one and a half feet; "personal distance," one and a half to four feet; "social distance," four to twelve feet; and "public distance," twelve feet and beyond (Beebe, Beebe, and Redmond 231). Intimate distance, as the name suggests, is generally reserved for those people closest to us. Lovemaking, hugging, and holding small children all occur in this zone. The exception to this rule comes when we extend our hand to perfect strangers in greeting, allowing them to briefly enter our intimate space with a handshake. Personal distance, while not as close as intimate, is still reserved for people we know well and with whom we feel comfortable. This zone usually occupies an area relatively close to us. It can at times be applied, however, to include objects we see as extensions of ourselves. For instance, while driving, we may feel our personal space being invaded by a car following behind us too closely. We see our own car as an extension of ourselves and extend our "personal bubble" to include it. Social distance is often considered a respectful distance and is used in many professional business settings as well as in group interactions. There is a public distance between a lecturer and a class, or someone speaking publicly from a podium and his or her audience.

In positioning ourselves in relation to others—especially in choos- 6
ing nearness or distance—we communicate respect or intimacy, fear
or familiarity. We can improve a friendly relationship simply by using
a warm, personable distance, or drive potential friends away by seeming cold and distant, or getting quite literally too close for comfort.
We can put people at ease or make them uncomfortable just by our
proximity to them. The study of nonverbal communication, and specifically proxemics, demonstrates the truth of the old adage, "Actions
speak louder than words."

WORKS CITED

Axtell, Roger E. *Gestures: The Do's and Taboos of Body Language Around the
World.* Wiley, 1998.
Beebe, Steven A., Susan J. Beebe, and Mark V. Redmond. *Interpersonal
Communication: Relating to Others.* 2nd ed., Allyn, 1999.
Buhler, Patricia. "Managing in the 90s." *Supervision,* vol. 52, no. 9, Nov.
1991, pp. 18–21. *EBSCOhost,* AN: 9611204565.
Jordan, Sherry. "Embodied Pedagogy: The Body and Teaching Theology."
Teaching Theology and Religion, vol. 4, no. 2, Dec. 2002, pp. 98–101.
Wiley Online Library, doi:10.1111/1467-9647.00100.
Sielski, Lester M. "Understanding Body Language." *Journal of Counseling
& Development,* vol. 57, no. 5, Jan. 1979, pp. 238–42. *Wiley Online
Library,* doi:10.1002/j.2164-4918.1979.tb05155.x.

Supervolcanoes: A Catastrophe of Ice and Fire

Jonathan Potthast

University of California, Riverside
Riverside, California

Jonathan Potthast approaches his essay from the assumption that although his audience may be completely unfamiliar with his subject—supervolcanoes—they will almost certainly be familiar with the concept of regular volcanoes. He begins his essay with a discussion of the more familiar phenomenon to introduce readers to the processes and effects that are shared between the two volcano types before building on this knowledge to explore the differences inherent in supervolcanoes. When readers are able to relate to a portion of the topic, they find it easier to engage with new information. How effective do you think Potthast is in guiding readers through the complexities of his topic? Consider how the title of this essay frames his discussion.

Possibly the most destructive natural disaster, short of a large asteroid   1
impact, would be the eruption of a supervolcano. Supervolcanoes are volcanoes that produce eruptions thousands of times the size of ordinary volcanoes. Like hurricanes, the power of volcanoes is measured using an exponential scale (see the *Volcanic Explosivity Index,* or *VEI,* in fig. 1).

A brief synopsis of the effects of regular volcanoes can provide   2
clues as to how destructive the eruption of a supervolcano would be. Volcanic eruptions feature several dangerous physical effects, including pyroclastic flows, pyroclastic surges, lahars, tephra falls, and massive amounts of fine ash particles in the air. Pyroclastic flows, which are dense superheated mixtures of ash, rock, and gas, are the most deadly feature of volcanoes. They are often as hot as 1,400 degrees Fahrenheit and flow at rates of hundreds of miles per hour, making

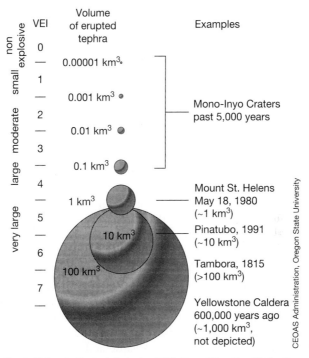

Fig. 1. Volcanic Explosivity Index (VEI). From "Eruption Styles." *Volcano World*. Dept. of Geosciences, Oregon State U and Oregon Space Grant Consortium, 2014. Web. 22 Dec. 2014.

prior evacuation the only possible means of escape. Driven by gravity, pyroclastic flows destroy everything in their path, and "they pose lethal hazard from incineration, asphyxiation, burial, and impact" ("Pyroclastic"). In the wake of the May 18, 1980, Mt. St. Helens eruption, a pyroclastic flow "swept down the mountain, flattening forests, overtaking escaping vehicles and killing several people who stood absolutely no chance of moving out of its path" ("Lahars").

In addition, by rapidly heating phreatic (underground) water, volcanic eruptions can trigger violent steam-driven explosions. The water from these phreatic eruptions can then combine with lava from pyroclastic flows to create devastating mudslides called *lahars*. (Rainwater or melting snow can also combine with lava flows to form lahars.) Lahars flow with enough force to uproot trees, carry away cars, and flatten buildings ("Lahars"). They flow much faster than humans can run, and can kill people instantly. When cooled, they solidify into a sort of concrete. For example, the eruption of Mt. Vesuvius in AD 79 produced lahars large enough to bury the entire city of Pompeii in what quickly became solid volcanic rock ("Lahars"). The most dangerous aspect of lahars, however, lies in their ability to form long after a volcanic eruption has apparently ceased, even after evacuated inhabitants have returned to their homes.

Pyroclastic surges, another devastating feature of many volca-   4
noes, are composed of gas and particles of volcanic ash, which move as quickly as pyroclastic flows but are less dense. P. J. Baxter, a physician specializing in occupational and environmental medicine at Cambridge University and a consultant to the World Health Organization on volcanoes, notes that humans exposed even briefly to pyroclastic surges face serious burns as well as risks of asphyxia (suffocation) and hypoxia (oxygen deprivation to body tissue). The extreme heat of the surges, if not hot enough to kill a person instantly, can kill a person by burning their lungs, throat, and windpipes so severely that those organs swell to the point of preventing any air from getting in.

Tephra falls, or showers of pieces of volcanic rock ejected from   5
a volcano, can also be deadly to those nearby. The sheer force of a tephra "rain" can cause roofs to collapse and people without shelter to be battered to death ("Hazards"). While tephra presents an immediate and short-lived danger, however, fine ash particles in the air cause more lasting damage. Heavy ash deposits can destroy vegetation, causing widespread famine and suffering to animals that depend on those plants for food. Inhaling fine volcanic ash can cause silicosis, an irreversible lung disease ("Hazards"). Ash particles also cause damage to moving parts in machinery and vehicles.

Aside from the obvious immediate destruction of these physical   6
effects, a volcanic eruption can also have a surprising aftermath. For example, following the 1996 Soufriere Hills volcano, hydrogen sulfide and sulfur dioxide (gases produced in the eruption) combined to form sulfuric acid; this, mixed with the rainwater, destroyed acres of cloud forest (Brosnan). Coral reefs could be destroyed in a similar manner.

Even more astounding, ash in the air after a volcano can tempo-   7
rarily cause dramatic changes to the climate. For instance, in the years following the eruption of Tambora in Indonesia on April 5, 1815, fine particles of volcanic ash and aerosols created a fog-like layer in

the atmosphere that blocked some of the sun's rays and led to temporary global cooling of about five and a half degrees Fahrenheit ("Mount Tambora"). In Europe and North America, 1816 became known as "the year without a summer"; the New England states, for example, experienced a "killing frost through June, July, and August" ("Mount Tambora"). Although "enough grains, wheat, and potatoes were harvested to prevent a famine," crops such as corn, beans, and squash were destroyed before they could be harvested, hay crops were meager, and "there were reports of people eating raccoons, pigeons, and mackerel" (Foster). Other recent major volcanoes, such as Krakatoa in 1883, have produced similar cooling effects: "On the average, temperature dropped by as much as 1.2°C in the succeeding year. In the years that followed, global climates were very erratic, stabilizing only 4 years after" (Villanueva).

Luckily, no supervolcano has erupted in recorded history. Several supervolcanoes exist today, but most are under the ocean, and all are considered dormant or extinct. According to the National Parks Service, a catastrophic eruption would probably provide a good deal—maybe even years—of advance warning, and other geologic events ("strong earthquake swarms and rapid ground deformation") would occur within days or weeks of the eruption (United States). 8

A dormant supervolcano close to home is in Yellowstone National Park. According to Joel Achenbach, a reporter on science and politics for magazines and newspapers such as *National Geographic, Slate,* and the *Washington Post,* three super-eruptions have occurred there, with one just 640,000 years ago (a blink of an eye in geologic terms). Even more powerful was a super-eruption 2.1 million years ago that "[left] a hole in the ground the size of Rhode Island" (Achenbach 1). The caldera, or crater, of the Yellowstone supervolcano is about 45 miles across, and over time, has been eroded and covered by glaciers and forests; part of the caldera's rim is invisible, hidden beneath the surface of Lake Butte. 9

It was thought that the volcano was extinct, but activity is making scientists rethink that view (Achenbach 2). A huge magma chamber lies deep under the volcano's caldera. When shifted by earthquakes and pressed by hot rock, the land above it rises and falls. An earthquake swarm in the mid-1980s made Yellowstone drop, so that it was about eight inches lower ten years later (Achenbach 2). More recently, "portions of the caldera have surged upward at a rate of nearly three inches a year, much faster than any uplift since close 10 observations began in the 1970's" (Achenbach 3). Such activity indicates a live volcano.

Although a catastrophic eruption is far from imminent, one is possible. If a supereruption were to occur here, the results would be devastating: A Yellowstone eruption, for example, could deposit a 10-foot layer of ash that would destroy vegetation 1,000 miles away. Toxic gases would sweep across much of the nation, making "two-thirds of the U.S. ... uninhabitable ... forcing millions to leave their homes" (Bates). Burning plants would generate vast amounts of carbon dioxide that would increase the greenhouse effect and ultimately contribute to global warming, but the immediate effect of a supervolcanic eruption would be dramatic global cooling. While Tambora created a "year without summer," a supervolcanic eruption would "potentially plunge the Earth into years of 'volcanic winter'" (Achenbach 2). According to science writer Charles Choi, a supervolcanic eruption would have an impact comparable to that of a mile-wide asteroid, killing many millions of people and changing the entire global landscape.

11

WORKS CITED

Achenbach, Joel. "When Yellowstone Explodes." *National Geographic*, Aug. 2009, pp. 1–3.

Bates, Daniel. "Is the World's Largest Super-Volcano Set to Erupt for the First Time in 600,000 Years, Wiping Out Two-Thirds of the U.S.?" *Daily Mail*, 25 Jan. 2011, www.dailymail.co.uk/scienceandtech/article-1350123/World's-largest-volcano-Yellowstone-National-Park-wipe-thirds-US.html.

Baxter, P. J. "Blast, Burns, Asphyxia and Hypoxia: How Do Pyroclastic Surges Damage Humans?" *Montserrat Volcano Observatory*, Michigan Tech. U, Dept. of Geology, www.montserratvolcano.org/humans.htm. Accessed 6 May 2014.

Brosnan, Deborah M. "Ecological Impacts of the Montserrat Volcano: A Pictorial Account of Its Effects on Land and Sea Life." *Sustainable Ecosystems Institute*, www.mona.uwi.edu/cardin/virtual_library/docs/1007/1007.pdf. Accessed 5 May 2014.

Choi, Charles Q. "Supervolcano Not to Blame for Humanity's Near-Extinction." *LiveScience*, TechMedia Network, 29 Apr. 2013, www.livescience.com/29130-toba-supervolcano-effects.html.

Foster, Lee. "1816—the Year Without Summer." *Climate Corner,* NOAA, Eastern Region Headquarters, www.ncdc.noaa.gov/rcsd/eastern/1816 -year-without-a-summer. Accessed 6 May 2014.

"Hazards Associated with Soufriere Hills." *Hazards Associated with Soufriere Hills,* vwsindia.org/6214/hazards_associated_with_soufriere_hills. Accessed 6 May 2014.

"Lahars and Pyroclastic Flows." *The Geography Site,* www.geography-site .co.uk/pages/physical/earth/volcanoes/pyroclastic%20flows.html. Accessed 5 May 2014.

"Mount Tambora." *Encyclopaedia Britannica,* 16 Oct. 2015, www.britannica .com/place/Mount-Tambora.

"Pyroclastic Flow Hazards at Mount St. Helens." *USGS: Volcano Hazards Program—Mount St. Helens Hazards,* U.S. Geological Survey, 22 Jan. 2013, volcanoes.usgs.gov/volcanoes/st_helens/st_helens_hazard_77.html.

United States National Park Service. "Yellowstone Volcano: Frequently Asked Questions." *National Park Service, U.S. Dept. of the Interior,* 29 Apr. 2014, www.nps.gov/yell/learn/nature/volcanoqa.htm.

Villanueva, John Carl. "Mount Krakatoa." *Universe Today,* 18 Sept. 2009, www.universetoday.com/40601/mount-krakatoa.

Therapeutic Cloning and Embryonic Research

Etoria Spears

University of California, Riverside
Riverside, California

Is it possible to explain a controversial topic without allowing personal biases to show? When Etoria Spears explains the concept of "embryonic research," she asks her readers to consider a newborn baby who has contracted an incurable disease. Is this introduction meant to establish some sensitivity toward the benefits of embryonic research, or is it intended to open dialogue? Spears also presents reasons one might oppose the concept. As you read, consider how you might have written about a multifaceted issue such as this. If you were writing about a controversial topic, what focus might you take, and how might you establish your authority on the subject without appearing biased?

Imagine the joy of having your first child. Hundreds of emotions run through your mind as you hold the tiny newborn in your arms. You wonder many things: Will I be a good parent? Can I support my child properly? Will I be able to give her all the love and attention she needs and deserves in order to grow into a strong adult? Such questions are common when it comes to raising a child. However, few can bring themselves to consider how they would feel if they learned their infant had a life-threatening disease for which there was no known cure.

Unfortunately, this was the case for Roger and Helen Karlin, whose daughter Lindsay Faith was diagnosed with the unique and fatal Canavan disease at the young age of three months. Canavan is a neurological disease in which the brain deteriorates at such an alarming rate, its victims usually die before reaching their teen years (Donegan). Upon discovering there was no known cure for their daughter's condition, the Karlins turned to gene therapy treatment to save their daughter's life. The treatment was intended to replace damaged brain cells with replicated ones created from stem cells. However, this would prove difficult because "scientists have had unexpected difficulty getting healthy genetic material to transfer successfully and remain functional in the living cells of patients suffering from genetic diseases" (Donegan). The odds of success were very slim, but they decided to pursue the treatment in hopes of buying Lindsay some time (Donegan).

The story of the Karlin family's struggle with Lindsay's disease is just one of many cases that consider therapeutic cloning as medical treatment. "Therapeutic cloning" is defined as the cloning of human embryos in order to acquire stem cells for medical research. Stem cells, also called "master cells," are essentially blank slates with the ability to take the form of any type of cell present in a tissue. For example, a stem cell that is introduced to the tissue of the liver would take the form of a liver cell. Scientists hope to use cloned cells to replace damaged or dying cells in the human body. The ability to do so has the potential to cure hundreds of diseases, including Alzheimer's, Parkinson's, and diabetes. This form of cloning is very different from reproductive cloning, which is intended for creating new beings. However, the process of harvesting the stem cells required is exactly the same. Stem cells are obtained via somatic cell nuclear transfer, also called SCNT. An egg is stripped of its genetic material by removing DNA from the nucleus. The desired DNA is then inserted into the egg, which is given an electric shock to promote cell division. After about four to five days, the egg reaches the blastocyst stage and stem cells can be harvested by destroying the embryo (Hansen). Although the research could contribute a great deal of knowledge to the scientific field, many find it controversial due to the destruction of the embryo to reach the stem cells within.

It is not uncommon for groundbreaking research such as therapeutic cloning to raise a few eyebrows. Despite the possible benefits that could be gained, many people are hesitant to support this technology, mainly because of the debate over the moral status of an embryo. In general, there are three different views on this matter: the no-moral-status view, the middle view, and the equal-moral-status view (Chan 107). The aim of presenting the three views is to explain each of them respectively, not to grant authority to one view over another (107).

The no-moral-status view holds that the embryos created for 5
therapeutic cloning have absolutely no moral status whatsoever
(Chan 108). One argument supporting this view suggests that
these specific embryos lack key traits of human embryos that would
develop into actual people, namely the fact that they are unfertilized
(108). Therefore, not only is this kind of embryo exempt from the
moral status of a human being, but it has even less moral status than
a fertilized embryo. Its purpose is for research, proponents of this
theory say, not for producing life, so there is no room to argue if it
has any moral status at all (108).

The middle view offers an understanding between those of no 6
moral status and equal moral status. The middle view suggests that
although an embryo does not share the same status as a human
being, it still deserves respect as a form of human life (Chan 110).
This view permits distinction from an embryo and a person because,
unlike people, supporters of the middle view say, there is no evidence
that embryos can think or feel (110). At the same time, it can be
said that embryos are a form of life and should be regarded as such,
not merely things to be used at our disposal (110). With that in
mind, some may still not be convinced it is morally permissible to use
unfertilized embryos for research.

The final view is that of equal moral status. In this case, regard- 7
less of the fact that an unfertilized embryo will never be a person, the
embryo still has complete moral status as if it were a living, breath-
ing, human being. For advocates of this view, there is no question
as to the ethics of embryonic research: It is absolutely unacceptable.
Under no circumstances would scientists have a right to destroy an
embryo, fertilized or not, for the sake of research or advancements in
medicine. Some even go so far as to call it murder.

How one regards the moral status of the human embryo varies 8
based on one's personal beliefs and choices. In the past decade, scientific discoveries have advanced our knowledge in leaps and bounds.
The new information we have gained has brought us one step closer
to curing some of the most devastating diseases known to man.
However, as innovative as this technology may be, there is constant
disagreement over if and how it should be used. Regarding the use of
therapeutic cloning to treat illnesses, the main issue is the moral status of the human embryo. Some claim it has no moral status, others
feel it deserves our respect as a form of human life, and still others
believe it's the same as a person and should not be used for research.

While the debate rages on, people around the world will continue to suffer until a verdict is reached or another solution is found.

WORKS CITED

Chan, Jonathan. "Therapeutic Cloning, Respect for Human Embryo, and Symbolic Value." *The Bioethics of Regenerative Medicine,* edited by King Tak Ip, Springer, 2008, pp. 107–16.

Donegan, Craig. "Gene Therapy's Future." *CQ Researcher,* vol. 5, no. 46, Dec. 1995.

Hansen, Brian. "Cloning Debate." *CQ Researcher,* vol. 14, no. 37, Oct. 2004.

The Disorder That Hides Within

Max Wu

University of California, Riverside
Riverside, California

Max Wu approaches his essay from the assumption that although his subject—mental illness—might be difficult for his audience to identify with, they will almost certainly understand the nerves associated with public speaking. Wu then compares this common fear with its more extreme version, social phobia. When readers are able to relate to this disorder, they become curious and want to understand it better. Once Wu has engaged his readers' interest, he considers current scientific research in the field. How effective do you think Wu is in narrowing such a large concept? Consider how the title of this essay frames Wu's discussion.

Are you afraid of speaking in front of an audience? Do you get jitters and "butterflies in your stomach" as you approach the stage with weak knees? "Yes," he says. "Of course, all the time," she replies. Do you feel that your general social performance in the world is so inadequate that you escape any and every instance where you might face public scrutiny? Ask this question and the room goes quiet. The fact of the matter is, most people get nervous and loathe the idea of public speaking, but some people feel nervous in every social situation. This fear of social scrutiny is referred to by mental health professionals as "social phobia." What separates common stage fright from social phobia is that social phobia is a crippling disorder that can obstruct a healthy lifestyle. However, it is easily treated once the individual realizes he or she needs help.

Social phobia is difficult to diagnose because of the way patients seem to subconsciously mask their abnormal behavior and practices. In an article written for the *Irish Times,* Marie Murray describes in great detail the actions that many patients practice that make it hard for the outside world to spot a problem. A clinical psychologist at University College Dublin, Murray has observed many students with social phobia and has made some breakthrough discoveries that have helped doctors around the world deal with the mystery surrounding social phobia. An unfortunate facet of social phobia that Murray observes is that "people become trapped by their false belief of how they appear to other people and . . . are unable to see evidence of when they are being successful in social encounters" (11). People with social phobia have a distorted view of the world that develops over time to a point where they become clinically depressed and believe that the world is against them. This hazy view of the world grows day by day as normal conversation becomes interpreted as personal attacks time and time again.

Murray also observed that patients with social phobia engage in activities that they feel make them more confident but in reality distance them from others and end up hurting their own psychological well-being. Murray knows this disorder is incredibly difficult to cope with and feels that the most important step in curing these people is to allow them to identify their own fears and understand that these fears are common and possible to be overcome. 3

J. A. den Boer, a professor of psychiatry and author of an article on social phobia in the *British Medical Journal,* has dedicated a large part of her career to research about social phobia. Through her numerous studies, she concludes that "social phobia is a poorly investigated and misunderstood condition" (796). She finds that social phobia starts when a child is under five years old and "may abruptly follow a stressful or humiliating experience" (797). After years and years of these unfortunate experiences, "the course of the disease is lifelong and unremitting unless treated" (797). Many patients who suffer from the disorder do not realize that the pain they have to endure is that of social phobia and thus further delay their treatment, which den Boer claims leads to increased risks of suicide (798). 4

Social phobia has not been well documented in the past or well diagnosed, but proper diagnosis and treatment are possible. In order to properly diagnose a patient, doctors need to pay close attention to the patient's medical history for any sign of events that might have triggered symptoms of the condition. *The Diagnostic and Statistical Manual of Mental Disorders,* or *DSM-III-R,* published by the American Psychiatric Association, issues criteria that must be met to diagnose social phobia. Drawing from the *DSM-III-R,* a doctor would 5 ask questions about how the patient would deal with certain social situations and the responses would determine the severity of the disorder.

After a patient realizes that something must be done to free his or her life from social phobia, what treatments are available? What can be done to free a mind from deep-seated nervousness and fear of humiliation that it has grown to accept? One promising form of treatment is being developed in Australia by Professor Gavin Andrews, the head of the clinical research unit at St. Vincent's Hospital (Fallon 16). Andrews invented a character named John, a first-year college student with social phobia. John has trouble going to class and surviving at school because of the overwhelming case of social phobia that haunts his daily life. By using this generic character in an online treatment program, Andrews manages to help those who feel trapped in their lives but would never have surfaced to receive treatment for their crippling disorder. Using "online exposure therapy, computer-aided training programs, virtual reality technology and enhanced cognitive behavioral therapies," Andrews successfully treated the almost 550 patients he received in the first year of his online treatment program, curing half of them completely (Fallon 17). It can be difficult for sufferers to seek treatment. In a study Andrews conducted in 2004, he found that 24 percent of Australians with agoraphobia (the fear of public places) and 7 percent of Australians with social phobia surfaced to receive medical attention from professionals (Fallon 17). The disorder is not difficult to cure, but sufferers must first confront their fears before they can find lasting relief.

Although social phobia was not well documented or often diagnosed in the past, doctors are becoming increasingly aware of how to identify and treat the disorder. Today, numerous treatment strategies exist, and sufferers are finding relief. Hopefully soon, the excessive fear of social situations will plague only a scarce minority.

WORKS CITED

den Boer, J. A. "Social Phobia: Epidemiology, Recognition, and Treatment." *British Medical Journal*, vol. 315, no. 796, Sept. 1997. *BMJ*, doi:10.1136/bmj.315.7111.796.

Fallon, Mary. "When Fear Takes hold." *Sydney Morning Herald*, 1 June 2009, www.smh.com.au/education/when-fear-takes-hold-20090528-bodw.html.

Murray, Marie. "Anxiety Disorder Leaves You in Fear of Social Situations." *The Irish Times*, 1 Apr. 2008, www.irishtimes.com/news/health/anxiety -disorder-leaves-you-in-fear-of-social-situations-1.908814.

The Art and Creativity of Stop-Motion

William Tucker

University of California, Riverside
Riverside, California

For this assignment, William Tucker knew that he wanted to write about film or animation, but he realized that both "film" and "animation" were far too broad to cover in one essay. Instead, Tucker narrowed his topic to "stop-motion animation," a subcategory that caught his interest. Although stop-motion animation is one of the oldest techniques in film animation, it is still popular both on the big screen and on YouTube. Tucker explains the concept by defining it, explaining its history, narrating the process used to make stop-motion films, and providing examples of popular stop-motion films. The enthusiasm for stop-motion Tucker developed while writing this essay ultimately led him to make his own film. Consider whether Tucker's enthusiasm is contagious: Does his explanation of stop-motion animation inspire you to try your own hand at it?

Cinematography and filmmaking are present everywhere today. It is 1
virtually impossible to go about your day without occasionally seeing a motion picture, whether it is a sitcom, an advertisement, or an instructional video. The process of producing films has changed in the past century, and many techniques have been invented and perfected. One style of film in particular has proven to stand the test of time. The style can be seen in popular productions such as *Gumby*, *Chicken Run*, *Fantastic Mr. Fox*, and the original *Godzilla* and *King Kong* movies. It played a key role in the origin of film and continues to be a relevant art form in the filming community, used both by famous Hollywood directors and by independent film students alike. It inspires creativity. This style, stop-motion film, is a critical part of film and cinematography.

Stop-motion, also known as frame-by-frame film production, is   2
an animation technique in which a still camera photographs an object
that is moved very small distances at a time. When these still images are
played back quickly, they create the illusion of movement. The frame
rate, or FPS (frames per second—the speed at which the individual
photos are shown during the sequence), varies. The original stop-motion films usually never reached over 20 FPS because of the limitations
of older technology (Johnson). However, today most stop-motion films
vary from 25 FPS to as high as 30 FPS, depending on how quickly the
director wants the inanimate object to appear to move (Johnson).

The technique of stop-motion is nearly as old as the motion pic-   3
ture itself. Albert E. Smith and J. Stuart Blackton are credited with
being the first to use the technique in their 1898 film, *Humpty
Dumpty Circus,* where toys and puppets appear to come alive on screen
(Delahoyde). Stop-motion grew in popularity, as it allowed directors
to depict fantasy and imagination while still providing realistic-looking
scenes. For example, before computer-generated imagery (CGI), if a
director wanted to make a dinosaur movie, the director could dress
humans in dinosaur costumes, hire animators to create a hand-drawn
animated film, or use stop-motion with clay dinosaur figurines. Using
dinosaur costumes would be easier than using stop-motion, but it
would more often than not make the dinosaurs look tacky and unreal.
Hand-drawn animation is lovely, but two-dimensional. A stop-motion
film takes a long time and meticulous work to create, but it capti-
vates audiences with its more authentic and "real" look. During the
beginning years of animated film, stop-motion was critically acclaimed,
winning many Oscars in the animated-film categories.

Stop-motion animators soon began to use clay figurines as the   4
main focus in stop-motion films; this technique is now known as
claymation. Clay figurines allow inanimate objects to take on human-
like characteristics and are easy to manipulate quickly between individual photographs. Famous claymation stop-motion films include
the hit 1970s television show *Gumby* and the short film *Vincent,*
which helped a young Tim Burton attract the attention of Walt
Disney Studios (Delahoyde). Burton would go on to revolutionize
the stop-motion industry by crafting feature-length stop-motion
films, such as *The Night-mare before Christmas, James and the Giant
Peach,* and *The Corpse Bride.*

Stop-motion requires not only creativity but also patience and   5
precision. With stop-motion films now playing back at as high as

30 FPS, nearly nine thousand individual photographs are needed for just five minutes' worth of footage. Because of this, most stop-motion films, even those with a professional crew, are in production for as long as three years (Delahoyde). Stop-motion directors begin each scene by choosing an inanimate object to be the focus point of the scene. After the object is chosen, it is photographed and moved less than an inch between individual photographs. The camera is placed in a stationary position (a tripod is almost a necessity in order to keep the camera focusing on the same exact location for each photo) (Delahoyde). A major problem that stop-motion enthusiasts face is making sure that the backgrounds of frames are similar to one another. If the background is not exactly the same for each frame, noticeable errors like splotches and blurs can occur. Also, if the background is inconsistent, the film will look less convincing and may even give the audience headaches from the lack of visual consistency. For this reason, most creators shoot inside and make their own backgrounds, either by drawing one or by making a CGI-based background ("Stop Motion Filming Technique").

Those brave enough to shoot a stop-motion film outdoors must 6 take into account all the variables that can hurt the overall presentation of their film. If the film is being shot in a crowded place, the creator cannot allow pictures to be taken with people in the background. People in the background of the shot will cause inconsistency in the frames that will appear as colored splotches in the film, especially if the frame rate is extremely high ("Stop Motion Filming Technique"). Stop-motion directors must also take into account the weather and brightness of the outdoors. Since the process of taking photos for a stop-motion film takes an exorbitant amount of time, people making films may have to plan on being outdoors shooting a scene for many hours. Lighting changes as the sun moves throughout the day. If the outdoor scene doesn't have consistent lighting because of the sun's movements, the scenes may suffer from unwanted shadows and different lighting at separate points in the scene. Consistency and attention to detail are the foundations of stop-motion film. They are perhaps the most important factors separating professional stop-motion films from amateur films.

Stop-motion still plays a key role in the filming world today. It 7 has inspired new film art forms that are heavily used. For example, time-lapse photography is a well-known technique used in film to quickly show the passing of time. Stop-motion helped lead to the time-lapse technique by stringing together individual photographs in order to represent movement and time ("Introduction"). The time-lapse process does take longer than typical stop-motion. In time-lapse photography, a camera focuses on an object for as long as a year, taking pictures periodically of the slow changes that occur. Then the many pictures are played in quick succession to show the changes. Popular subjects include the growth and blooming of a flower, a day and night's worth of city traffic, and the movement of the sun and moon. These scenes in nature take anywhere from a day to an entire year to take place, but with time-lapse/stop-motion the entire process can be viewed in as little as ten seconds, which creates an interesting illusion for the audience.

Although newer forms of cinematography are constantly being invented and revised, stop-motion will forever be important in the film community. Although CGI has become the industry standard for movie animation, stop-motion is still flourishing. Popular sites such as YouTube allow creators to post original stop-motion videos; they can then be viewed by a wide audience. Some of the most popular films on the Internet today are stop-motion films, receiving hundreds of thousands of views daily. This art form will forever captivate viewers and inspire ingenuity, whether it is used for a simple amateur video or a feature-length film of epic proportions.

8

WORKS CITED

Delahoyde, Michael. "Stop-Motion Animation." *Dino-Source,* Washington State University, public.wsu.edu/~delahoyd/stopmo.html. Accessed 19 Mar. 2018.

"Introduction to Stop Motion Animation." *Dragonframe,* www.dragonframe .com/introduction-stop-motion-animation. Accessed 20 Mar. 2018.

Johnson, Dave. "Make a Time-Lapse Movie." *Washington Post,* 9 Nov. 2005, www.washingtonpost.com/wp-dyn/content/article/2005/11/08 /AR2005110800094.html.

"Stop Motion Filming Technique." *Animation 101,* ThinkQuest Library, 1999, wayback.archive-it.org/3635/20130831143030/http://library .thinkquest.org/25398/Clay/tutorials/stopmotion.html. Accessed 20 Mar. 2018.

"Tim Burton Talking about Animation." *Tim Burton Dream Site,* Minadream.com. Accessed 6 Nov. 2015.

Analyzing and Synthesizing Opposing Arguments 5

Every day, high-stakes issues fill the airwaves and the Internet and crowd the pages of newspapers and magazines. Most issues we only glance at, while a few may engage us deeply—either because we are curious or because we recognize that the outcome of those issues is important to us personally: Should college athletes be paid to play? Should candy-flavored e-cigarettes be banned? Should social media sites share users' data with researchers or businesses? Should phone and cable providers be able to charge Web users differently for different levels of service?

By definition, a controversial issue is unsettled, unresolved. A debate swirls around it. As we read or listen to this debate, we may be inclined at first to take sides. Often, however, if we pay closer attention, we realize that the issues aren't as black and white as they sometimes seem. In order to truly understand what's at stake and take a responsible position on an issue, we need to take some preliminary steps: Specifically, we need to analyze and explain the debate and then synthesize the various existing positions to forge connections and find common ground. We need to *explain* a topic to an audience, rather than taking a particular side.

The *analysis* and explanation of debates can be informative to readers who want to understand issues of the day. They can also clarify and even help resolve immediate dangers or crises in a business or corporation; inform debate in an elected governing body, like a city council or the U.S. Senate; or introduce newcomers to an ongoing debate among experts over an important academic discipline, like those from which you choose your college courses.

However, simply explaining the debate is not always enough. If we can identify points on which the stakeholders might be able to agree, we can move beyond analysis and toward *synthesis*. Essays that synthesize do not simply explain both sides or make arguments in support of one side or another; instead, they analyze the concerns shared by those who argue on either side and discuss ways in which seemingly irreconcilable positions might in fact be amenable to compromise or consensus, at least in part.

In "Analyzing and Synthesizing Opposing Arguments," you're asked to think more deeply about conflicting opinions. Instead of asking you to merely understand and then write about both sides of the issue, we encourage you to take a closer look into what each side has in common. If they truly had nothing in common, there would be nothing to argue about. What motivating forces are at work? What is at stake? And what shared values are driving the parties to argue? Essays that successfully analyze and synthesize employ certain basic features of the genre: an informative introduction to the issue and opposing positions; a probing analysis; a fair and impartial presentation; and a clear, logical organization.

You will encounter many disciplinary debates in your college career. By attempting to find the common ground behind these debates, you will hone your analytical skills and broaden your perspective, allowing you to imagine new solutions and acquire greater understanding of your field. Practice in explaining, analyzing, and synthesizing different positions will allow you to join the debate, arguing vigorously and responsibly in support of a position of your own.

Use the guidelines in the Peer Review Guide that follows to practice peer review using the essays in this chapter.

A Peer Review Guide

AN INFORMATIVE INTRODUCTION

Has the writer explained the issue and opposing positions clearly and in a way that will engage readers' interest?

Summarize: Briefly tell the writer what you understand the issue to be and what the opposing positions are.

Praise: Indicate where the writer does a good job explaining the issue, introducing the authors, or engaging readers' interests.

Critique: Describe any confusion or uncertainty you have about the issue, about why it is important, or about the positions the essays being analyzed take.

A PROBING ANALYSIS

Is the writer's analysis of the points of disagreement interesting and insightful?

Summarize: Tell the writer what you understand to be the points of disagreement and the areas of potential agreement.

Praise: Identify one or two passages where the analysis seems especially effective—for example, where the opposing arguments are shown to be based on similar motivating factors, such as a shared value or a common concern.

Critique: Identify places where additional details, an example or an illustration, or more explanation would make the analysis clearer. Let the writer know if you detect any other motivating factors that might be used to establish common ground.

A FAIR AND IMPARTIAL PRESENTATION

Has the writer represented the opposing arguments in a balanced, unbiased way?

Summarize: Circle the words used to describe the proponents, and underline the words used to describe their views.

Praise: Note any passages where the writer comes across as being especially fair and impartial.

Critique: Tell the writer if the authors and their positions are being presented unfairly or if one side seems to be favored over the other. Identify passages that seem critical of the proponents or their views, and suggest ways the writer could make those points less negatively, such as by using quotations to state criticisms or replacing negative words with neutral ones.

A CLEAR, LOGICAL ORGANIZATION

Is the essay clear and readable?

Summarize: Underline the thesis, and circle key terms that forecast the topics the essay will focus on. Then circle those key terms when they appear elsewhere in the essay.

Praise: Pick one or two places where the essay is especially clear and easy to follow—for example, where the writer has repeated key terms or synonyms for them effectively, or where the writer has used comparative transitions, such as *both* or *as well as* to signal similarity and *whereas* or *although* to signal differences.

Critique: Let the writer know where the readability could be improved—for example, where a topic sentence could be clearer or where a transition is needed. Suggest a better beginning or a more effective ending.

Gambling and Government Restriction

Luke Serrano

University of California, Riverside
Riverside, California

Discussions of governmental regulation versus personal auton-
omy can often become heated. In the case of gambling, is it the
government's role to prevent gambling addiction, or is it a matter
of personal responsibility? In this essay, Luke Serrano successfully
presents both sides of the argument as offered by a pair of psychologists and a financial analyst, but also finds a common thread: a
belief that compulsive gambling is real—and serious. As you read,
think about how harmful something has to be before you believe
the government should ban or regulate it.

People often look for sources of entertainment to temporarily take   1
their minds off responsibilities and problems. While some people
are satisfied with a simple game or television show, others have the
desire to make their entertainment even more interesting by investing money in it. Having something at stake in a game provides people with a rush that does not come from simply playing the game.
Archaeological evidence suggests that gambling dates as far back as
2300 bc to ancient China, India, Egypt, and Rome ("The History of
Gambling" 1). However, almost as long as there has been gambling,
there have been people trying to put an end to it. Authority figures have noticed that gambling can serve as a distraction that keeps
people away from what they are supposed to be doing. In medieval
England, gambling was outlawed when King Henry VIII discovered
that his soldiers were spending more time gambling than working on
drills and marksmanship (1). In the United States, gambling was outlawed in Nevada until 1931, when casino gaming was legalized and
Las Vegas began its rise as one of the largest gambling hot spots in

the world (1). It now brings in over $30 billion in revenue each year (Dunstan 2). Two main views have arisen concerning the influence gambling has had on people. Both sides believe government regulation has a great effect on gamblers, and that gambling addiction is a real problem that requires treatment. Their viewpoints diverge because one side believes that gambling causes serious problems and should be illegal; the other believes that gambling is not a problem and that restrictions do more harm than good.

Those who argue that gambling is a problem point to the personal and social issues created by those who gamble too much. Arnie and Sheila Wexler are both certified compulsive gambling counselors in New Jersey. Sheila developed the compulsive gambling treatment program at the New Hope Foundation in Marlboro, New Jersey (Wexler and Wexler 1). The Wexlers firmly believe that compulsive gambling is a disease similar to drug and alcohol addiction. They argue that "the disease can be much more insidious [than drug or alcohol addiction] because it is more difficult to detect and can have a more devastating effect on friends and families" (2). The devastating effects compulsive gambling can have on people have led the Wexlers to call for the outlawing of gambling in the United States.

Some people, however, believe that compulsive gambling is not a pressing issue. Quantitative analyst Guy Calvert represents a Wall Street firm and is an adamant believer that the growing prevalence of compulsive gambling is just an exaggeration (Calvert 1). In his essay "The Government Should Respect Individuals' Freedom to Gamble," Calvert says, "Individuals should not be prohibited from gambling just because some people find it addictive," and he claims the "dangers of prohibiting gambling outweigh the benefits" (1).

The argument for the prohibition of gambling is centered on the detrimental effects that gambling can have on people. The Wexlers argue that compulsive gambling is "a progressive disease" that goes through phases (3). The first phase of gambling addiction is the phase in which the gambler reports a series of wins or streaks. This phase can reoccur throughout the gambling addiction, but the initial win streak is the hook that draws the gambler in (3). This hook gives the gambler a taste of wealth and the illusion that the wealth and luck will continue. The next phase of compulsive gambling is the losing phase. The losing phase is the phase in which gamblers lose the money that they might have won and begin to chase their losses (3). At this point, the gambler begins to borrow money to cover bets that he or she cannot pay. This is when the desperation phase begins; it is the last phase, at which point the gambler will do anything to put down the next bet (3). Family, friends, and work no longer matter. The desire to get the same rush as from the first big win is the only thing that matters. Families are destroyed, friendships are ruined, and careers are lost because the gambler cannot go without betting long enough to take care of responsibilities. Studies estimate that "the number of compulsive gamblers in this country is between 10 million and 12 million, approximately 5 percent of the general population" (5). The sheer number of compulsive gamblers and the devastation that comes with them are the reasons that the Wexlers believe the only viable action is the prohibition of gambling.

In contrast to the prohibition argument, the no-restrictions argument says the prohibition of gambling would be detrimental to the United States. Calvert argues that measures to suppress gambling would "usher in a new era of public corruption, compromising the integrity of government officials, judges, and the police" (2). He gives the prohibition of alcohol as an example of what would happen if gambling became illegal (1). Crime would rise because of the underground lifestyle that is brought with illegal gambling. In addition to being harmful, Calvert says, the prohibition would be unnecessary because most people do gamble responsibly. Most people who go to casinos "are not crazed, welfare-dependent casino desperadoes; they are in many respects better off than the average American." Studies show that the average household income of casino players is 28 percent higher than that of the U.S. population (4). Gambling is used the majority of the time as a source of entertainment, not as a fix for the compulsive gambler. Furthermore, banning gambling would not deter the truly compulsive gambler (2). It is the nature of an addict to find the next fix no matter what the cost. Illegality would do nothing to stop the compulsive gambler, just as heroin's being illegal does nothing to stop the junkie. Like an alcoholic or a drug addict, a compulsive gambler has to want to get help to get better.

Although the two parties disagree on whether the government should regulate gambling, they do agree that compulsive gambling is a problem and an addiction. In one instance described by the Wexlers, a man came to a treatment center and seemed to be having withdrawal symptoms after a gambling binge. He had dilated pupils, he was sweating and shaking, and he suffered severe mood swings (2). The similarities between compulsive gambling and drug and alcohol addiction are undeniable. Calvert agrees, saying, "Pathological gambling can and sometimes does result in genuine human misery" (5). Both parties agree that this is a problem that needs to be solved.

People who have gambling problems need treatment because without it there is no stopping the addiction.

In 1996, members of an estimated 32 percent of all U.S. house-   7
holds gambled at a casino, amounting to about 176 million visits to
casinos (Calvert 2). In 2013, a report from the American Gaming Association indicated that 34 percent of Americans had visited a casino at
least once in 2012 ("2013 State of the States" 3). These staggering
numbers show that gambling has a great effect on Americans, whether it
is positive or negative, and it is here to stay. The arguments both for and
against gambling bring forth valid points. On the one hand, the prohibition argument claims compulsive gambling is a serious problem and
the only way to stop it is by prohibiting gambling completely. On the
other hand, the progambling supporters argue that gambling is a legitimate institution that provides entertainment and economic growth for
the United States; moreover, this party argues that the prohibition of
gambling would cause more harm than good for the American people.
Despite the different opinions that exist about gambling, it is a large part
of American recreation and is an issue that should not be taken lightly.

WORKS CITED

"2013 State of the States: The AGA Survey of Casino Entertainment."
    American Gaming Association, 31 May 2013, www.americangaming
    .org/research/reports/state-states-14.
Calvert, Guy. "The Government Should Respect Individuals' Freedom to
    Gamble." *Gambling,* edited by James D. Torr, Greenhaven P, 2002.
    Excerpt from "Gambling America: Balancing the Risks of Gambling
    and Its Regulation." *Policy Analysis,* no. 349, 18 June 1999. *Opposing
    Viewpoints Resource Center,* www.cato.org/publications/commentary
    /the-government-should-respect-individuals-freedom-to-gamble.
Dunstan, Roger. "Pivotal Dates in Gambling History." *American Gaming
    Association.* American Gaming Association, 2003, www.americangaming
    .org/newsroom/press-releases/pivotal-dates-in-gambling-history.
"The History of Gambling." *Gambling PhD,* 2003, gamblingphd.com
    /the-history-of-gambling.
Wexler, Arnie, and Sheila Wexler. "The Hidden Addiction: Compulsive
    Gambling." *Legalized Gambling,* edited by Mary E. Williams,
    Greenhaven P, 1999. Contemporary Issues Companion Ser. Rept. of
    "The Hidden Addiction." *Professional Counselor,* June 1997. *Opposing
    Viewpoints Resource Center,* ic.galegroup.com/ic/ovic/ReferenceDetails
    Page/introduction-to-addiction.

Virtual Reality?

Chris Sexton

University of California, Riverside
Riverside, California

In the past three decades, video games have evolved from simple side-scrolling, two-dimensional, eight-bit entertainment for children into cinematic, realistic, completely engaging environments for players young and old. As the quality of the technology has increased, so have the violence level and emotional intensity of many popular games. Parents and critics have been left to wonder whether this increased realism will blur the line for children between fiction and reality, and whether it could lead to real-world violence. And, although psychologists have studied the effects of video games on children, their results have been inconclusive.

In his essay, Chris Sexton presents the opposing viewpoints about video-game violence, and particularly about the *Grand Theft Auto* franchise. He outlines the history of the controversy and the range of opinions about violent video games. Although the sides disagree, he finds that they all support increased parental awareness of the content of video games. As you read, notice the variety of stakeholders that Sexton cites, and think about what their motivations might be.

A car whizzes through rush-hour traffic with the ferocity of an 1 uncaged lion, barreling over pedestrians like a student driver knocks around traffic cones. Following this car is a steadily growing armada of police cars. The driver of the car makes a series of sharp turns at a pace that would make a NASCAR racer jealous, knocking cars aside like tumbleweeds in the road. More and more police are joining the fray, and on the horizon, they have set up a roadblock to put an end to this rampage. The driver of the car tries to double back, but he is soon caught in a storm of twisted metal. He takes off in any direction he can go at lightning speed, and hits an oncoming car with extreme force. The police surround the car, and it is not long before the game ends and the perpetrator is shot dead.

This is not a scene from a car chase on the news but from a video game. Depending on your perspective, this is either compelling entertainment or a frightening depiction of murder and crime. A debate has raged on for over a decade now, with some claiming that video games like this have a detrimental effect on the development of children. Others believe that games are not behavior-altering and are an acceptable form of entertainment. While they have different perspectives on how violent games affect people, both sides of this issue agree on the need for a strong ratings system and parental responsibility.

Video-game violence came to the forefront of the news after the shooting at Columbine High School in 1999. When the perpetrators of this horrible crime were discovered to have been fans of the first-person shooter *Doom,* a violent science-fiction game with blood and gore, many were concerned that this game was the cause of it all. While both shooters had a variety of psychological issues, the fact that they were avid video-game players stuck out in the minds of many. Concerned parents believed there had to be a correlation between playing violent games like *Doom* and committing real-life violence. When *Grand Theft Auto III* was released in 2001, the issue got even more attention. Set in a fictional New York City, the game allowed players the freedom to kill civilians and police officers. Taking video-game violence from a science-fiction setting like *Doom* into a reality-based setting like *Grand Theft Auto* made parents' concerns even stronger.

The idea that video games are dangerous and cause violence, however, may be a misconception. According to a study from Swinburne University of Technology in Melbourne, Australia, only children who were already more predisposed to aggression reacted in a negative manner to video games ("Most Kids"). The researchers studied the behavior of 120 children aged eleven to fifteen after exposure to the violent game *Quake II,* and did not see adequate evidence that video games are a major factor in affecting behavior. In fact, as Professor Grant Devilly says, hyperactive children actually became less aggressive while playing violent games, and most children showed no negative or positive effects from the video games at all ("Most Kids"). In regard to the notion that video games cause violence, Devilly notes, "It's the only message parents have ever received and it's just not accurate" ("Most Kids").

Other studies have conflicted with this one, though. Research by Iowa State University psychologists showed that violence in the media, and specifically video games, had a behavioral effect on children ("ISU Psychologists"). They tested 161 nine- to twelve-year-olds, as well as 354 college students, and found that even depictions of cartoon violence could cause negative effects on brain development. They concluded that the act of intentionally harming another character in a game could affect behavior in the real world as well. While movies have for a long time shown graphic violence, the participant role that video games give players can affect their behavior in a way that movies and music do not. This study supports the notion that young children can become more aggressive in real life due to excessive video-game playing. However, research has not completely proven yet whether or not video games make young people more violent.

The video game depicted in the introduction of this essay is *Grand Theft Auto V,* released in 2013 by Rockstar Games for the Xbox 360, PlayStation 3, and PC. Games in the *Grand Theft Auto* series are "sandbox games," games that let players roam the virtual world and complete missions and objectives in any order they want. Players can do missions for a variety of people throughout the massive in-game city and do side quests (missions not essential to the main story), such as street races and vigilante hunts. Unfortunately, giving players this much freedom in a game where violence is necessary to complete missions also allows them to commit heinous crimes against innocent in-game bystanders. The series is acclaimed by video-game players and critics, but this acclaim has not come without controversy.

The *Grand Theft Auto* series has for a long time been the target of scorn from a range of critics, from concerned parents to former secretary of state Hillary Clinton. In Clinton's 2005 speech to the Kaiser Family Foundation, she bemoaned the "demeaning messages about women" in games like *Grand Theft Auto,* and said that the game "encourages violent imagination and activities." Clinton was concerned that the omnipresence of the media is detrimentally affecting children. Their "steady diet" of violent material is desensitizing them to violence. She does not single out video games, however, also criticizing the Internet for giving children easy access to violent and pornographic material. She acknowledges that parental responsibility is an important solution to this problem, but claims that parents cannot do everything by themselves: "Parental responsibility is crucial but we also need to be sure that parents have the tools that they need to keep up with this multi-dimensional problem" (Clinton).

David Trend, a professor at the University of California, Irvine, does not see the correlation between fictional and real-life violence. Trend, author of *The Myth of Media Violence,* explains that exposure to violence is nothing new. Violence is "deeply ingrained in our culture," and is an important part of storytelling in anything from television shows to religious texts like the Bible and the Koran (Trend 3). Video-game violence is no different from the violence that is a central part of human history. Trend believes that eliminating forms of violent entertainment is not a feasible plan: "Getting rid of offerings like *Fear Factor* and *The Amityville Horror* on the basis of violence alone would also rule out important films like *Saving Private Ryan, Schindler's List,* or *Hotel Rwanda*" (4). While *Saving Private Ryan* is a movie that shows intense violence, it is also mostly historically accurate and conveys an important message about war and sacrifice. Would it be right to shield people from a movie that many agree is a classic just because it shows us the unfortunate truth of war? 8

This argument can be applied to video games as well. *The Call of Duty* series is a good example of this. The series explores conflicts from World War II all the way up to the current unrest in the Middle East. It shows players an in-depth look at the horrors of war, and that includes graphic violence. Although violent, games like this are often surprisingly historically accurate and can be a learning experience for the player. 9

Although people on both sides of this issue seem to be set in their opinions, they both see the need for parents to be informed about the video games their children play. Both sides support the ESRB, the Entertainment Software Ratings Board, which provides ratings for video games that are much like the ratings for movies. Retailers like Target and Walmart, who are on the ESRB Retail Council, have a strict policy against selling Mature-rated games (the equivalent to an R-rated movie) to people under seventeen years old without a parent present ("ESRB Retail Council"). While this policy is not required by law, it is widely supported because it gives parents a way to monitor the games that their children are playing at home. 10

Parental responsibility is an important part of the issue of video- 11
game violence. While some people act like violent games like *Grand
Theft Auto* and *Call of Duty* just fall out of the sky into the hands of
children, it is ultimately up to parents to decide what is and is not
allowed. If parents believe that their child is not mature enough to play
violent games, it should not be the game developer or government's
job to keep the game out of the house. Instead, the parents should
closely monitor the games they are buying for their family. Every game
has a rating on the front and back of the box, as well as descriptions of
exactly why the game got this rating. For example, the Mature-rated
game *Gears of War 3* is rated M for "Blood and Gore, Intense Violence,
and Strong Language." Parents can see this just by looking at the box,
allowing them to easily decide if the game is right for their family.

Both sides of this contentious issue acknowledge that parental 12
responsibility is extremely important, and the ESRB ratings system
makes things easier on parents. Since research has not proven either
way whether video games are harmful to children, it is still a judgment
call for parents. The more information is readily available about video
games, the fewer misconceptions there will be about their effects.
More resources for parents will hopefully make video games less of a
scapegoat in the future and satisfy people on both sides of this issue.

WORKS CITED

Clinton, Hillary. "Speech to Kaiser Family Foundation Upon Release
of Generation M: Media in the Lives of Kids 8 to 18." Kaiser Family Foundation, 8 Mar. 2005, Washington, DC, votesmart.org
/public-statement/83593/senator-clintons-speech-to-kaiser-family
-foundation-upon-release-of-generation-m-media-in-the-lives-of-kids
-8-to-18#.WrvfoIjwaUk.

"ESRB Retail Council." *Entertainment Software Ratings Board,* www.esrb
.org/retailers/retail_council.aspx. Accessed 17 Nov. 2015.

"ISU Psychologists Publish Three New Studies on Violent Video Game
Effects on Youths." Iowa State University, 22 Mar. 2007, www.news
.iastate.edu/news/2007/mar/vvg.shtml.

"Most Kids 'Unaffected' by Violent Games." *Sydney Morning Herald,* 1 Apr.
2007, www.smh.com.au/news/National/Most-kids-unaffected-by-violent
-games/2007/04/01/1175366055463.html.

Trend, David. *The Myth of Media Violence: A Critical Introduction.*
Wiley-Blackwell, 2007.

Are Laissez-Faire Policies to Blame?

Matthew Chrisler

University of California, Riverside
Riverside, California

The following essay does a great job of both clarifying an often confusing topic—laissez-faire economics—and investigating two differing perspectives on a frequently debated issue. Matthew Chrisler wrote this piece shortly after the financial crisis of 2008. Notice how, despite widespread frustration at the time, Chrisler was able to consider two opposing viewpoints without injecting his personal opinion—his tone remains balanced and thoughtful throughout. Because Chrisler remained impartial, his readers trust that he is presenting both sides accurately. After reading his essay, consider whether you think Chrisler was successful at maintaining a logical approach and refraining from taking a position on this issue.

Due to the recent collapse of credit and other economic troubles, 1 many scholars have devoted themselves to analyzing the roots of the current market problems. Two papers illuminate polar points of view on the issue of whether "laissez-faire" economics is responsible for the current credit crisis. George Reisman's blog entry "The Myth That Laissez-Faire Is Responsible for Our Financial Crisis" argues that laissez-faire systems are not responsible because they do not exist; "The Conservative Origins of the Sub-Prime Mortgage Crisis," an article by John Atlas, argues that laissez-faire is indeed the reason we face the current global crisis. The two papers touch on what constitutes laissez-faire economics, government regulation and deregulation, subprime mortgages, the Federal Reserve, and congressional acts, as well as historical trends in the economy.

"Laissez-faire," or *hands-free* in French, is the economic school 2 of thought that promotes little to no government interference in an economy. Taking the definition literally, George Reisman asserts that laissez-faire market conditions do not exist in the modern economy. In contrast, Atlas argues that any movement toward less regulation, or the act of deregulating an industry, is laissez-faire in principle, and the ideal laissez-faire economy does not have to exist for an action to be considered as such. In support of his claim, Reisman's main argument is that after the Great Depression and the creation of governmental banking regulations, increased taxes, farm subsidies, apartment rent controls, and a veritable alphabet soup of regulatory agencies, America ceased to be a laissez-faire nation in any sense of the word. Conversely, Atlas, building off their argument that a move toward deregulation is laissez-faire economics, assert that America has had a long tradition of regulation tied with economic prosperity until the 1980s, during which deregulation of industries caused a period of economic distress. Reisman conflicts with Atlas on many levels because of differing opinions on what it means to be "laissez-faire."

The two articles present opposing perceptions of the magnitude and benefits of government interference in markets. Reisman places blame for the recent financial crisis on the increased meddling of government in the market, while Atlas argues that it was the deregulating of certain markets that led to today's crisis. According to Reisman, much of the crisis was caused by a combination of the Community Reinvestment Act and the government guarantee on loans. The Community Reinvestment Act mandated that banks make loans to low- and moderate-income borrowers who would normally not qualify for a loan. In addition, the government would guarantee the mortgages of these low-income borrowers, creating a perfect niche for the subprime lenders. Because these bad loans were guaranteed by the government, subprime lenders sought profits by making loans at exceedingly high interest rates, using bait-and-switch tactics and devious contracts to entice low-income borrowers to take out loans. On the other hand, Atlas gives evidence that deregulation is responsible for the rise of the housing crisis, which spawned the financial crisis. In the 1980s, banks lobbying Washington were able to push back the regulations that prevented banks from investing in private markets and making loans. After this deregulation occurred, a massive increase in loans was recorded, leading to a bust. Because no regulations were enforced, banks were able to make high-risk, high-interest loans to those who would normally be excluded, leading to the take-off of the subprime market. According to Atlas, a plethora of banks—including Countrywide, Washington Mutual, and Lehman Brothers—were responsible for almost two-thirds of subprime loans. Atlas shows that large banks, as the backers of these loans, are not blameless.

Using different information, the two articles present differ- 4 ent arguments regarding the government's role in the crisis. Reisman asserts that through overregulation of the housing market, the government inadvertently caused the current crisis. However, Atlas argues that because the government deregulated the banking industry in the 1980s, the subprime lenders were left free to practice predatory lending.

Separate from government, which controls monetary policy, 5 are the actions of the Federal Reserve, which controls fiscal policy. Criticism coming from both sides focuses on the actions of the Federal Reserve and its chair, Ben Bernanke. They differ mainly in their opinion of whether it was laissez-faire or regulatory policy that was responsible for the Reserve's recklessness. Reisman bases his argument on the Federal Reserve's control of the nation's banking interest rates, which is essentially the interest rate at which banks lend one another money. Reisman asserts that the actions of the Federal Reserve were extremely irresponsible, because its use of the federal interest rate is responsible for much of the credit crisis. In the years just before the crisis, the Federal Reserve continually lowered the federal interest rates in order to encourage people to take out money. The Fed also lowered the Federal Reserve ratio, or the percentage amount banks had to guarantee on a given deposit. The Federal Reserve hoped to increase the overall amount of capital in the market by means of the money multiplier. When there are low interest rates, and the Federal Reserve ratio is low, more capital, or credit, is available at a lower cost, which leads to a marked increase in loans. As Reisman explains, "In recent years, the Federal Reserve has so encouraged this process that checking deposits have been created equal to fifty times the actual cash reserves of the banks, a situation more than ripe for implosion."

However, when the federal interest rate decreased to the point 6 where the overall increase in prices, or inflation, was greater than the interest rate, banks started losing money on loans, because they would be paid back in money that was worth less. Combined with the rapid bust of the real estate market, banks became fearful of lending money to large businesses and private investors because the loans would usually end in foreclosure or a net loss for the bank. According to Reisman, this led to the large freeze in loans, which in turn contributed to the current chaos in today's markets. Much in the same vein as their other arguments, Atlas argues that the lowering of the interest rate is not government regulation but the absence of enforcement of the spirit of regulation. Again they stress that a move toward deregulation is a move toward laissez-faire economics, therefore reflecting the blame onto proponents of hands-off economics. On this subject the two articles do not contest information but instead provide different perspectives on the same data.

The question of whether or not laissez-faire economics is responsible for the current economic crisis is one that cannot be decided in two articles, or even through a detailed study of the current economy. Reisman and Atlas presents convincing arguments on both sides of the question but leave a lot of questions unanswered. Most important to many millions of people in the United States is, Where do we go from here? Both articles agree that while the causes are muddled, an answer needs to be forthcoming, and soon. Because their views are informed by different values and different information, they understandably differ on what that solution should be. However, as with the aftermath of the recent election, there is no time for division, recrimination, or revenge; the authors of these papers all agree that a unified solution based on sound economic principles rather than ideological positions should be implemented to relieve the economic pressures on the United States.

WORKS CITED

Atlas, John. "The Conservative Origins of the Sub-Prime Mortgage Crisis." *The American Prospect,* 17 Dec. 2007, prospect.org/article /conservative-origins-sub-prime-mortgage-crisis-0.

Reisman, George. "The Myth That Laissez-Faire Is Responsible for Our Financial Crisis." *George Reisman's Blog on Economics, Politics, Society, and Culture,* Blogspot, 21 Oct. 2008, georgereisman.com/blog/2008 /11/myth-laissez-faire-responsible-our-present-crisis-or.html.

Criminal DNA Databases: Enhancing Police Investigations or Violating Civil Rights?

Brittany Koehler

Oakland Community College, Orchard Ridge
Farmington Hills, Michigan

To capture reader interest and establish the timeliness of her topic, Brittany Koehler frames her essay with a reference to popular TV crime shows, then attempts to show her audience the relevance of this subject by detailing how these fictional scenarios may be more true-to-life than readers realize. When writing an essay that analyzes two opposing viewpoints, it is important to use quality research that equally represents both sides of the debate. Does Koehler succeed in finding common ground? How might additional information about the authoritative sources she cites make her essay more effective?

On television today, crime shows have captivated viewers' attention. 1
The ratings of shows like *CSI: Las Vegas, New York,* and *Miami; True Detective;* and all the *Law & Order* spin-offs that circulate on television have skyrocketed in recent years. On these shows, criminals are easily apprehended when police investigators enter fingerprints and DNA samples collected at a crime scene into a computer that matches them to a suspect's DNA or fingerprints in the computer's database. However, many people don't realize that having a DNA database is a very controversial issue.

DNA "fingerprinting" is a technique that police often use in their 2
investigations. A DNA sample is extracted from someone suspected of being involved in a crime; this is generally done by the removal of

cells from the cheek with a cheek swab. Police compare the DNA of a suspect with any genetic material removed from the scene of a crime. From here, police create profiles of the evidence collected from a crime scene or from the DNA samples removed from a suspect (Weekes 1).

In the United States, the profiles compiled by police investiga- 3 tors are added to the Combined DNA Index System (CODIS), a central database containing over a million DNA profiles. Created in 1994 with the DNA Identification Act, CODIS allows forensic pro- files to be inserted by every state in the United States of America. Not only are profiles added to CODIS, but police investigators are also able to search the database for possible matches to DNA col- lected from crime scenes ("Genetic" 7).

In the years since the creation of the DNA database, those peo- 4 ple who support the existence of CODIS have been pushing for its expansion. In 2003, President George W. Bush called for profiles to be created from all arrestees, including juveniles and illegal immigrants (Driscoll 2). However, there are many who feel that a DNA database is a violation of citizens' civil rights. The Electronic Privacy Informa- tion Center (EPIC) and the American Civil Liberties Union (ACLU) are two of the most vocal groups who strongly disapprove of CODIS.

John Pearson offers support in favor of DNA databases through- 5 out his essay "Counterpoint: The New Fingerprint: The Effectiveness of DNA Profiling." Sally Driscoll's essay "Point: DNA Profiling Is a Threat to Civil Rights" provides support for an opposing outlook on the debate. Both essays agree on the benefits that a DNA database would provide; however, they stand on opposing sides regarding the reliability of DNA in criminal cases and the efforts needed to protect the privacy of citizens.

The benefits of a DNA database are recognized on both sides of 6 the debate. Pearson claims that having a database of DNA profiles improves the "ability [of] investigators to track criminals" (3). He cites many benefits that have come from the creation of CODIS; for example, with the profiles from the database "about 7,000 previously unsolved criminal cases nationwide" have had suspects identified, and the Innocence Project "claims to have exonerated 131 people using DNA evidence as of August 2003" (4). Similarly, Driscoll agrees that there are benefits to having a criminal database of DNA. She admits that CODIS is "a proven crime-fighting tool" and has "helped bring closure to crime victims, their families, and the wrongly accused" (2). Both sides agree that acquitting the "wrongly accused" and solving previously unsolved cases are benefits of having a DNA database. However, while the benefits of a DNA database are great in number, the reliability of DNA in criminal cases comes into question.

The essays strongly disagree on how reliable DNA is in criminal 7 cases. Pearson deduces that DNA fingerprinting is more reliable than classic fingerprinting. He argues that DNA "degrades very slowly" and DNA evidence can be found in the form of any bodily fluid, skin, or hair—even teeth or bone (2). After declaring that DNA evidence can be extracted from "nearly any organic source," he points out that fingerprints "have to be isolated on a smooth surface to allow for a good impression" (2). Pearson also contends that criminals can easily avoid leaving fingerprints by wearing gloves, whereas an "offender would have to wear something akin to hazmat . . . to prevent any contact that would shed hair or skin cells or draw blood" (2). Pearson argues that police investigators are more likely to collect DNA samples at a crime scene than a usable fingerprint.

In contrast, Driscoll asserts that DNA evidence is not as reliable 8 as many people seem to believe it is. With DNA there is always the possibility for "corruption" and "misuse" (4). For support, Driscoll cites a research study performed by Stanford University that established that "as much as 3 percent of DNA samples have been mishandled" (4). She also states that not only can DNA be mishandled, but it can "easily be planted at a crime scene," whereas it is much more difficult to plant a fingerprint (4). These are not the only ways that Driscoll shows that DNA is not very reliable. She cites a case where an innocent citizen was implicated with DNA: "In one 'cold hit' DNA taken from a rape victim matched DNA in a database, except that it belonged not to the rapist, but to a man with whom the woman had consensual sex prior to the crime" (4). The collections of planted DNA, corrupted DNA, or DNA of innocent bystanders are all possible scenarios that would force one to question the reliability of DNA. How one feels about the reliability of DNA in criminal cases can factor into how one feels about the possible invasion of privacy that a DNA database could create.

Both sides have different ideas of how to protect the privacy of 9 citizens who could possibly be invaded through the establishment of a DNA database. Pearson mentions that "strict guidelines" were instituted to protect the "privacy of individuals" with the DNA Identification Act of 1994. According to Pearson, privacy is already extremely protected with "stiff criminal penalties facing those who would use such materials in violation of established laws" (3). He also argues that the DNA profiles are developed only "to the extent required for identification" (3). Those who would abuse the privacy of U.S. citizens with what little information is included in the DNA profiles entered into the DNA databases would be severely punished by the judicial system. However, Pearson admits that "at some point in the future . . . additional regulation in regard to individuals and corporations will be needed" (3).

On the other hand, Driscoll argues that the DNA database "infringes on [U.S. citizens'] constitutional . . . right to privacy" (2). Driscoll cites a court case that supports her claim: "In 2006, a Minnesota Court of Appeals determined that the routine collection of DNA from citizens who had been charged with crimes, but were either not convicted or proved to be innocent, is in violation of the Fourth Amendment to the U.S. Constitution" (2). The Fourth Amendment protects citizens against unreasonable searches and seizures, which are an invasion of a person's privacy; the Minnesota Court of Appeals felt that the DNA of those who had been arrested but not convicted fell under the protection of the Fourth Amendment. 10

Nevertheless, while there are differences of opinion on the reliability of DNA in criminal cases and the invasion of privacy that a DNA database would cause, both sides agree that having a DNA database would be beneficial. And as the debate of whether or not to have a DNA database continues, the techniques depicted on the crime shows *CSI* and *Law & Order* are currently becoming realities. 11

WORKS CITED

Driscoll, Sally. "Point: DNA Profiling Is a Threat to Civil Rights." *Points of View: DNA Profiling,* Points of Views Reference Center. *EBSCO,* 2007, www.ebsco.com/research-databases/points-of-view-reference-center /point/DNA profiling/driscoll.

"Genetic Privacy." *Electronic Privacy Information Center,* 8 Apr. 2008, www .epic.org/privacy/genetic.

Pearson, John. "Counterpoint: The New Fingerprint: The Effectiveness of DNA Profiling." *Points of View: DNA Profiling,* Points of View Reference Center. *EBSCO,* 2007, www.ebsco.com/research-databases /points-of-view-reference-center/point/DNA profiling/Pearson.

Weekes, Rob. "DNA Database for Criminals." *International Debate Education Association,* 4 Oct. 2001, idebate.org/debate-tags/dna-database.

Online Piracy: A David and Goliath Debate

Adam Hood

University of California, Riverside
Riverside, California

In this essay, Adam Hood takes a historical look at the origins of the debate over online piracy, exploring its origins in the music industry. As you read, notice how Hood presents the debate (and the debaters) to his readers in paragraphs 1–4 and avoids even a hint of which position he favors. Hood then goes on to explain the differences between the two positions in terms of the ethics of file sharing, the definition of music itself, and the consequences of attempting to prevent file sharing. He ends by connecting this early debate to the current state of online piracy. No mystery here — just impartial comparison and contrast of the major points he has identified in the two opposing positions.

———————————

Just six months after eighteen-year-old Shawn "Napster" Fanning   1
created the Internet file-sharing program that would rock the music world, his small start-up company was sued by the Recording Industry Association of America, whose claim was later backed by the United States 9th Circuit Court of Appeals (Ante). From the beginning, the file-sharing debate was a battle waged between the little guy and the big guy, and that has not changed since pirated movies and television joined music as likely candidates for file-sharing online. Both sides saw it this way, but in slightly different terms. From the standpoint of those who defended the practice of swapping files, the fight was between the "industry" and the common listener. From the perspective of those who opposed the practice, the fight was between defenders of justice and lawbreakers.

The debate also pitted the young and the old. According to the Pew Internet & American Life Project, it was young adults and full-time students who were—and are—among the most likely to download or share files—and the least likely to say they care about copyright (Madden and Lenhart). And it is college administrators and professors who have ended up joining forces with the courts and the media industries to control these file-sharing upstarts.

Enter Matthew Scrivner, a little guy (DOB 1976), and Graham Spanier and Cary H. Sherman, big guys (and graybeards). Scrivner, author of "In Defense of Music Downloading: Why Internet File-Sharing Is Necessary for the Survival of Music," did tech support by day and spent the rest of his time "hanging out"—reading, listening to music, watching movies, and playing Dungeons and Dragons—by his own account. Spanier and Sherman, coauthors of "Thou Shalt Not Pirate Thy Neighbor's Songs," were presidents: Spanier of Penn State University and Sherman of the Recording Industry Association of America.

The little/big, young/old split was not just a surface divide—it also extended to argumentative styles, if Scrivner's "In Defense" and Spanier and Sherman's "Thou Shalt Not" can be taken as representative approaches to either side of the debate. Scrivner argued as an underdog would, wrestling every point to the ground and seeming to make himself breathless with the effort to get his points across. Spanier and Sherman, on the other hand, argued from the secure vantage point of righteousness: They devoted more time to convincing their audience of university professors and administrators to take action against file-sharing on campus, and to showing them how, than to arguing explicitly against file sharing. Much of their argument was implicit.

Whether file sharing is unethical is central to the debate. Both Spanier and Sherman on the one hand and Scrivner on the other acknowledged the question's importance by addressing it right away, with Spanier and Sherman essentially saying "Of course it's unethical" and Scrivner protesting "Not so fast." Spanier and Sherman treated the question with cool confidence in their first paragraph, asserting that there had lately been "a new level of clarity"—the implication is moral clarity—on the issue of file sharing. They presented their case evenly and without embellishment: Thanks to a June 2005 ruling from that ultimate arbiter of ethics, the Supreme Court, the "message" on file sharing was officially more "straightforward" than ever: File sharing was "wrong," plain and simple (par. 1).

Recognizing that the appeal to ethics was one of his opponent's strongest hands, Scrivner set it up and knocked it down right away. His first two sentences got right to the point: "The record industry is lying to you. At the 46th Grammy Awards this month they announced a new initiative that would promote an 'ethical viewpoint about music downloading'" (par. 1). Notice how Scrivner located the ethical stance not in the ruling of the highest court in the land, as Spanier and Sherman did, but in the mouth of the record industry, where the "message" suddenly seemed nothing other than a public relations line. With this tactic, and by relating the industry to concepts such as "power" and "control" and pitting it against the average music listener ("you"), Scrivner managed to portray the music industry as a control-hungry behemoth with questionable motives. We would do well to have a healthy suspicion of its message, Scrivner seemed to be saying, and that early skepticism carried over into the debate as it continues to rage. A visit to a college campus today will find numerous students streaming pirated versions of the latest episode of *Game of Thrones* without the least bit of moral concern that they might be "stealing" from a powerful corporation.

With the underdog's typical all-out effort, Scrivner sweated to   7
establish a definition of music, stringing example to example and scenario to scenario in an attempt to communicate that music was just information, that tunes were just memes—germs of "intellectual infection," as he put it, passing through networks of people. Gathering momentum, he asks:

> A hundred years ago, if I heard a song at church, and rode my horse home and found myself humming it, I was stealing? And fifty years ago, if I heard a song on the radio, and it was so catchy that I found myself singing it out loud later on while I cooked dinner, I committed theft? And ten years ago, when I waited hours for the top 40 count down to play that one song just so I could tape it to cassette for my girlfriend, I was taking something that wasn't mine? (par. 6)

In establishing his definition of music (both here and elsewhere),   8
Scrivner keeps the focus on the listener and avoids mentioning those behind the music—composers, songwriters, singers—thus skirting the question of creative authorship.

At the outset of the debate, Spanier and Sherman (like Scrivner) also avoided addressing the question of creative authorship. Instead, they assume that the question of creative authorship had already been settled. When they asserted that "Stealing intellectual property is wrong" (par. 1), they assumed that readers already equated music with intellectual property. When they spoke of the necessity of fostering "an environment that respects all creative work" (par. 6), they assumed readers already thought of music as a form of creative work. They acknowledged no other viewpoints—perhaps it did not occur to them that they needed to. Like soft-spoken lecturers who hold sway over their students by sheer self-possession, Spanier and Sherman quietly bully their readers into sharing their definition of music.

Modern critics are more straightforward, and the question of   10 authorship and artistry has been brought to the fore more recently by anti-piracy advocates such as Harrie Tholen of NexGuard (a digital watermarking company), noting that "piracy also affects the unsung, talented, hard-working individuals behind today's box office hits" (qtd. in Strauss). The argument has evolved from rules for the sake of rules to rules for the sake of protecting artists and other contributors.

The counterpoint of the modern file-sharer has evolved as   11 well. Instead of making a simple point about freedom, the stance has become one of access. "If you force someone to go and find content," says Gavin Mann, managing director of broadcast for Accenture, "and they find pirate versions, all you are really doing is educating them into finding it illegally again next time. It's better to make it easily available" (qtd. in Strauss). Access (and ease of access) has replaced the vagueness of Scrivner's original doomsaying: "[Music] cannot be contained or controlled. Doing so kills it, and leaves us in nothing but silence" (par. 7). Unfortunately, the tension between artistry and access is still present, and so the debate continues, though perhaps more complicated for having spanned so many years and for having the roots of the conflict buried so far in the past.

Since Spanier, Scrivner, and Sherman first took up the file-sharing   12 debate about music, the debate not only has not been resolved but has expanded to include other media, such as movies, television, and images. Exploring the origins of the debate, however, might help each side better understand the foundational perspectives that are driving the conflict. Perhaps if each side acknowledges what matters most to the other, both sides will stop overcompensating with prophecies of the end of the world as we know it and be able to find a reasonable compromise.

WORKS CITED

Ante, Spencer E. "Shawn Fanning." *Business Week*, 15 May 2000, www .businessweek.com/2000/00_20/b3681054.htm.

Madden, Mary, and Amanda Lenhart. "Music Downloading, File-Sharing and Copyright: A Pew Internet Project Data Memo." *Pew Internet & American Life Project,* 31 Jul. 2003, www.pewinternet.org /2003/07/31/music-downloading-file-sharing-and-copyright.

Scrivner, Matthew. "In Defense of Music Downloading: Why Internet File-Sharing Is Necessary for the Survival of Music." *2 Walls Webzine,* 15 Feb. 2004, www.2walls.com/Music/defense_of_downloading.asp.

Spanier, Graham, and Cary H. Sherman. "Thou Shalt Not Pirate Thy Neighbor's Songs." *Chronicle of Higher Education,* 2 Dec. 2005, chronicle .com/weekly/v52/i15/15b02401.htm.

Strauss, Will. "Game of Thrones: Winter Is Coming . . . and So Are the Pirates." *IBC,* 13 July 2017, www.ibc.org/delivery/game-of-thrones -and-the-fight-against-illegal-streaming/2066.article.

Arguing a Position 6

If you're like most people, when you think of an "argument," you probably think of a disagreement. A constructive and reasoned argument, however, is something else altogether. A constructive argument is more thoughtful and less dramatic than the heated exchanges people have when they are upset; building such an argument can be both challenging and enjoyable.

The purpose of an argument essay is not to "win" but to present a thoughtful case that clearly supports your logic. In writing a reasoned argument, you must first examine all sides of the issue you're discussing: As you gain knowledge of your issue, you will move beyond what you've perhaps always thought about it, expanding your perspective in order to understand its advantages, drawbacks, and ambiguities. When you fully understand all aspects of your subject (including opposing viewpoints), you are better equipped to present a logical argument. By anticipating other positions, accommodating those you find plausible, and refuting those you find flawed or weak, you construct an effective argument.

When you have strong feelings about an issue, it can be easy to overlook or dismiss positions that differ from your own. A good argument, however, demonstrates that it is possible to respect those who hold different views, even if you hope to convert them to your way of thinking. By using well-supported reasons to justify your position, and in thoughtfully addressing readers' potential objections, you present yourself as informed and reasonable. Your careful consideration of both sides of an issue and your use of authoritative sources to support your claim helps readers trust your argument. And when readers see the validity of your position, you can make a difference. In fact, inserting your views into the debates that swirl around contested issues is one of the most valuable and satisfying contributions to American life and culture that an educated person can make.

Reasoned argument is always more effective when it is addressed to particular readers. Your goal in addressing this specific audience is to challenge their thinking without ridiculing their values or beliefs. You should assume that whomever you are addressing is informed and intelligent and can understand and empathize with a reasonable argument.

The student writers in this chapter use certain basic features of the genre to build their positions: a focused, well-presented issue; a well-supported position; an effective response to opposing views; and a clear, logical organization. They offer facts, statistics, and expert testimony, in addition to using writing strategies such as narration, description, exemplification, and comparison and contrast to present their arguments. Mary Hake, for example, calls attention to the unseen hardships of migrant farmworkers by citing facts and statistics, but she puts this data in context by narrating the history of migrants' presence in the United States and by comparing their population to the population of several states. Tan-Li Hsu uses facts, statistics, and abundant examples to show how marketers are selling potentially dangerous energy drinks directly to teenagers.

Writing an argument like those presented here may cause you to question your own beliefs and assumptions, but this uncomfortable confrontation will expand both the boundaries of your thinking and your ability to effectively communicate what you truly believe. So take a position. Study the issue. Consider likely differences between your viewpoint and your readers'. Speak out reasonably. The world is waiting to hear from you.

Use the guidelines in the Peer Review Guide that follows to practice peer review using the essays in this chapter.

A Peer Review Guide

A FOCUSED, WELL-PRESENTED ISSUE

How well does the writer present the issue?

Summarize: Tell the writer what you understand the issue to be. If you were already familiar with it and understand it differently, briefly explain.

Praise: Give an example from the essay where the issue and its significance come across effectively.

Critique: Tell the writer where more information about the issue is needed, where more might be done to establish its seriousness, or how the issue could be framed or reframed in a way that would better prepare readers for the argument.

A WELL-SUPPORTED POSITION

How well does the writer argue in support of the position?

Summarize: Underline the thesis statement and the main reasons.

Praise: Give an example in the essay where the argument is especially effective; for example, indicate which reason is especially convincing or which supporting evidence is particularly compelling.

Critique: Tell the writer where the argument could be strengthened; for example, indicate how the thesis statement could be made clearer or more appropriately qualified, how the argument could be developed, or where additional support is needed.

AN EFFECTIVE RESPONSE TO OPPOSING VIEWS

How effectively has the writer responded to others' reasons and likely objections?

Summarize: Identify where the writer responds to a reason others use to support their argument or an objection they have to the writer's argument.

Praise: Give an example in the essay where a concession seems particularly well done or a refutation is convincing.

Critique: Tell the writer how a concession or a refutation could be made more effective, identify a reason or an objection the writer should respond to, or note where common ground could be found.

A CLEAR, LOGICAL ORGANIZATION

How clearly and logically has the writer organized the argument?

Summarize: Find the sentence(s) in which the writer states the thesis and forecasts supporting reasons, as well as transitions and repeated key words and phrases.

Praise: Give an example of how or where the essay succeeds in being especially easy to read, perhaps in its overall organization, clear presentation of the thesis, clear transitions, or effective opening or closing.

Critique: Tell the writer where the readability could be improved. Can you, for example, suggest better forecasting or clearer transitions? If the overall organization of the essay needs work, make suggestions for rearranging parts or strengthening connections.

Animal Rights
Liam Hwang
Boston College
Chestnut Hill, Massachusetts

In most arguments, the stance of the author is present from the beginning, serving as a useful foundation upon which to make the case. Liam Hwang, however, uses a subtler approach. He first presents a balanced examination of both sides of the argument—whether animals should be granted "personhood"—before ultimately choosing a side. This strategy allows the reader to follow the same learning and decision-making processes that Hwang himself went through, making agreement with Hwang's ultimate conclusion feel more natural than if Hwang had openly taken a side earlier in the essay. How effective do you find his strategy? What are the potential downsides?

In an unprecedented move, PETA filed a lawsuit against SeaWorld   1
with killer whales as the plaintiffs on October 26, 2011 (Mears and Cohen). The case sparked debate over the issue of whether the Thirteenth Amendment of the United States Constitution, which outlaws slavery, extends to cover animals as well as humans. While there is no specific mention of human beings in the Thirteenth Amendment, there has never been a case in which a nonhuman entity sued for a violation of constitutional rights. The case was dismissed by the judge, who stated that "orcas had no standing to seek the same constitutional rights as people" (Dobuzinskis).

This particular lawsuit to save the killer whales of SeaWorld, while   2
new in its approach, is but one of many to protect animals. While some may consider this lawsuit to be a rather radical method, nearly everybody believes, to a certain degree, in the necessity of the protection of animals. However, there are two sides as to how this protection should be achieved. One side believes that animals should be given actual rights and should be seen as more than just property. The other

argues that giving animals rights solves nothing and only creates more problems. This essay will address and explain the arguments that each side has to offer before taking a stance on which is the most valid.

One of the main arguments used by advocates for the elevation of animals from property to beings with rights is that the current status of animals does not sufficiently protect them. For example, in *American Legal Defense Fund (ALDF) v. Espy*, it was ruled that the ALDF did not have the standing to sue the United States Department of Agriculture for excluding birds, mice, and rats from the Animal Welfare Act (United States Court of Appeals for the District of Columbia Circuit). This was because the animals in question were considered property, and thus it was difficult to assert that an injury had occurred. As standing must include the three factors of (1) an injury in fact, (2) a causal connection between the alleged injury and the conduct in question, and (3) the ability of the alleged injury to be redressed by a judicial remedy, these factors are difficult to assert if the animals are considered to be property (Kelch). As a result, many animals that are subject to experiments and slaughter for food are simply the property of the owner and are thus easily exploited.

What advocates of animal rights maintain is that animals cannot be classified as property because they are conscious, feeling, living beings (Plass). In fact, the situation concerning the property status of animals is compared to the situation of slaves. Although slaves were clearly conscious, living beings, they were still subjected to atrocities and considered to be property that people could own. Animal rights advocates state that the inhumane treatment of human beings was remedied in part by granting them personhood status instead of status as property, and that the granting of personhood status to non-human beings would be a step in the right direction (Plass).

Those opposed to the bestowing of rights to animals claim that animals are fundamentally different from human beings and cannot operate under the same laws or be treated in the same way. For one, there are countless species of animals, and animal rights advocates seem to focus only on a select few (Duckler). They do not realize that if all nonhumans were granted rights, many human activities essential for survival would become illegal, as they would bring harm to the animals. When advocates lump all animals together, from the elephant to the termite, it becomes impossible for humans to do anything at all. Separating each animal is another problem in itself: From all the species, how is one to create laws that tailor to each type of animal

(Duckler)? Attempts were made to create groups for animals by level of consciousness, but that proved to have problems (Cupp). Aside from the large variety of different opinions on how consciousness should be defined in animals, to bring that to a courtroom would create levels of complexity and uncertainty that nobody is willing to undertake.

Another problem is that humans are very different from all other animals in that the manner of thought that produces language appears only in humans (Duckler). Rights are embodied in linguistic expression, and only humans are capable of the complexity of that kind of language. There is a difference between communication, which animals are perfectly capable of, and language, which animals cannot grasp. This means that animals are not able to be responsible for their own actions and can only be accorded protections, not rights.

Also, if animals are granted rights, then they will be required to follow the societal rules of humans as well. As they are unable to understand language, it is hard to see how they will be able to manage this. They do not have rights, but correspondingly, they do not have responsibilities in human society (Cupp). If an animal kills a human being, it is not committing a crime because it does not know the difference between right and wrong. There is no moral compass to guide an animal; it simply does what it does. Therefore, to give an animal rights would be irrational.

At this point in time, it is very unlikely that animals will be granted rights. As in the instance with the killer whales, there are other cases that deny that animals can be treated like human beings. In *Kihlstadius v. Nodaway Veterinary Clinic,* a judge stated, "[T]he court is aware of no authority establishing civil rights in the dog" (United States, District Court for the Western District of MI). Considering all the problems that would inevitably come with granting animal rights, it is doubtful that there will be any change in policy in the near future. While increased protection of animals in factory farms or in experimental labs is completely possible, the status of animals as property should remain unchanged.

WORKS CITED

Cohen, Tom, and Bill Mears. "PETA Lawsuit Alleges SeaWorld Enslaves Killer Whales." CNN, 26 Oct. 2011, www.cnn.com/2011/10/26 /justice/killer-whale-lawsuit/index.html.

Cupp, Richard L., Jr. "A Dubious Grail: Seeking Tort Law Expansion and Limited Personhood as Stepping Stones Toward Abolishing Animals' Property Status." *Southern Methodist University Law Review,* vol. 60, 2007, pp. 3–54.

Dobuzinskis, Alex. "Judge Dismisses Suit Accusing SeaWorld of Enslaving Killer Whales." Reuters, 9 Feb. 2012, www.vancouversun.com/news /Judge+dismisses+suit+accusing+SeaWorld+enslaving+ killer+whales/6126247/story.html.

Duckler, Geordie. "Two Major Flaws of the Animal Rights Movement." *Animal Law Review,* vol. 14, no. 2, 2008, pp. 179–200.

Kelch, Thomas G. "Toward a Non-Property Status for Animals." *New York University Environmental Law Journal,* vol. 6, no. 3, 1998.

Plass, Stephen A. "Exploring Animal Rights as an Imperative for Human Welfare." *West Virginia Law Review,* vol. 112, 2010, pp. 403–31.

United States Court of Appeals for the District of Columbia Circuit. *American Legal Defense Fund (ALDF) v. Espy.* 23 F.3d 496, 20 May 1994.

United States District Court for the Western District of MI. *Kihlstadius v. Nodaway Veterinary Clinic.* 697 F.Supp. 1087 (1988).

Fracking: Drilling Toward Disaster

Heather Nickell

Murray State College
Tishomingo, Oklahoma

Some argue that hydraulic fracturing, or fracking, has been an important source of economic growth and has even been beneficial for the environment, as the natural gas that results is cleaner to burn than coal. However, Heather Nickell argues that these benefits do not justify the damage that fracking causes and makes an ethical argument for ending the practice. Using evidence drawn from the Environmental Protection Agency, she details the risks associated with fracking. As you read, notice how she addresses opposing viewpoints, and consider whether she has done so sufficiently.

"Drill baby, drill." This is a common phrase in the American oil and gas industry. There are two ways to interpret this phrase. To those working in the oil and gas industry, it is a phrase that represents the enthusiasm of striking oil and getting rich. To those who are concerned about the environment, it is a daunting expression, for it means that drilling must happen no matter what the consequences. Drill the land until it bleeds black gold. This phrase means that no man, woman, plant, animal, or natural disaster will stand in the way of the almighty drill bit. Fracking is dangerous to the health and safety of the American people, and it should be stopped.

Hydraulic fracturing, or "fracking," is a method of drilling for oil and natural gas. By pumping large quantities of chemically treated water at very high pressures into rock or shale formations, the natural gas and oil trapped inside the rock are stimulated. This causes previously unavailable oil and natural gas to break free from the cracks in the rock and shale, which is then pumped to the surface of the Earth (United States, EPA, "Process"). Hydraulic fracturing was developed in the 1940s to help stimulate underperforming oil and natural gas wells. The modern style of fracking that uses steerable drill bits was developed in the 1990s ("Fracking").

Hydraulic fracturing poses two major threats to public safety. One of these threats is contaminated water. The water used to break the rocks open is treated with chemicals, with hydrochloric acid and ethylene glycol being among the most frequently used (United States, EPA, "Hydraulic"). This would not pose a threat to public safety if the water was always properly disposed of after its use. A common practice in disposing of hydraulic fracturing water is to pump the used water into underground storage tanks called injection wells (United States, EPA, "General"). The Environmental Protection Agency's final investigative report on fracking states, "The EPA found scientific evidence that hydraulic fracturing activities can impact drinking water resources under some circumstances" (United States, EPA, "Hydraulic"). In the movie *Gasland,* citizens living near drilling sites reported that their tap water was so contaminated with chemicals and gases that it could literally be set on fire. 3

A second dangerous side effect of hydraulic fracturing is man-made earthquakes. Earthquakes have been on the rise in states where fracking takes place, such as Oklahoma and Pennsylvania. The rise of hydraulic fracturing in Oklahoma started in the 2000s. Coincidently, the number of earthquakes started rising after the boom began. The number of 3.0+ magnitude earthquakes in Oklahoma in the year 2013 was 109. In 2014, that number rose to 579. In the year 2015, that number rose even higher, to 915 ("About Us"). It is understood that underground injection wells that store fracking wastewater are to blame for the rise in man-made earthquakes in the United States ("Fracking"). 4

While there are very serious consequences to fracking, there are also benefits. Hydraulic fracturing changed the way that oil and natural gas is obtained. More importantly, it made it easier and more efficient. Before the modern technique of fracking was developed, a lot of oil and natural gas was left underground because drills were unable to extract it. Fracking helped create the oil and gas boom of the 2000s, thus creating thousands of jobs and stimulating the economy (Hassett and Mathur). Oil and gas companies create many well-paying jobs all over the country. Without fracking, many citizens would be without work. 5

In conclusion, hydraulic fracturing is a double-edged sword. The 6
benefit of creating jobs and stimulating the economy are extremely
important for citizens of this country. There are many Americans
who depend on the process of fracking to feed their families. While
this may be true, the process of fracking is damaging to the planet.
The benefits of fracking do not outweigh the consequences. The
people of this planet have a responsibility to take care of the land that
we live on. Fracking is slowly, but surely, tearing apart the earth. It
is also creating dangerous situations for the plants and animals that
make their homes here. Fracking must be banned. The oil and gas
industry should stop putting profit over ethics and develop a safer
way to drill for oil.

WORKS CITED

"About Us." *Earthquakes in Oklahoma,* earthquakes.ok.gov/about-us.
"Fracking." *Encyclopedia Britannica,* 22 Nov. 2016, www.britannica.com
/technology/fracking.
Hassett, Kevin A, and Aparna Mathur. "Benefits of Hydraulic Fracking." *AIE,*
4 April 2013, www.aei.org/publication/benefits-of-hydraulic-fracking.
United States, Environmental Protection Agency. "General Informa-
tion about Injection Wells." *EPA,* 6 Sept. 2016, www.epa.gov/uic
/general-information-about-injection-wells.
---. "Hydraulic Fracturing for Oil and Gas: Impacts from the Hydraulic
Fracturing Water Cycle Drinking Water Resources in the United States
(Final Report)." *EPA,* 15 Nov. 2017, cfpub.epa.gov/ncea/hfstudy
/recordisplay.cfm?deid=332990.
---. "The Process of Unconventional Natural Gas Production." *EPA,* 9 Jan.
2017, www.epa.gov/hydraulicfracturing/process-hydraulic-fracturing.

Energy Drinks

Tan-Li Hsu

University of California, Riverside
Riverside, California

In this essay, Tan-Li Hsu considers such weighty concerns as ethical marketing and consumer deception. However, rather than getting lost in such a large issue, Hsu investigates something much smaller: He offers a focused look at energy drinks, including how they are marketed and their potential effects on health. Hsu cites news articles reporting studies about caffeine abuse in teenagers; he also cites the American Beverage Association, which defends its labeling practices. By bringing his opposition into the debate and refuting their claims, Hsu strengthens his own position. Like many of Hsu's other readers, you may have never thought about caffeine levels in energy drinks or the dangers of caffeine. As you read, think about how Hsu presents the issue to his readers, and consider his strategies for convincing them of his argument.

Ever since Red Bull energy drink was introduced in the United States in 1997, the market for energy drinks has been continually expanding. Roland Griffiths, a professor of psychiatry and neuroscience at Johns Hopkins University School of Medicine and author of a study published in the journal *Drug and Alcohol Dependence,* estimates that the market for energy drinks now totals at least $5.4 billion a year (Doheny). These popular drinks are packed with caffeine, a stimulant that is able to freely diffuse into the brain and temporarily increase alertness. Although the Food and Drug Administration places a limit on how much caffeine food products can contain—71 milligrams for each 12-ounce can—energy drinks are considered to be dietary supplements and not food products, allowing the caffeine content of these drinks to remain unregulated (Roan). As a result, hundreds of brands of energy drinks with ridiculous amounts of caffeine not specified on labels flourish in the market.

1

Furthermore, marketers intentionally target teenagers, who are   2
more susceptible to drinking multiple cans because they tend to live
active lifestyles that leave them sleep deprived. It's no wonder that
"[t]hirty-one percent of U.S. teenagers say they drink energy drinks,
according to Simmons Research. That represents 7.6 million teens"
("Teens"). With the increased use of energy drinks combined with
the lack of caffeine content warning labels on cans, emergency room
doctors and poison control centers are reporting more cases of caffeine intoxication (Seltzer). Energy drink manufacturers are putting
teenagers in danger by not clearly indicating the amount of caffeine on labels and by marketing highly caffeinated energy drinks to
teenagers.

All energy drinks list caffeine as an ingredient on labels, but many   3
don't specify how many milligrams of caffeine are in the drink. Some
brands, like Wired and Fixx, have 500 mg of caffeine per 20-ounce
serving, about ten times the caffeine found in cans of soda (Doheny).
Another ingredient, guarana, is a source of caffeine that adds to the
drinks' already high caffeine content. Unsuspecting teens who crave
a buzz by drinking several cans of energy drinks are unknowingly
putting themselves at risk for the irregular heartbeat and nausea associated with caffeine intoxication. In rare cases, such as that of nine-
teen-year-old James Stone, who took "two dozen caffeine pills for
putting in long hours on a job search," intoxication may even lead to
death by cardiac arrest (Shute).

It is possible to promote responsible consumption of energy   4
drinks by including possible health hazards along with caffeine content on can labels that encourage drinking in moderation. The reason
why such warning labels don't already exist is because marketers are
more concerned with money than the health of consumers. "Vying
for the dollars of teenagers with promises of weight loss, increased
endurance and legal highs [. . .] top-sellers Red Bull, Monster, and
Rockstar [. . .] make up a $3.4 billion-a-year industry that grew
by 80 percent last year" ("Teens"). By warning about the possible health hazards of drinking too much caffeine, manufacturers of
energy drinks risk a decrease in purchases. Maureen Storey, a spokes-
woman for the American Beverage Association, argues that "most
mainstream energy drinks contain the same amount of caffeine, or
even less, than you'd get in a cup of brewed coffee. If labels listing
caffeine content are required on energy drinks, they should also be
required on coffeehouse coffee" (Doheny). This argument has some

validity, but it fails to include ingredients in energy drinks that function as a hidden source of caffeine, such as guarana. Guarana is a berry that grows in Venezuela and contains a high amount of guaranine, a caffeine derived from the guarana plant. Assuming that energy drinks and coffee have the same amount of caffeine, the risk of caffeine intoxication from energy drinks is much higher because of the guaranine.

Marketers take advantage of teens by encouraging them to drink more with attractive brand names such as Rockstar, Monster, and Cocaine Energy Drink that promise to enhance performance. There are many reasons why marketers target teenagers instead of a more mature age group. The first is that teens are more easily tricked by claims that energy drinks will increase endurance and mental awareness. Also, teens are more enticed by the thought of an all-night party than adults are. It's no surprise that marketers are targeting exhausted teenagers who are more likely to purchase these drinks than an adult who makes sure he is in bed by 10 p.m. However, marketers fail to realize the consequences of such marketing techniques. A study led by Danielle McCarthy of Northwestern University showed "a surprising number of caffeine overdose reports to a Chicago poison control center" ("Teens"). "Although adults of all ages are known to use caffeine, it is mainly abused by young adults who want to stay awake or even get high, McCarthy said" ("Study"). 5

Another reason why marketers shouldn't incite teens to buy energy drinks is that the half-life of caffeine in a young body is significantly longer than in an adult's body (Shute). Half-life is the time required to remove half the amount of a substance to prevent accumulation in the body. With a longer half-life in teens, caffeine can accumulate more easily and increase the risk of caffeine intoxication. Preteens are getting hooked on caffeine as well: "A 2003 study of Columbus, Ohio, middle schoolers found some taking in 800 milligrams of caffeine a day—more than twice the recommended maximum for adults of 300 milligrams" (Shute). The problem for preteens is especially dire because "their body weight is low," as Wahida Karmally, the director of nutrition for the Irving Center for Clinical Research at Columbia University Medical Center, explains (Shute). Moreover, researchers do not know how such high levels of caffeine consumption affect a child's developing body. 6

Manufacturers argue that marketing to teenagers and preteens is acceptable because energy drinks can be part of a balanced lifestyle 7 when consumed sensibly. While convincing, this argument does not demonstrate a clear understanding of the scope of the problem. If a student drinks an energy drink while studying at night and can't sleep because of it, he might drink another in the morning to help wake up. According to Richard Levine, a professor of pediatrics and psychiatry at Penn State University College of Medicine and chief of the division of adolescent medicine and eating disorders at Penn State Milton S. Hershey Medical Center, "too much caffeine can make it harder to nod off, even when you're tired. Then you risk falling into a vicious cycle of insomnia caused by energy drinks followed by more caffeine to wake up" (Seltzer). Those who fall into this cycle become addicted to energy drinks, and this addiction threatens the very idea of sensible consumption. For example, fifteen-year-old Eric Williams explained that "he used to drink two to four energy drinks a day, and sometimes used them to stay awake to finish a big homework project" (Seltzer). The headaches he got when he didn't drink them convinced him to quit "although it took him two weeks" to break the habit (Seltzer). Teens shouldn't rely on energy boosters to achieve a balanced lifestyle; they should learn time management and get into the habit of a good night's sleep every day.

Exciting brand names, appealing promises of enhanced performance, and lack of clear warning labels have allowed energy drink manufacturers to intentionally target a younger audience. With these tactics, the energy drink market has grown into a billion-dollar industry. Although manufacturers are enjoying profits, consumers are placing themselves at risk for serious health problems associated with caffeine intoxication. The most susceptible to intoxication are teenagers who drink either to delay exhaustion or to get a buzz. Caffeine content and overdose warnings must be placed on energy drinks to make teens aware of the potential dangers of drinking too many of them.

WORKS CITED

Doheny, Kathleen. "Energy Drinks: Hazardous to Your Health?" *WebMD Health News*, 24 Sept. 2008, www.webmd.com/food-recipes/news/20080924/energy-drinks-hazardous-to-your-health#1.

Roan, Shari. "Energy Drinks Can Cause Caffeine Intoxication." *Booster Shots, Los Angeles Times*, 28 Sept. 2008, www.latimes.com/science/sciencenow/la-sci-sn-energy-drink-do-body-20151109-story.html.

Seltzer, Rick. "Heavy Use of Energy Drinks Can Threaten Teens' Health." *Atlanta Journal-Constitution,* 27 Aug. 2008, www.ajc.com/news /health-med-fit-science/energy-drinks-can-threaten-teen-health/ Hz9qj1RZ8rIwDWY08n8tjP.

Shute, Nancy. "Over the Limit?" *U.S. News,* U.S. News & World Report, 15 Apr. 2007, health.usnews.com/health-news/blogs /on-parenting/207/04/15/over-the-limit.

"Study: More People Abusing, Getting 'High' on Caffeine." *Fox News,* 24 Feb. 2009, www.foxnews.com/story/2009/02/24/study-more -people-abusing-getting-high-on-caffeine.html.

"Teens Abusing Energy Boosting Drinks, Doctors Fear." *Fox News,* 31 Oct. 2006, www.foxnews.com/story/2006/10/31/teens-abusing-energy -boosting-drinks-doctors-fear.html.

With Each Seed a Farmer Plants

Mary Hake

Pierce College
Lakewood, Washington

Farms are an important part of the United States' national self-image—we take for granted the "amber waves of grain" that provide food for us and for the world. Mary Hake writes about a grimmer side of this story: the plight of migrant farmworkers. By citing statistics and evoking reader sympathy for the migrant workers, she eloquently argues for rights for these workers. Hake claims that United States agriculture is a "broken system" that cannot survive without abusing the labor force it depends on. As you read, think about Hake's purpose in writing this essay, and what kinds of audiences she might have written it for. How effectively does Hake use her sources to support her claims?

When we sit to eat our meals and join in the family chatter Thanksgiving Day, many of us will have tables laden with food. Americans live in one of the richest nations on earth. We have fertile farmland, agricultural techniques that are modern and efficient, agreeable rainfall in many areas and irrigation provided by flowing rivers in others. Seeds are plentiful, orchards bloom and flourish, grains ripen each year. Yet within this framework are the harvesters of our bounty: the migrants who have fought for decades for a decent wage, livable housing, clean water, and enough food to feed their own children even as they pick our celebratory feast. As Edward R. Murrow referred to these people on Thanksgiving Day, 1960: "The under-educated, unprotected, under-fed and unclothed. The forgotten ones" ("Harvest"). How is it, then, that they can still be "forgotten" so many years later?

Living in a country that prides itself on its heritage of personal   2
freedom and individual rights, we have neglected an entire group of
people who are without the strength or the voice to demand otherwise from us. The same science that tells us that unclean water and
overcrowded living conditions breed disease, that great fatigue can
cause dangerous accidents in the field, and that poverty is a reason
why those who are sick or injured do not seek the medical care they
need to stop its spread, also tells us how to grow even more food in
less time, necessitating many more harvesters to do this dirty work
each growing season. With each seed a farmer plants, he grows two
things. One is a valuable crop; the other is poverty. Seen in this light,
every migrant farmworker who harvests food in the United States
should have equal access to the health care and basic human services
we deem to be our right as Americans, for to do anything less is to
put the nation's food supply in danger.

Our current use of a migrant workforce has its roots in the   3
1940s, when the United States government instituted a program to
provide cheap labor for the fruit and vegetable farmers (Reynolds
and Kourous). These farmers needed help picking their produce in
the limited amount of time they had before it began to rot in the
fields. Many of their previous helpers had been lost in World War II.
The cheapest and fastest way to provide these replacement laborers
was to go into Mexico and hire more than three million Mexican
nationals between 1942 and 1964 (Reynolds and Kourous). This
plan, named the Bracero Program, brought these workers across the
border by bus for the length of the harvest season. Then, without
ceremony, these farmhands were sent home again. For almost twenty
years, American agriculture sent for foreign help to harvest our food
in this revolving-door fashion and in relative secrecy.

By the 1960s, however, that began to change, largely through   4
the efforts of one man, Cesar Chavez. A farm laborer from the age of
ten, Chavez realized that American farmhands were being denied a
fair wage and safe working conditions (Wheeler 33). As businessmen,
the field owners wanted to increase their profits, a goal they accom-
plished by paying the lowest possible wage to the braceros. Some
farmworkers, like Chavez, were born in America of Mexican heritage,
while others were Mexican citizens who were bused across the border directly to the fields each growing season. Through a philosophy
of nonviolence and the action of "organized sit-down strikes in the
fields," Chavez worked to protest this situation (Wheeler 33). When

the braceros returned the next season, Chavez became convinced of the need to organize the farmworkers into a union that would eventually become known as the NFWA, or the National Farm Workers Association (Wheeler 36). In 1965, after much struggle, the NFWA reached its goal of a national boycott to call attention to the plight of the American migrant.

Migrant workers, as they will be defined for this essay, are farm   5 laborers who travel more than one day to reach their places of employment. Men, women, and children have historically performed this role, often from a very young age and for very little money. Some have been born into it, some forced by financial need to take any work they could find. An anonymous farmer speaking of his workers more than forty years ago said: "We used to own our slaves, now we just rent them" ("Harvest"). It is within this context that the modern American must examine how we pay for the food that we eat.

Most migrants have an income far below the poverty line and   6 are rarely in one place long enough to acquire the legal residence necessary to apply for aid. As writer Eric Schlosser states, "Migrants are among the poorest workers in the United States. The average migrant is a twenty-nine year old male, born in Mexico, who earns less than $7,500 a year for twenty-five weeks of farm work" (*Reefer Madness* 79). Many have no money at all and work only to feed themselves.

This transient life has a direct impact not only on the adult labor-   7 ers but on the entire family as well. Some have argued that migrants are culturally unable to sustain permanent residence, and that they actually enjoy moving with the seasons and would feel limited otherwise. There is absolutely no evidence to support this point of view. Moving as they must, the children are often malnourished owing to a lack of money to feed them and a lack of time to prepare meals. They have little or no warm clothing, and lasting friendships are unheard of. Educational needs cannot be met because no single teacher is in control of what is taught, thus completing a generational cycle of illiteracy. It is true, also, that small hands may be needed in the fields. Legally, children as young as ten years old may work as harvesters, side by side with adults. Molestation and sexual assault are very real threats, and when they occur, they are often unreported crimes (*Reefer Madness* 85).

Jill Wheeler's book *Cesar Chavez* recounts one migrant child's   8 difficulty attending school: "It was hard for the children of the farm workers to get an education because they were working to help their families. They constantly moved from one job to the next. As a child, Cesar attended nearly forty different schools" (Wheeler 14). The bright migrant child, under this burden of transience and without the continuity of curriculum, has little hope of academic success. He or she will never fully advance with the class, and indeed most migrant children do not continue their schooling beyond the sixth grade. With no high school diploma and no formal training, many barely able to speak English, they are ill-equipped for any work other than the fields. They cannot escape the patterns of the harvest, the same necessary and seasonal migration that trapped their parents before them. Similarly, without a decent wage earned or credit history established, many farm-workers are without the means to live in private quarters. At the mercy of their employers, they are often left with no choice but to sleep outside or in communal tents with strangers.

Journalist Carole Pearson notes: "A lack of adequate, affordable housing forces many seasonal migrant workers to live in deplorable conditions. Because growers are not required to provide accommodations for their employees, it's not uncommon to see workers camped along the river banks or in the orchards, living in shelters of discarded cardboard and plastic tarps" (4). Migrants are expected to work long hours, always outdoors, whether in pouring rain or blazing sunshine; they are also expected to sleep wherever they can. Some have roofs, but not all. Some have floors, but many do not. Most are in the midst of shanty towns, where clean running water is not guaranteed, bathroom facilities may not be available, and nothing stops the spread of contagious diseases (Pearson 6). 9

The possibility of a spreading epidemic, created by ignorance and poor hygiene among a mostly transient population, has frightening consequences for the general public. Estimates of the number of migrants working in the United States during any one harvest period vary, but all studies agree that there are at least 1.5 million people who work the fields under these circumstances. Some studies state that the number may be as high as 5 million individuals; 5 million chances for a disease to move (Carrasco-Mendoza 2). 10

By contrast, according to a recent census, more than half of these United States have less than 5 million residents ("Facts and Figures"). Colorado ranks as our twenty-second most populated state with a mere 4.7 million. Arkansas drops down to under 3 million. When added together, the populations of the states of Maine, Idaho, 11 and Hawaii do not equal the estimated number of migrant workers. Even taking the more conservative estimate of 1.5 million leaves us with a migrant group larger than the populations of Delaware, Hawaii, Idaho, Maine, Montana, New Hampshire, Rhode Island, Vermont, and Wyoming ("Facts and Figures").

Separated, unnoticed, and uncared for, this undeniably large   12 group of people is spread across every state's farmland. Touching every agricultural community, they bring their own risk factors with them. As Pat Hanson points out in the article "Migrant Farmers 'Suffering in Silence'": "Close to one third had never been to a doctor in their lives. Seventy-five percent had no health insurance" (3). Without health insurance, money becomes the most important obstacle to healing. Very few doctors will treat undocumented workers unless they are able to pay cash or provide a billing address. Additionally, cultural, educational, and language differences, as well as prejudice and discrimination, are cited as barriers to obtaining health care (Carrasco-Mendoza 2). Without money, the ability to understand what care is needed, or the ability to speak English fluently, many migrants are treated as undesirab'e aliens who must be turned away.

Many would argue that doc rs who will not treat indigent tran-   13 sient workers are simply protecting themselves and the entire health care industry from potentially hundreds of thousands of dollars or more in health care costs. For a system that is already overwhelmed by rising fees and an uncontrolled number of patients, adding the additional migrant population r'ight cause a final catastrophic collapse, in effect leaving all Americans without proper care. Additionally, this argument holds, for an individual farmer to insure each of his migrant workers would nearly bankrupt an already fragile agricultural system.

Both of these points, while valid, are solely based on economic   14 payout and overlook the need for each system as it currently stands to be overhauled. In essence, they state that we cannot afford to help the migrant living in poverty because it would break an already broken system. According to Wikipedia, "the generally high cost of treatment has led to the concept of doctors completing their *pro bono* work, although in practice even serious conditions are left untreated. Health insurance is expensive and medical bills are overwhelmingly the most common reason for personal bankruptcy in the United States" ("Health Care"). By contrast, government-funded health care systems such as Canada's can provide an equal opportunity for

treatment regardless of the patient's ability to pay. In America, however, it is still possible to die of an expensive disease.

Similarly, American agriculture is changing under severe pres-   15
sure from large corporations. Those who still own small family farms
have difficulty raising and selling enough crops to stay competitive.
Aggressive techniques are used to raise crop yields—bioengineering
more hardy and weather-resistant varieties combined with multiple
pesticide use. In the center of this David-and-Goliath battle is the
migrant farmworker. With a larger crop to harvest, smaller farms
must turn to outside help or lose their investment. Eric Schlosser
addresses this issue extensively in his book *Fast Food Nation:* "Family
farms are giving way to corporate farms that stretch for thousands of
acres. These immense corporate farms are divided into smaller hold-
ings for administrative purposes, and farmers who are driven off the
land are often hired to manage them" (118).

The argument, then, that paying for health care and providing   16
for the basic living needs of the harvesters would harm the individual farmer doesn't apply if the real wealth behind agriculture belongs
to large and often multinational corporations whose profits can be
measured in the billions of dollars. While it may hurt the smallest
independent farmer financially, it also follows that the least amount
of acreage would require the least help to manage it. If five men can
pick one hundred laden apple trees, only the largest orchard would
find this requirement unduly burdensome.

Another argument raised against providing for the migrants sim-   17
ply states that this kind of care and benefit should be reserved for
United States citizens alone, and that to treat those who are illegal
immigrants as equals is unjust to the American field hand. This point
of view refuses to acknowledge the migrants' contribution to the
American economy. The United States fruit and vegetable industry,
worth $28 billion annually, would lose both its function and its prof-
itability without the work of the migrant harvester (Schlosser 230).
The Thanksgiving table itself would have no harvest to celebrate; it
would be empty of both food and spirit. Indeed, the migrants' contribution to America cannot be separated from the United States
economy. Every day that is spent in the field supports this country
and its citizens. It seems only fair, then, that migrant workers should
receive something back.

Some writers state that to aid undocumented workers is to   18
reward them for breaking the law. This quote from William Triplett

puts forth that idea quite plainly: "Some farm bosses even have been convicted in recent years of enslaving workers, most of whom are illegal aliens afraid to speak out for fear of deportation. Human rights advocates say the only way to improve conditions is to give undocumented workers legal residency, but opponents say that would reward illegals for breaking U.S. immigration laws and ultimately spark more illegal immigration" (829).

This position implies that the United States is undeniably a better place to live than anywhere else, and that given any reason to do so, many more immigrants would come here to live illegally. It does not specifically address how that would be easier to do, or why many more people would wish to do so. At its heart, this argument is a form of national arrogance, but more than that, it seems to miss the most obvious point. Namely, the illegal immigrant as migrant worker has toiled and bled as little more than slave labor for over sixty years and should, indeed, be rewarded. It was the United States, after all, that created the Bracero Program and, in so doing, created an artificial reliance in both cultures, Mexican and American, on transient and low-paid work. It is in the interest of international justice to acknowledge our role in the creation and proliferation of our immigrant workforce, legal or otherwise.

As Americans, many of us are far removed from our own food chain. Most cannot grow enough to survive. Many have no idea how to pick different kinds of produce when they are ready to be harvested, and some do not even know how to prepare them. It cannot be wise, then, to treat those who do have that knowledge so poorly. The migrant workers among us are the silent, movable backbone of our agriculture. Intricately tied to our ability to feed ourselves and, by extension, the world, they play an irreplaceable role in our economy. Even so, their lives are endangered daily by ignorance, prejudice, poverty, and disease. If the state population of Colorado cried out in one tormented voice of great distress, thousands across the nation would hasten to answer. It cannot be, and must not be, any different when the voices come from the farms, in every direction, and speak in Spanish.

But ours is a land of nomad harvesters.
They till no ground, take no rest, are homed nowhere.
Travel with the warmth, rest in the warmth never;
Pick lettuce in the green season in the flats by the sea.

Lean, follow the ripening, homeless, send the harvest home;
Pick cherries in the amber valleys in tenderest summer.
Rest nowhere, share in no harvest;
Pick grapes in the red vineyards in the low blue hills.
Camp in the ditches at the edge of beauty.

—from "The Nomad Harvesters"
by Marie De L. Welch (Sackman, xii)

WORKS CITED

Carrasco-Mendoza, Rachel. "Migrant Farm Workers Significant to America's Way of Life." *La Voz,* 27 Aug. 1997, p. 3. *ProQuest.*

"Facts and Figures, United States Populations by State." *FactMonster.com.* Fact Monster/Information Please Database, 2005.

Hanson, Pat. "Migrant Farmers 'Suffering in Silence': California Groups Look at Problems and Solutions." *The Hispanic Outlook in Higher Education,* vol. 12, no. 17, 2002, pp. 28–32. *ProQuest.*

"Harvest of Shame." *CBS Reports,* narrated by Edward R. Murrow, WCBS, 25 Nov. 1960. Fox Video, 1992.

"Health Care in the United States." *Wikipedia,* 14 Nov. 2006.

Pearson, Carole. "A Case of Apples: Mexican Farm Workers in Washington." *Our Times,* vol. 20, no. 2, 2002, p. 21. *ProQuest.*

Reynolds, Kathleen, and George Kourous. "Legislation and Regulation Favor Agribusiness: An Overview of Health, Safety and Wage Issues." *Border Lines,* vol. 6, no. 8, 1998. *ProQuest.*

Sackman, Douglas C. Foreword. *Factories in the Fields,* by Carey McWilliams, Archon, 1969.

Schlosser, Eric. *Fast Food Nation.* New York: Houghton, 2002.

———. *Reefer Madness.* Houghton, 2003.

Triplett, William. "Migrant Farmworkers." *CQ Researcher,* vol. 14, no. 35, 2004, pp. 829–52. *CQ Researcher.*

Wheeler, Jill C. *Cesar Chavez.* MN: ABDO & Daughters, 2003.

Proposing a Solution 7

Problem solving requires a questioning attitude—a refusal to accept things as they are simply because they've always been that way. It invites creative effort—time spent imagining how things might be improved. When you identify a problem that has long existed or notice that old solutions are failing because they're outdated, you take a step toward positive change. As a student, you are in an enviable position to identify and solve problems. Studying and writing, you have been practicing a stance that problem solving requires—thinking skeptically and creatively. And you have the luxury of time to notice problems and think hard about solutions.

Don't be afraid to research problems that are new to you—an outsider's fresh, unbiased point of view is often very valuable. But remember to consider problems from an insider's perspective too: problems of your town and city, neighborhood and dormitory, athletic team and booster club. If you volunteer time and effort on behalf of political parties, religious or cultural groups, or social justice organizations, this experience with specific groups uniquely qualifies you to examine their limitations. What's more, a proposal to solve a local problem may well have national implications.

In addition to giving you a say in your community, practice in presenting problems and proposing solutions will expand your professional-writing repertoire. If student writer Kati Huff pursues a career in management, applies for a job directing a nonprofit, or volunteers to work for a local political organization, she will have demonstrated her ability to notice and analyze problems and suggest ways to fix them, while acknowledging the concerns of the people who would have to carry them out—in this case, school administrators who create cafeteria policy and the cafeteria employees who would have to learn new rules and techniques if existing policies were changed.

It can be frustrating to work diligently on a proposal for a problem that you know you have little power to solve; no matter how well argued, many proposals are never carried out. People who are quite insightful about solving problems may be hampered or thwarted by economic constraints or aggressive opposition from prominent stakeholders. But this shouldn't deter you from proposing a solution to a problem, especially when you choose a local problem in which you have a personal interest and about which you can talk to people in your community and get their views on the issue.

Don't underestimate the power of interviewing people affected by the problem you intend to solve and approaching others who have the power to change it. Interviews with those who have first-hand experience with the problem can help you anticipate objections to your solution and allow you to test it with an audience that's directly involved. Scheduling an interview with someone who has the power to solve the problem may help you anticipate and counter resistance to your proposal. Use the basic features of the genre as a guide for your own writing. Essays that propose a solution feature a focused, well-defined problem; a well-argued solution; an effective response to objections and alternative solutions; and a clear, logical organization.

You are ready to add your voice to the conversation about problems on your campus; in your town; at your job; or with college, government, or corporate officials, whose policies affect your life and the lives of your family and friends. If your proposal can convince readers to consider and perhaps implement your solution, you will have succeeded in altering the conditions of your world.

Use the guidelines in the Peer Review Guide that follows to practice peer review using the essays in this chapter.

A PEER REVIEW GUIDE

A FOCUSED, WELL-DEFINED PROBLEM

Has the writer framed the problem effectively?

> **Summarize:** Tell the writer what you understand the problem to be.

Praise: Give an example where the problem and its significance come across effectively, such as where an example dramatizes the problem or statistics establish its significance.

Critique: Tell the writer where readers might need more information about the problem's causes and consequences, or where more might be done to establish its seriousness.

A WELL-ARGUED SOLUTION

Has the writer argued effectively for the solution?

Summarize: Tell the writer what you understand the proposed solution to be.

Praise: Give an example in the essay where support for the solution is presented especially effectively—for example, note particularly strong reasons, writing strategies that engage readers, or design or visual elements that make the solution clear and accessible.

Critique: Tell the writer where the argument for the solution could be strengthened—for example, where steps for implementation could be laid out more clearly, where the practicality of the solution could be established more convincingly, or where additional support for reasons should be added.

AN EFFECTIVE RESPONSE TO OBJECTIONS AND ALTERNATIVE SOLUTIONS

Has the writer responded effectively to objections or alternative solutions?

Summarize: Tell the writer what you understand to be the objections or alternative solutions that he or she is responding to.

Praise: Give an example in the essay where the writer concedes or refutes a likely objection to the argument effectively, and where reasons showing the limitations of alternative solutions are most effectively presented.

Critique: Tell the writer where concessions and refutations could be more convincing, where possible objections or reservations should be taken into account or alternative solutions should be discussed, where reasons for not accepting other solutions need to be strengthened, or where common ground should be sought with advocates of other positions.

A CLEAR, LOGICAL ORGANIZATION

Is the proposal clearly and logically organized?

Summarize: Underline the sentence(s) in which the writer establishes the problem and proposes a solution. Also identify places where the writer forecasts the argument, supplies topic sentences, uses transitions, and repeats key words and phrases.

Praise: Give an example of how the essay succeeds in being readable—for example, in its overall organization, its use of forecasting statements or key terms introduced in its thesis and strategically repeated elsewhere, its use of topic sentences or transitions, or an especially effective opening or closing.

Critique: Tell the writer where the readability could be improved—for example, where using key terms would help or where a topic sentence could be made clearer, where the use of transitions could be improved or added, or whether the beginning or ending could be more effective.

The Social Security Problem

Max Moore

University of California, Riverside
Riverside, California

In this essay, Max Moore effectively uses research to explain a complex current issue, Social Security, then offers a possible solution. For an issue that is the result of many factors, Moore acknowledges that his might not be a very popular solution; however, he has done such a thorough job of considering various aspects of the problem—smoothly weaving authoritative sources throughout—that the reader is inclined to grant his suggestion serious consideration. As you read, take heart in knowing that even the most complicated social issues become easier to manage when careful research guides your writing.

It is hard to be nineteen years old and give any thought to retirement. Why would anyone begin saving money for a time that exists so far in the future? It can be easy to forget about retirement in the competitive and fast-paced world we live in today. This is why Social Security is such an important program for many Americans. President Franklin D. Roosevelt created Social Security in 1934 to protect the elderly and handicapped from the widespread poverty of the Great Depression (Cooper 793). Each year, every working citizen in the United States pays a tax that helps finance Social Security checks for the elderly. Starting in the 1970s, various experts and officials began warning that the Social Security system was soon going to be bankrupt. Today, the U.S. Department of the Treasury predicts that if the Social Security program continues functioning the way it is, there will be insufficient funds by 2041 (7). It is clear that some type of action must be taken to save Social Security, or else the program will be lost within the next thirty years.

The concept of Social Security would have been quite difficult 2 to explain to most people a hundred years ago. Until the twentieth

1

century, most people worked until they died. Today, it is uncommon for people to work past the age of 65 (Gendell 14), even if they are still healthy (Gendell 19). In the 1950s, the average age of retirement for men was 68.5; since then, it has dropped to 62.6 (Gendell 14). Social Security is faced with a larger burden as more people decide to leave the workforce earlier. Most experts agree that demographic changes and the country's shrinking workforce are the main causes of the Social Security problem (Gruber and Wise 1). These two opposing factors are slowly creating a perfect storm that will quickly drain the money in the Social Security fund.

Based on various demographic trends, the elderly population will   3 continue to increase for the next fifty years. When Social Security was created, the fertility rate in the United States was 3.7 children per woman (Brain 239). Today, the fertility rate is 2.1, and experts expect that it will continue to drop (Glazer 964). A declining fertility rate means that each future generation is smaller than the last, and with a smaller younger generation, there are proportionately more elderly people that must be paid for. Death rates have also been steadily declining (Brain 239). With declining fertility and death rates, the percentage of elderly people compared to the total population is rapidly increasing. One model estimates that by 2050, the elderly population will make up 20 percent of the total population, compared to 7 percent when Social Security was first created (Cliquet and Thienpont 28; Brain 240). Another factor contributing to the Social Security problem is the decreasing workforce. In the 1950s, there were 15 workers for every Social Security beneficiary; today, there are only 3.3 workers for every beneficiary (Cooper 788). In the years to come, each worker will have to support a larger fraction of retired elderly. Based on the population differences of the elderly and changed retirement trends, it is easy to see why the future budget of Social Security is in jeopardy. There is no way that the current tax structure can support the predicted increase in the number of elderly citizens.

Without reform, Social Security is clearly on a downward slope.   4 However, solutions to the problem become complicated, because there is no practical way to increase the birth and death rates. One popular proposed solution that has brought much debate came in 2001, when President George W. Bush boldly tried to tackle the growing financial issue facing Social Security. He was not alone in the debate over Social Security reform. In 1982, President Ronald Reagan had to call for an emergency commission to fix the impending

Social Security deficit at hand. The commission raised taxes and retirement age requirements, which solved the deficit problem for only the short term (Benavie 15). Ever since then, various reforms have been brought to the continuing debate, but most politicians are afraid that pushing Social Security reform would be committing political suicide (Benavie 37). Bush proposed that the best way to fix Social Security was to make it partially privatized.

    Privatization of Social Security, under Bush's reform, is a system 5 in which younger workers have the choice to invest a portion of their payroll tax into a personal retirement account (Benavie 37). This retirement account would consist of various stocks that each person has chosen to invest in. In the long run, these retirement accounts would hypothetically accrue much higher returns than the present trust fund system does (President's Commission 26). The basic idea of privatization is that the higher returns made from the privately invested accounts would reduce the cash deficit of the Social Security trust fund. Bush has explained that over the long term the yields from a balanced stock portfolio are around 6 percent; he compares this yield to the return on retirement benefits, which is only around 2 percent (Benavie 40, 41). The system in place now is referred to as the "pay as you go" system (U.S. Dept. of the Treasury 6). This means that "each generation's taxes finance the benefits of the generation that preceded it" (U.S. Dept. of the Treasury 6). Under privatization, each generation saves its own money for retirement (U.S. Dept. of the Treasury 6). The differences between the two systems are quite large, which means that implementing a privatization system would mean a complete renovation of Social Security. This is where the first issue with Bush's reform comes into play.

    If privatization is used to fix the Social Security problem, a large 6 "transition cost" will have to be paid by the first few generations using the new system (Benavie 42). In the initial stages of privatization, the government still has to pay benefits to prior generations that did not partake in the privately invested accounts. As the present workforce begins privatization, there is less money in the Social Security program (Benavie 42). The resulting deficit in the system is referred to as the transition cost. This large deficit in Social Security is largely unavoidable and can usually only be fixed by more government spending (Edwards and Edwards 9). The President's Commission to Strengthen Social Security, created by President Bush, tried to estimate the transition cost needed to sustain a privatized system;

the lowest cost was $0.4 trillion and the highest was $1.1 trillion (92). It appears privatization creates only a larger deficit in the near future. Supporters of privatization would argue that various taxes could be used to pay for the transition (Kotlikoff 19), but an increase in taxes is what people are trying to avoid. The higher-yielding benefits received by the first few generations using the privatized system will be significantly diminished by the transition cost they'll have to pay for (Benavie 42). In the end, there is no real advantage to higher-yielding accounts if the government has to increase taxes anyway.

Not only are the personal accounts used in privatization more risky, but they contradict the ethics involving Social Security. Under this plan, people can choose to invest in more risky portfolios if they wish to receive a higher yield, as privatization leaves it up to workers to exercise judgment with their retirement money (President's Commission 143). Is increased risk what U.S. citizens need for their retirement funds? Today, after market plunges and corporations abandoning their 401k plans, Social Security is the only source of retirement income for many Americans (Cooper 784). It may not offer very high benefits, but it is fairly reliable. Franklin D. Roosevelt said that the Social Security program was meant to "give some measure of protection to the average citizen . . . against poverty-ridden old age" (U.S. Dept. of the Treasury 2). Bush's plan does not seem to protect the average citizen. By allowing citizens to invest in risky stocks, privatization creates a less safe environment for the average citizen's retirement plan (Benavie 43). Social Security is fundamentally intended to function as an insurance against poverty, not as a risk-involved retirement plan. Trying to privatize Social Security is economically and fundamentally illogical in our current situation. Privatizing Social Security would create a large transition cost and would also create a more unstable environment for citizens' retirement plans. It is clear that something must be done to fix Social Security, but President Bush's proposed reform is not the solution.

Solving the Social Security problem is certainly not easy: Factors such as demographic changes are very hard to maneuver around. Also, radical changes to the existing structure of Social Security, like privatization, create more problems than originally existed. Therefore, the best way to keep Social Security solvent for the next few generations is to increase both taxes and the retirement age. Most Americans treat increased taxes like the plague, and the last thing senior citizens want is to wait longer to receive their retirement checks. Even though my proposed solution may have some negatives, this remains the best way to fix the Social Security problem.

Increasing the retirement age would better represent the economic and demographic structure of today. Currently, the age at which a person can start receiving full benefits is 66 (U.S. Dept. of the Treasury 3). Since 1935, the age requirement to receive benefits has only gone up one year. This does not correspond to the three-year increase in life expectancy since 1935 (Benavie 29). Social Security laws should stay consistent with the surrounding demographics. If government programs are to remain solvent for more than a century, updates must be made to keep the programs relevant to the times. The elderly are much different today than they were when Social Security was created. The amount of elderly living at the poverty level has dropped 20 percent since 1955 (Brain 242).

Society as a whole has changed dramatically since the Great Depression. Due to the automation of industry and globalization, the job structure in the United States is radically changing (Reich 214). Most people no longer find themselves unable to work at the age of 65 after a lifetime of hard manual labor. Today, many people can continue working as long as their mind permits it. We can predict only that these economic and demographic changes will continue into the twenty-first century. Increasing the retirement age would reflect only the current changes in the elderly today. There is no way that the workforce of the future can support the growing elderly population without help. By making the retirement age older, it is highly likely that people at the ages of 65 to 70 will remain in the workforce. This would ease the burden of Social Security payments. We cannot reduce the elderly population, but we can redefine what it means to be elderly. Raising the retirement age proportionate to the average life expectancy is the best way to keep Social Security afloat. Another factor that would complement an increased retirement age is increased taxes. No one likes raising taxes. On the other hand, no one likes elderly people living at the poverty level. As time goes on, people will decide a fair balance between age and tax increases. The issue will continue to be a hot topic for debate in the years to come; although this solution is not perfect, it is the best possible option. Every generation that replaces the last must tackle the various hurdles Social Security poses. In the next fifty years, we will see if Franklin D. Roosevelt's progressive plan will survive or fail.

WORKS CITED

Benavie, Arthur. *Social Security Under the Gun*. Palgrave Macmillan, 2003.

Brain, Charles M. *Social Security at the Crossroads*. Garland Publishing, 1991.

Cliquet, Robert, and Kristiaan Thienpont. *Population and Development: A Message from the Cairo Conference*. Kluwer Academic Publishers, 1995.

Cooper, Mary H. "Social Security Reform." *CQ Researcher*, vol. 14, no. 33, 2004, pp. 781-804, library.cqpress.com/cqresearcher/document .php?id=cqresrre2004092400.

Edwards, Alejandra Cox, and Sebastian Edwards. "Social Security Privatization Reform and Labor Markets: The Case of Chile." *National Bureau of Economic Research*, May 2002, www.nber.org/papers/w8924.

Gendell, Murray. "Retirement Age Declines Again in 1990s." *Monthly Labor Review*, Oct. 2001, pp. 12-21.

Glazer, Sarah. "Declining Birthrates." *CQ Researcher*, vol. 18, no. 41, 2008, pp. 961-84, library.cqpress.com/cqresearcher/document.php?id=cqresrre 2008112100.

Gruber, Jonathan, and David A. Wise. "Social Security Programs and Retirement around the World: Fiscal Implications." *National Bureau of Economic Research*, National Institute on Aging, Apr. 2005, www.nber .org/papers/w11290.

Kotlikoff, Laurence. "Privatization of Social Security: How It Works and Why It Matters." *National Bureau of Economic Research*, Sept. 1996, www.nber.org/papers/w5330.

Presidential Statements: George W. Bush — 2001. Social Security Online, www .ssa.gov/history/gwbushstmts.html.

President's Commission to Strengthen Social Security. *Strengthening Social Security and Creating Personal Wealth for All Americans*. Washington, D.C., 2001, www.ssa.gov/history/reports/pcsss/Final_report.pdf.

Reich, Robert B. *The Work of Nations: Preparing Ourselves for 21st Century Capitalism*. Random House, 1991.

U.S. Dept. of the Treasury. *Social Security Reform: The Nature of the Problem*, 2007, www.treasury.gov/resource-center/economic-policy/ss-medicare /Documents/post.pdf.

Cracking Down on Lighting Up

Monica Perez

The Catholic University of America
Washington, D.C.

In a proposal essay, even the most well-publicized problem bears repeating, and Monica Perez does this well by solidifying the risks of smoking and the benefits of quitting with statistics and expert testimony. Having readied readers for her proposal by refreshing their memories about the horrors of the "nasty habit," Perez outlines a three-part action plan to "help push smoking out of society" and successfully responds to possible objections to her proposal from tobacco companies, states, and bar and restaurant owners. As you read, pay attention to Perez's tone, which reveals both her disgust with smoking and her determination to crack down on it. How effective is that tone as a call to action? Does it anger you? Inspire you?

On March 19, 2014, zombies roamed the halls of Muskegon High 1
School in Michigan. Well, they weren't real zombies. They were students in full makeup with ripped clothes. Most of the "zombies" were limping, groaning, and carrying signs . . . and for what? No, it wasn't related to Halloween or candy. This was an organized campaign to inform the local community of the dangers of smoking and to show teens what could happen if they keep smoking cigarettes. The "zombies" at Muskegon were just one of the many events organized as a part of "Kick Butts Day," an antismoking effort from the Campaign for Tobacco-Free Kids. Across the country, students are encouraged to start their own campaigns and post them on social media with the hashtag #KickButtsDay or #NotAReplacement. This event is another addition to the decades-long movement to educate the public about the dangers of smoking.

Smoking is a nasty habit that is the leading cause of many types 2
of cancer; these include cancer of the kidney, cervix, bone marrow,
pancreas, and stomach, to name a few. Some of the more obvious diseases caused by smoking include lung, oral, and throat cancers, along
with chronic lung disease. Studies have also linked smoking to heart
disease, osteoporosis, and cataracts. Secondhand smoke is another
side effect of smoking, but this affects not smokers but the bystanders
who happen to be around smokers. According to the Environmental Protection Agency, secondhand smoke is a "Class A carcinogen,"
meaning that it causes cancer and that it is not safe to be exposed to at
any level or for any amount of time. One estimate stated that environmental tobacco smoke kills "53,000 Americans every year" (Clark).

Thankfully, many of the harsh effects of smoking can be reversed. 3
By quitting smoking, you can reap the healing benefits. According
to About.com, after twenty-four hours of not smoking, blood pressure decreases, body temperature increases, carbon monoxide and
oxygen levels return to normal, and the chance of a heart attack
decreases. After two days, nerve endings begin to regrow, and there
is an improvement in one's ability to taste and smell. Soon, former
smokers may have a new lease on life: in as little as a month, there
is significant improvement in coughing, fatigue, shortness of breath,
and sinus congestion (Martin, "Quit Smoking Benefits"). The question isn't, however, why should people quit smoking, but how do we
get them to do so? How do we help change society's mentality on
smoking? We should start with continuing prevention and treatment
programs, implementing clean-air laws and smoke-free policies, and
continuing to increase cigarette sales taxes.

The best way to get people to quit smoking is to make sure that 4
they never start. "Prevention is a far better investment" than treatment simply because it is so much harder to rid people of an addiction than it is to keep them from falling victim to one ("Smoking
Kills"). When it comes to prevention, education is key. We must
continue to target younger audiences and teach them the risks of
lighting up. If we start to educate children as soon as they enter
the school system, there is a much better chance they will not be
influenced later on. We must also focus our attention on teens. As a
group, teenagers and young adults have one of the highest growth
rates of new smokers, with three thousand young people beginning
every day ("Smoking"). To reduce the number of teens who start
smoking, we need to change smoking's image. It doesn't help that

our society is bombarded by continual advertisements and positive images of smoking in movies and television shows. An internal tobacco company marketing report from 1989 said, "We believe that most of the strong, positive images for cigarettes and smoking are created by cinema and television" ("Facts"). We must teach the next generations to filter out these false images. There are thousands of different organizations, like The Truth, that can help. But it must be a cooperative effort; parents must speak to their kids, and teachers must act as role models and continue to stress the dangers of cigarette smoking. We also cannot forget that young smokers need extra support and encouragement to quit.

Implementing or strengthening clean-indoor-air laws and smoke-free policies state-by-state is another way to help reduce smoking nationwide. These policies include prohibitions against smoking in public places, such as bars, restaurants, and the workplace. It is important that the public know that clean-indoor-air laws "prompt more smokers to try to quit; increase the number of successful quit attempts; reduce the number of cigarettes that continuing smokers consume," and have a strong, documented "positive impact . . . on preventing children and adolescents from ever starting" to smoke (Barry, "Smoke-Free Laws"). The *American Journal of Public Health* reviewed nineteen studies on smoke-free workplaces and found that all reported either declines in daily cigarette consumption by continuing smokers or reductions in smoking prevalence after bans on smoking in the workplace were introduced (Barry, "Smoke-Free Laws"). Smoke-free homes and workplaces also significantly lower adolescent smoking rates. And smoke-free policies are also good for nonsmokers. According to Charles S. Clark, "88% of Americans find cigarette smoke annoying." Some people have even developed allergies to smoke, especially those with asthma. Others just plain don't like the smell and certainly don't want to taste the smoke in their food. According to a report by the Campaign for Tobacco-Free Kids, "People are speaking up for their right to breathe clean, smoke-free air" ("Smoke-Free Laws"). Smoke-free policies will help protect nonsmokers and smokers alike, although perhaps for different reasons.

Like implementing smoke-free policies, raising the sales tax on cigarettes is another indirect way to encourage people to quit or to at least cut down on smoking. If you are a smoker, then you know just how expensive packs are becoming these days. As of 2015, the average price per pack, with all taxes, is about $6.18 ("Toll of Tobacco in the United States"). And that average has been rising, with cigarette taxes in many states going up. In New York, for example, one pack can now cost around $14 or $15. Results from surveys conclude that teen smoking decreases by 7 percent and overall smoking goes down by 3–5 percent for every 10 percent increase in the price of cigarettes ("Update from the States").

Opposition can be seen from every corner. The tobacco companies, the states, and bar and restaurant owners all have something to say. Tobacco companies are upset for the obvious reason that if measures such as these are taken, sales will go down and the number of new smokers will decline—which really isn't such a bad thing. One of the biggest misconceptions about smoke-free laws is that they harm business for restaurants and bars. Not only will these laws "help protect restaurant and bar employees and patrons from the harms of secondhand smoke," but there is overwhelming evidence—dozens of studies and hard economic data—that smoke-free laws can do this without harming business (Knox, "Smoke-Free Laws"). In March 2003, New York passed a citywide comprehensive smoke-free law. A year later, the city reported that "business receipts for bars and restaurants have increased, employment has risen, and virtually all establishments are complying with the law." Moreover, the 2004 Zagat Survey found that while 4 percent of New Yorkers surveyed were eating out less often because of the smoke-free law, a whopping 23 percent were eating out *more* often because of the law (Knox, "Smoke-Free Laws"). There will be the occasional bar that hurts because they depend more heavily on customers who smoke, but overall the positive effects far outweigh the negative effects. States worry about the loss of cigarette revenues and the fate of the tobacco farmer. I say, in this day and age, a health-savvy trend is sweeping the nation and especially the younger generations. It is only a matter of time before the number of new smokers drops so significantly that they cannot support the tobacco industry. States that rely on tobacco revenues should start switching their areas of income now. Tobacco farmers can help this transition by growing soybeans or corn instead. For those wary states, why not at least pursue a trial period of passing smoke-free laws or flat out banning smoking to see the results for yourselves? There will hardly be a "negative economic impact, so there are no valid reasons for . . . states not to pass similar laws" ("Study: Mass. Smoking").

According to Terry Martin, "Smoking remains the leading preventable cause of death in this country" ("Health Consequences of

Smoking"). Thousands of lives will be taken this year. Perhaps by implementing these suggested measures, a few may be saved. I can't think of a logical reason not to do everything within states' power to help push smoking out of society. The American community as a whole needs to join together in a collective effort to rid our country of the maladies smoking brings. Neither one person nor one state can do it alone.

WORKS CITED

Barry, Matt. "Smoke-Free Laws Encourage Smokers to Quit and Discourage Youth from Starting." Campaign for Tobacco-Free Kids, 1 July 2004, www.tobaccofreekids.org/assets/factsheets/0198.pdf. Accessed 10 Apr. 2015.

Clark, Charles S. "Crackdown on Smoking." *CQ Researcher*, 4 Dec. 1992, library .cqpress.com/cqresearcher/document.php?id=cqresrre1992120400.

"Facts." *truth*. Truth.com, www.thetruth.com/the-facts. Accessed 8 Apr. 2015.

Knox, Becca. "Smoke-Free Laws Do Not Harm Business at Restaurants and Bars." Campaign for Tobacco-Free Kids, 1 July 2004, www.tobacco freekids.org/assets/factsheets/0144.pdf. Accessed 10 Apr. 2015.

Martin, Terry. "The Health Consequences of Smoking." *Smoking Cessation*. About.com, 8 Sept. 2004, www.about.com/smoking-cessation-forum -moderators-2824797. Accessed 8 Apr. 2015.

————."Quit Smoking Benefits—One to Nine Months." *Smoking Cessation*. About.com, 8 Sept. 2004, www.about.com/smoking-cessation-forum -moderators-2824789. Accessed 8 Apr. 2015.

"Study: Mass. Smoking Ban Hasn't Dampened Business." *Morning Edition*, narrated by Steve Inskeep, National Public Radio, 5 Apr. 2005. www .npr.org/templates/story/story.php?storyId=4576608.

"Smoke-Free Laws: Protecting Our Right to Breathe Clean Air." Campaign for Tobacco-Free Kids, 5 July 2004, www.tobaccofreekids.org/what -we-do/us/smoke-free-laws. Accessed 8 Apr. 2015.

"Smoking Kills Millions Each Year." *Australian Nursing Journal*, vol. 12, no. 7, 2005, p. 27. *Proquest*, Proquest.com.

"Smoking: U.S. Won't Meet Smoking Goals." *Medical Letter on the CDC & FDA*, 10 Jan. 2000, p. 11. *Proquest*, Proquest.com.

"Toll of Tobacco in the United States." Campaign for Tobacco-Free Kids, 3 Feb. 2015, www.tobaccofreekids.org/problem/toll-us.

"Update from the States: Tobacco Taxes and Smoke-Free Policies in Action." American Heart Association, 28 Mar. 2005, www.heart.org/HEARTORG /Advocate/StateIssues/TobaccoControl/Tobacco-Control---State-Issues _UCM_458694_Article.jsp#.WrzeBowaUk. Accessed 8 Apr. 2015.

Adapting to the Disappearance of Honeybees

James Benge

University of California, Riverside
Riverside, California

Sometimes students who specialize in math and science don't always recognize that the techniques they've mastered in a composition course provide them with the structure and tools they need to support effective research in other disciplines. James Benge provides an excellent example of a more technical style that still maintains a clear purpose—solving a specifically defined problem—and offers a well-argued solution (while also considering potential flaws in the plan). Despite the scientific subject matter, Benge engages his readers with a clever introduction and a relatable tone as he considers several potential causes for the global decline in honeybees and then offers the best possible solution. As you read, consider who Benge assumes his audience to be: Are they laypeople unfamiliar with his subject, biologists knowledgeable about the issue, or some combination of the two? How might his tone or approach change with a different audience?

Let's talk about honeybees. They're loud, they sting, and they make honey. The end. If only it were that easy. Honeybees are probably the single most important component in almost all of agriculture. To get a grasp of the impact these little guys have, we just need to examine any one foodstuff and follow the trail it leaves. We spin the wheel and land on almonds. Every August, billions of farm-grown honeybees are released into the California Central Valley almond orchards by being deceived that it is springtime. The almonds are exported worldwide, bringing in billions of dollars; the husks are sold as topsoil; and the rest is sold as cattle feed, all thanks to the honeybee (Agnew). An article from *Annals of Botany* states that "70 percent of crops that

1

account for about 35 percent of all agricultural production depend to varying extents on pollinators" (Aizen et al., "How" 1585).

Unfortunately, a disturbing phenomenon is cropping up over the globe that is sending not only farmers but economists into a frenzied panic as this money-making godsend drops dead. Recent studies have shown a severe drop in honeybees around the world, and in the United States alone, losses have increased from "30 to 60 percent on the West Coast" to "as much as 70 percent in parts of the East Coast and Texas" (Sylvers). Scientists are not entirely sure as to what the source of the problem is, but accusations have ranged from "mobile telephones" to "nanotechnology" (Neumann and Carreck 3). Most of these claims have been debunked, and much of the drivel has been weeded out as scientists have narrowed the biggest causes down to three: stress, mites (Bjerga), and disease (Neumann and Carreck).

The scientific community has coined a term for this phenomenon, calling it "colony collapse." The article "Does Infection by *Nosema ceranae* Cause 'Colony Collapse Disorder' in Honey Bees (*Apis mellifera*)?" presents at least one of the possible scenarios that could cause this problem, and Robert J. Paxton has analyzed and theorized that the pathogen *Nosema ceranae* is "potentially serious on the individual [honeybee] and the colony." He admits that his hypothesis is unlikely to be the main cause of CCD (colony collapse disorder) in North America, but possibly is in Spain. *N. ceranae* are a microsporidia (impossible to detect without a microscope) that infect hives within about eighteen months, in turn leading to colony collapse (Paxton). Climate change is moving this once temperately isolated pathogen to farther regions of the globe. So the problem may not seem as widespread as the next suspect for CCD, but it is worth further observation (Paxton).

Mites pose what could be a more serious cause of CCD. *Varroa destructor,* a mite capable of rendering honeybees flightless, is the second biggest factor of colony collapse. Though not globally ferocious enough to be the leading cause of CCD, they could prove to be the longest-lasting progenitor of this catastrophe. As mentioned in the article "The Almond and the Bee," "Mite treatments only work for a while before the mites reproduce resistant strains, and render the chemicals useless" (Agnew). While pathogens like *N. ceranae* can be eliminated through pesticides, mites are far more adaptive, and need to be handled more locally, as each case of mite-caused CCD could be different.

Unfortunately, *Nosema ceranae* and *Varroa destructor* are just two of many speculated contributors factoring into the cause of CCD. The biggest suspect, by far, is the Israeli acute paralysis virus. The United States Department of Agriculture (citing several studies done on the virus) found that 96.1 percent of hives that suffered from CCD also were found to have been infected with the Israeli virus. They also discovered that the Israeli virus can also be carried by the Varroa mite. Despite the compelling evidence, in a quote from the USDA's cited article "Genetic Survey Finds Association Between CCD and Virus," Jeffery S. Pettis admits that "what we have found is strictly a strong correlation of the appearance of IAPV and CCD together. We have not proven a cause-and-effect connection" (Kaplan). 5

Let us pretend for a moment that all the honeybees have disappeared from the face of the earth. Disease, a declination of local habitat (Winfree et al.), and millions of years of nonstop work have finally caught up to the honeybees. Without them, the world as mankind knows it teeters on the brink of collapse as orchards can no longer be pollinated, thus leaving no fruits, vegetables, or nuts for people to eat, no husks or shells to supply to farms for food, potentially eliminating both the meat and the dairy departments. Fortunately, that is not something we have to endure (as far as honeybees are concerned), for we have alternatives. 6

If we wanted to go down the route of flat-out replacing the honeybee, then its relatives are the first place to look. *Hymenoptera*, the order name for bees and wasps, along with ants and termites, is the largest order of anything to ever crawl, walk, scuttle, swim, or fly on Earth since day naught. The blue orchard bee, the wild squash bee, and a wild berry pollinator called the *osmia agalia* are seen as the next in line for desperate beekeepers (Bjerga). They are just as reliable, and the diversity would be vital. However, as the exchange rate goes, blue orchard bees, along with most of the other wild bees, are a more expensive property than the honeybee, even with their own rising price, but that is a short-term wall that could be overcome through proper management. 7

Bees alone are not the only viable successors that scientists are looking at. Oddly enough, crickets, from a different order entirely, are being examined for their pollination abilities. The discovery is recent, but as *Annals of Botany* shows, a nocturnal and undescribed species of raspy cricket is capable of pollinating orchids (Micheneau et al.). This may seem a little too niche for anyone to care, but there 9 is potential for domestication, expanding its pallet for what it can pollinate. This could take years, and since there is no natural colony mind-set in crickets, there will need to be managerial techniques for managing the crickets as well.

The United States Department of Agriculture started its action plan to combat CCD back in 2007. Enclosed in the document is a scientifically driven, $7.7 million investigation (CCD Steering Comm. 2). The USDA is attacking the heavyweight causes head-on, despite the proposed causes being simply correlative at the moment. Under "Topic 4: Mitigative and Preventative Measures," several immediately accessible and financially reasonable solutions are presented to fight these known causes, such as high concentrations of ozone sprayed into hibernating beehives during winter to kill pathogens and pesticides, localizing honeybees to reduce stress, and studying local bumblebees, due to their similar ancestry, to determine local causes for CCD (CCD Steering Comm. 22). 8

These are well-reasoned and intelligent solutions to the disappearance of the honeybees, but it is hiding the real problem at hand, and that is the homogeny of the pollinator industry. Honeybees are not going to be around forever, yet the agricultural industry is becoming more dependent on pollinators every year. Since 1961, the American honeybee hive has been in decline by about 1.79 percent per year even before the outbreak of CCD (Aizen et al., "Long-Term" 1573). The only viable solution for beekeepers and other farmers dependent on the honeybee is to expand resources to cover multiple species of bees, as well as other pollinators. If the true cause of CCD does lie somewhere with the Varroa mite, the Israeli virus, or stress, the honeybee's salvation will not come overnight, if it even comes at all, and while the USDA's proposal can help preserve currently living honeybees, diversity is the key to the survival of the industry. 10

WORKS CITED

Agnew, Singeli. "The Almond and the Bee." *The San Francisco Chronicle*, 14 Oct. 2007. United States Department of Agriculture National Agricultural Library, www.nal.usda.gov.

Aizen, Marcelo A., et al. "How Much Does Agriculture Depend on Pollinators? Lessons from Long-Term Trends in Crop Production." *Annals of Botany*, vol. 103, no. 9, 2009, pp. 1579-88, doi:10.1093/aob/mcp076.

————. "Long-Term Global Trends in Crop Yield and Production Reveal No Current Pollination Shortage but Increasing Pollinator Dependency." *Current Biology,* vol. 18, no. 20, 2008, pp. 1572-75, doi:10.1016/j.cub.2008.08.066.

Bjerga, Alan. "Blue Orchard Bees Find Favor in Colony Collapse Disorder Peril." *Bloomburg.com,* 19 Oct. 2007. United States Department of Agriculture National Agricultural Library, www.nal.usda.gov.

CCD Steering Committee. *Colony Collapse Disorder Action Plan.* United States Department of Agriculture, 20 June 2007, www.ars.usda.gov/is /br/ccd/ccd_actionplan.pdf.

Kaplan, Kim. "Genetic Survey Finds Association Between CCD and Virus." United States Department of Agriculture National Agricultural Library, 6 Sept. 2007, www.nal.usda.gov.

Micheneau, Claire, et al. "Orthoptera, a New Order of Pollinator." *Annals of Botany,* vol. 105, no. 3, 2010, pp. 335-64, doi:10.1093/aob/mcp299.

Neumann, Peter, and Norman L. Carreck. "Honey Bee Colony Losses." *Journal of Apicultural Research,* vol. 49, no. 1, 2010, pp. 1-6, doi:10.3896 /IBRA.1.49.1.01.

Paxton, Robert J. "Does Infection by *Nosema ceranae* Cause 'Colony Collapse Disorder' in Honey Bees (*Apis mellifera*)?" *Journal of Apicultural Research,* vol. 49, no. 1, 2010, pp. 80-84, doi:10.3896/IBRA.1.49.1.11.

Sylvers, Eric. "Case of the Disappearing Bees Creates a Buzz." *The New York Times,* 22 Apr. 2007. United States Department of Agriculture National Agricultural Library, www.nal.usda.gov.

Winfree, Rachel, et al. "A Meta-Analysis of Bees' Responses to Anthropogenic Disturbance." *Ecology,* vol. 90, no. 8, 2009, pp. 2068-76, doi: 10.1890/08-1245.1.

Unhealthy Lunchrooms: Toxic for Schoolchildren and the Environment

Kati Huff

Lake Michigan College
Benton Harbor, Michigan

Kati Huff takes on two problems in this essay: unhealthy food and the generation of excessive waste. Two solutions in one essay is a tall order, but Huff shows the link between these issues. Both the food and the waste are unhealthy—for us and for the environment—and unsustainable for the future. Huff cites her sources in APA style and provides an annotated bibliography at the end of her essay, where, instead of just listing her references, she briefly describes each source, telling what information it contains and who produced it.

America's waistline is bulging over its belt, and the environment is [1] slowly wasting away. The cause of both of these problems lies in the most unlikely of places. This is a place where all schoolchildren have roamed, gossiped, and played, and where they have been conditioned to gorge themselves on fat-ridden food while disregarding Mother Nature. Where is this nightmare taking place? In tens of thousands of elementary, junior, and senior high cafeterias across the nation. Fried foods and foam trays are prevalent in almost all public schools. Schoolchildren, especially in elementary schools, are oblivious to what they are putting into their bodies and into the garbage cans that fill up landfill after landfill. Feeding children deep-fried corn dogs and grease-saturated french fries on nonbiodegradable trays is doing nothing for two of the biggest concerns this country has: obesity and the environment. By using reusable trays and being provided with healthy food, students may become more environmentally conscious as well as aware of what they are putting into their bodies. Landfills and the ozone layer will be less affected by the production and disposal of thousands of foam trays, and students will get the nutrition their growing bodies need.

As elementary school students, my friends and I used to have 2 contests to see who could squeeze the most grease out of their cheese pizza on pizza Fridays. Usually, whoever ended up with the juicy middle piece of the pizza won. Because we were children, and we were hungry, we would set the grease puddle aside and continue to eat the pizza. This is not the type of food that should be infecting future school kids' stomachs. Schools need to change the way kids eat. In a *Newsweek* article published in 2005, it becomes apparent that the meals schools serve often consist of French fries, breaded patties, and some sort of canned vegetable. This, in turn, makes kids want to buy cookies and other snacks that the à la carte section of the cafeteria may offer, instead (Tyre & Staveley-O'Carroll, 2005). Though public schools are now offering healthier items, some of the schools still have too many unhealthy foods weighing them down (Ramirez, 2007).

Unfortunately, the cost of healthy food is skyrocketing. In a 3 2005 article in the *Food Service Director* (2007), C. Atwell, a director from California, says that he supports the use of healthy foods, and making the transition to them is not the problem. California schools are required to ban fatty and sugary foods from their schools. And a state program gives school districts 10 cents per meal served when the lunchroom offers two vegetable and fruit options (Shalfi, 2007). However, the cost of food has "risen 25% over the last four years while [funding] increases from the state and federal governments came in at about 13%. The difference seems to grow wider every year" (as cited in Shalfi, 2007, p. 24). Even with some help from the government, schools have trouble affording healthy food for all their students.

If students could choose healthier foods at lunch, they would 4 still be putting the food on foam lunch trays. The food might be better, but what about the environment? Schools need to change the food they serve and also the kind of trays they are serving food on. Though the foam trays are often called Styrofoam trays, the name Styrofoam is a trademark of Dow Chemical Company. Dow (2007a) states that Styrofoam is not the substance used for these foam trays, cups, or containers. Polystyrene, a substance much like Styrofoam but less durable and less insulating, is used for school lunch trays (Dow Chemical Company, 2007b). According to an editorial written by members of the Committee for the Preservation of Wildlife of Northern Illinois University (2005), 1,369 tons of products made with polystyrene are carelessly dumped into our landfills every day in the United States. This number is only increasing due to the excessive use of polystyrene trays in schools. For example, there are approximately 600 students at Berrien Springs High School, a public school in Southwestern Michigan. Every day the cafeteria serves lunch to roughly 400 students. If they used 400 trays a day for five days a week, that would be 2,000 polystyrene foam trays waiting to be dumped somewhere at the end of the week. This number is only for the high school. The elementary schools and junior high in the Berrien Springs School District also use foam trays. The number of foam trays being dumped every day is astronomical.

P. Evans, the food service director for Berrien Springs Public   5
Schools, stated that almost every school district in the area uses polystyrene foam trays. The reason, she says, is that using foam trays is more economically feasible. "We buy foam trays in cases of 500 that are about three to four cents apiece," said Evans. "Buying these disposables [trays] is much cheaper than the labor we would have to pay for employees to wash dishes" (personal communication, November 15, 2007).

Another benefit to the disposable polystyrene trays is that they   6
are sanitary. With disposable trays, districts do not have to worry about cleaning trays two or three times to make sure they are up to code to serve food on again. However, an article by the Committee for the Preservation of Wildlife (2005) reports that polystyrene is made with petroleum and benzene. Both of these are known cancer-causing elements. In 1986, the EPA National Human Adipose Tissue Survey said that they had found styrene residues in 100% of samples of human tissues. Styrene (a part of polystyrene) exposure has been found to cause fatigue, low hemoglobin values, carcinogenic effects, and nervousness (Committee for the Preservation of Wildlife, 2005). If these side effects from styrene exposure have been proven, why do schools continue to serve children food on trays made from those very elements? Schools must come up with a better solution.

One solution would be to use disposable trays that are better   7
for the environment. Unfortunately, this plan has many problems. P. Evans said that the Berrien Springs School District had looked into buying more ecologically friendly trays. However, "Go Green" lunch trays cost three to four times as much as the foam trays, and few districts could afford that. The Boise, Idaho, schools tried to use trays

made of sugarcane fiber, even though the trays cost three times as much as the foam ones. This school district was willing to stretch the extra penny and try them. However, the trays needed to be composted in humidity and high heat, which is not likely weather in Idaho (Allen, 2007).

To reduce the number of trays in landfills, the foam trays that schools use now could be recycled. However, recycling polystyrene is not an easy process and is extremely costly (Myron, 1995). Schools would lose money trying to recycle every single tray they use. P. Evans stated that if the Berrien Springs School District were to recycle the foam trays, they would need to be washed and cleared of food debris before the recycling company would take them. This would defeat the purpose of using the trays—they would still need people to wash them. And the process to make polystyrene produces chemicals that pollute the ozone, so it would still be bad for the environment (Myron, 1995). 8

Extra labor, special facilities, and healthy foods are certainly not cheap. Though these costs seem outrageous, they can be managed. When using reusable trays, schools have to pay once for the trays and also for occasional replacement trays. There are ways to eliminate extra labor as well. The Berrien Springs School District food service program is trying out touch screens that will let students order their meals. This will eliminate the time it takes for cafeteria workers to fill out an order slip for each student. With this extra time, cafeteria workers will have time to wash dishes without going into overtime (personal communication, November 15, 2007). According to M. Shalfi of *Food Service Director* (2007), a school district in Ohio is looking at investing in a combi-oven. The oven cooks with steam and adds crispness without deep frying. Since they won't be deep frying, the school will not have to pay for oil or wash out fryers. They say that the oven will pay itself off in time because they will be saving about $3,000 a year. Another option for washing the trays would be to use students. Students at the high school level are, in most states, required to complete a certain number of community service hours. What better way to get those hours in than during the lunch period without taking the time to leave campus? Also, incentives for helping, such as a free lunch, can be used to get students to help wash the trays. In this way, there would be no extra cost for cafeteria labor. 9

While food service directors are trying to find a cost-effective, "green" approach to the trays, they must also try to get students to eat 1 healthier. Sneaking new ingredients into foods is one option. Unfortunately, students sometimes turn away from foods that look the same as the unhealthy ones but taste different. According to a report by the UK's Liberal Democrats, 250,000 fewer meals are eaten in secondary schools after mandating nutrition guidelines (Druce, 2007). Requiring a course on nutrition might help students make better food choices at lunch, but hiring and training new teachers would be costly, and students might not make the right decisions anyway.

There is, however, a light at the end of this toxic tunnel. It is   11 simple to get students to eat healthier food. Slowly introducing fresh fruits and vegetables is a great way to start. Offering a well-balanced meal with a touch of the old food is the way to get students to eat new foods. Children do not like change, so the transition to healthier foods needs to be a slow and continual process. Skim milk, fresh fruits and vegetables, and whole grains should be easily accessible at each meal. The main course does not have to be made of soybeans, but healthy options need to be available for students to fill up their reusable trays with. If done properly, at a slow and steady pace, healthy foods will catch on and become just as popular as grease-pizza Friday.

By implementing this simple and effective plan, several groups   12 of people will benefit. Food services will save money and time by not having to buy foam trays or pay for labor. Schoolchildren will be making the right food choices and will have less chance of becoming obese in the future. Finally, the environment will be cleaner and less affected by millions of polystyrene foam trays polluting it. Although these solutions would require some changes to the current school food system, they would be worth it for their benefit to students and to the environment.

ANNOTATED BIBLIOGRAPHY

Allen, A. (2007, October 30). Boise schools pushing for eco-friendly lunch trays: Community urges schools to use materials that can be recycled or composted. *Idaho Statesman.* Retrieved from http://www.idahostatesman.com The Boise School District shows its concern about foam trays used in the school cafeteria. Some of the schools in the district are equipped with facilities to use plastic trays, while others tried a new tray made of sugarcane fiber that can be composted. Although these trays cost three times as much as the foam ones, students seemed to prefer them. Problems like recycling or composting the fiber trays arose. PTO groups are now offering to put dishwashers into the schools. Alternatives to the foam trays are still being discussed.

American Chemistry Council Plastics Food Processing Group (PFPG). (2007). *Polystyrene facts*. Retrieved from http://www.americanchemistry.com
The Plastics Food Processing Group is a business group of the American Chemistry Council and supplies the public with resin and polystyrene while responding to inquiries from the public. The PFPG explains why polystyrene is sanitary, sturdy, efficient, economical, and convenient. The PFPG advocates the use of polystyrene products while relating them to our daily lives. The arguments for using polystyrene products are clearly stated here.

Committee for the Preservation of Wildlife. (2005, February 11). Students should choose Styrofoam alternative. *Northern Star*. Retrieved from http://www.star.niu.edu
This article, written by members of the Committee for the Preservation of Wildlife, explains some dangers of the use of polystyrene. The article ties in the dangers of its use with students' lives at the northern Illinois campus. This article also reflects students' views of the foam trays.

Dow Chemical Company. (2007a). *What is STYROFOAM?* Retrieved from http://www.dow.com
Dow Chemical explains that Styrofoam is not used in plates or trays that are commonly used in school cafeterias. Styrofoam is a trademarked name.

Dow Chemical Company. (2007b). *Polystyrene*. Retrieved from http://www.dow.com
Dow Chemical explains what polystyrene is and what it is used for.

Druce, C. (2007, September 3). Future of school meals looks bleak without intervention. *The Caterer*. Retrieved from http://www.thecaterer.com/articles/315858
This article discusses a report by the UK's Liberal Democrats that highlights the negative impact of new health food regulations on secondary schools in England.

Hackes, B., & Shanklin, W. (1999). Factors other than environmental issues influence resource allocation decisions of school food service directors. *Journal of the American Dietetic Association, 99*(8), 944–946. Retrieved from http://www.adajournal.org
Respondents to an extensive survey give insight into school food service recycling programs. Also, recommendations are made to conserve environmental resources and cut down on pollution.

Myron, H. (1995). *Polystyrene foam recycling*. Retrieved from http://www.newton.dep.anl.gov/newton/askasci/1995/environ/ENV138.HTM
"Ask a Scientist" offers some insight into recycling and alternatives to polystyrene (used for foam trays in school cafeterias). Recycling the foam

is costly, and not many companies are interested in buying back the recycled material. Also, ozone-destroying chemicals are used to make foam products.

Ramirez, E. (2007, August 16). Do school cafeterias make the grade? *U.S. News & World Report.* Retrieved from http://www.usnews.com
Creative ways to bring in more healthy foods to schools and the expenses of those healthy foods are discussed.

Shalfi, M. (2007, August 15). Taking back school lunch: Operators meet the challenges of the increased costs of healthier foods with creative solutions and an outcry for federal funding. *Food Service Director, 20*(8), 24–27. Retrieved from http://www.fsdmag.com
Transitioning to healthier lunch items is something that all schools agree on, but healthy food is expensive, and not all school districts get the funding for it. "Sneaking" healthy foods into entrées has proven successful, but nutrition education in the schools is still missing. Creative solutions such as buying combi-ovens, bringing back salad bars, creating more ethnic cuisines, and using whole grains are presented.

Tyre, P., & Staveley-O'Carroll, S. (2005, August 8). How to fix school lunch: Celebrity chefs, politicians, and concerned parents are joining forces to improve the meals kids eat every day. *Newsweek, 146,* 50.
As the number of children who are obese or have diabetes grows, it is becoming apparent that school kitchens need to be reevaluated. Meals provided by untrained workers in understaffed cafeterias do not give children the nutrition they need. Also, money from vending machine sales has declined because of the implementation of healthy foods; therefore, schools find it hard to pay for fresh fruits and vegetables.

8 Justifying an Evaluation

You are already very familiar with evaluations. In fact, if you're like most of us, you depend on evaluations on a daily basis. Before spending money to dine out, you probably ask for suggestions from friends who know the local restaurant scene or read restaurant reviews online or in your local newspaper. And you probably don't watch movies cold; instead, you're more likely to go to the theater on a friend's recommendation or read brief descriptions of what's playing on a movie-review site before buying a ticket. For a major purchase like a car or truck, a cell phone, a digital camera, or even a pair of running shoes, you're likely to look for a recent, authoritative review of the product, perhaps in *Consumer Reports*—a magazine whose comprehensive evaluations have catapulted its parent organization, the Consumers Union, into the national consciousness.

Obviously, reviews are wide ranging. Student writers in this chapter evaluate quite different subjects: a movie, a book, and even satellite radio. However, each writer employs the same basic features to justify his or her evaluation: a well-presented subject; a well-supported judgment; an effective response to objections and alternative judgments; and a clear, logical organization. Like any reviewers, these writers judge their subjects, but they go well beyond just giving them a thumbs-up or thumbs-down: They give reasons for their judgments and then support each reason with definitions, examples, descriptions, and comparisons to similar subjects. They may even anticipate readers' reservations or alternative judgments.

Judgments are easy to make—so much so that they are sometimes referred to as "snap judgments." When you evaluate, you test your snap judgments, turning them into reasoned evaluations. In doing so, you develop your powers of attention to details and the ability to discriminate among them. When evaluating a subject and writing up your evaluation of it, you must look closely and attentively, think hard and rethink, and justify—all the while extending and refining your understanding of the subject you are evaluating. To evaluate, then, is to engage in thoughtful, responsible, discriminating work—work that is worth your time.

Use the guidelines in the Peer Review Guide that follows to practice peer review using the essays in this chapter.

A PEER REVIEW GUIDE

A WELL-PRESENTED SUBJECT

Has the writer presented the subject effectively?

Summarize: Tell the writer what you understand the subject of the evaluation to be, and identify the kind of subject it is.

Praise: Point to a place where the subject is presented effectively—for example, where it is described vividly and accurately, where it is named, or where it is clearly placed in a recognizable genre or category.

Critique: Tell the writer where readers might need more information about the subject, and whether any information about it seems inaccurate or possibly only partly true. Suggest how the writer could clarify the kind of subject it is, either by naming the category or by giving examples of familiar subjects of the same type.

A WELL-SUPPORTED JUDGMENT

Has the writer supported the judgment effectively?

Summarize: Tell the writer what you understand the overall judgment to be, and list the criteria on which it is based.

Praise: Identify a passage in the essay where support for the judgment is presented effectively—for example, note particularly strong supporting reasons, appeals to criteria readers are likely to share, or especially compelling evidence.

Critique: Let the writer know if you cannot find a thesis statement or think the thesis is vague or overstated. Tell the writer where the evaluation could be improved—for example, suggest another reason that could be added, propose a way to justify one of the criteria on which the evaluation is based, or recommend a source or an example that could be used to bolster support for the judgment.

AN EFFECTIVE RESPONSE TO OBJECTIONS AND ALTERNATIVE JUDGMENTS

Has the writer responded effectively to objections and alternative judgments?

Summarize: Choose an objection or an alternative judgment about the subject, and explain it in your own words.

Praise: Identify a passage in the essay where the writer responds effectively to an objection or an alternative judgment. An effective response may include making a concession—for example, agreeing that a subject the writer is primarily criticizing has some good points, or agreeing that the subject has weaknesses as well as strengths.

Critique: Tell the writer where a response is needed or could be made more effective—for example, suggest a likely objection or alternative judgment that should be taken into account, help the writer understand the criteria behind an alternative judgment, or offer an example that could be used to refute an objection.

A CLEAR, LOGICAL ORGANIZATION

Is the evaluation clearly and logically organized?

Summarize: Briefly describe the strategies used to make the essay clear and easy to follow.

Praise: Give an example of where the essay succeeds in being readable—in its overall organization, in its clear presentation of the thesis, in its effective opening or closing, or by other means.

Critique: Tell the writer where the readability could be improved. Can you, for example, suggest a better beginning or a more effective ending? If the overall organization of the essay needs work, make suggestions for rearranging parts or strengthening connections.

Watchmen
Matthew Fontilla
Chaffey College
Rancho Cucamonga, California

Watchmen, a 2009 movie based on Alan Moore's graphic novel by the same name, is about a group of superheroes in an alternate-reality version of New York City in 1985. In this brief, exuberant review, Matthew Fontilla expresses his admiration for the style, characters, and overall intensity of the film. His review is designed for an audience who might see the movie based on his enthusiasm, and perhaps also for one that will identify as either "intellectual" or "geek." As you read, notice how Fontilla supports his judgment in each paragraph of his essay. Does he succeed in making you want to see *Watchmen*?

The film *Watchmen* is a "must see" for intellectuals and geeks alike; its 1
visual style surpasses that of all other comic book films. There is never
a dull moment during the film because the cinematography is phe-
nomenal and the philosophy, although slightly arcane, is scathingly
profound; your eyes will never leave the screen, and your mind will
never stop deciphering the meaning of the film. A second viewing is
highly recommended if you wish to grasp all the information and the
metaphors; the only problem with this is the fact that you will have
spent six hours and twelve minutes watching it twice. However, if you
take a lesson from Doctor Manhattan, you should be able to regard
time as meaningless, which will allow you to appreciate this film without worrying about the hours passing by. *Watchmen* is a masterpiece
because of its elucidation of the plight of society, the pains of superi-
ority, and the limits of time. The characters illustrate these points by
their vigilance, noncompliance with authority, and wisdom.

 Watchmen alludes to fear in society being like a wildfire; it spreads 2
rapidly, and the masses do nothing to impede its spread. Only a few
vigilantes will, sometimes foolishly, put their lives on the line in an

effort to put a stop to something bigger than themselves. The Watchmen are these few vigilantes in a fire that is the fear of, among many other issues, a seemingly inevitable nuclear war. Vigilantes are not always heroes, though. This moral complexity is one of the reasons why *Watchmen* is such a great film. While the Watchmen are superheroes, their actions aren't always justifiable. A recurring theme in the film is the question: Who watches the Watchmen? This suggests that the public is not always grateful for the actions of the Watchmen. They are frequently violent, occasionally destroy public property, and cannot always help the society they are a part of.

A brilliant aspect of the film lies underneath the costumes; a certain 3
degree of noncompliance is at the heart of all vigilantes. Each one is reluctant to follow the rules of society or even to follow a leader within the group. Although the Watchmen have a history as a public group, they are not always willing to comply with the public's demands. At the time the film is set, their superpowers have been made illegal; only two Watchmen are active, with government approval. However, each member of the Watchmen exemplifies this noncompliance in his or her own way. Rorschach, the member of the Watchmen who narrates the film, is perhaps the least compliant of the group. He is an independent, hardly a member of the group at all. His bitterness about the immorality of society leads him to kill those whom he considers immoral; the viewer must consider whether his actions are morally just.

A notable quote from the film that will give some insight on 4
the wisdom of each character is: "My father was a watchmaker. He abandoned it when Einstein discovered time is relative. I would only agree that a symbolic clock is as nourishing to the intellect as a photograph of oxygen to a drowning man." (The "symbolic clock" in the quote is the nuclear doomsday clock, which indicates symbolically how close the world is to nuclear war.) The Watchmen have cultivated wisdom by analyzing the malice of society, and the people who contribute to it, throughout their decades of existence. Thus, fearful symbols like the doomsday clock mean little to them. They each hold steadfast beliefs on how to remake a malevolent society, even if that means destroying it.

If you are looking to view an intellectually stimulating thriller, 5
a compelling superhero action film, or both, watch *Watchmen*. The deep symbolism throughout the film will leave you in awe, and the action sequences will have your palms sweaty in no time. Your imagination will be grateful, as long as you are willing to dedicate your undivided attention to the screen for almost three hours.

Evaluation of Nickel and Dimed

Jane Kim

University of California, Riverside
Riverside, California

For this essay, Jane Kim chose to evaluate *Nickel and Dimed*, Barbara Ehrenreich's firsthand investigation into the lives of the working poor. In her very first paragraph, Kim presents the reader with enough information to understand her position on both the book and its argument. Then Kim easily leads us through her well-organized argument, using relevant quotations from the book to support her judgments. As you read, notice the criteria Kim sets up for evaluating Ehrenreich's work.

Barbara Ehrenreich, a journalist with a Ph.D. in biology, reports   1
her experience in the world of the working poor in her book *Nickel and Dimed*. As an investigative reporter and scientist, she creates an experiment, sets some limits, takes a few necessities, and detaches herself from the upper-class world, which she is familiar with, and inserts herself into the society of the impoverished. She gains firsthand experience in what it feels like to live on a barely livable wage, always hoping to have shelter and nourishment the next day. She works as a waitress, a maid, a dietary aide, and an employee of Walmart, while trying to sustain herself off just what she makes at these jobs, minus the advantages she came with in her experiment (car, extra cash, and health). Ehrenreich, through her hands-on experience, evinces the difficulty and almost impossibility of living off the wages such workers make (as of 2001). Overall, Ehrenreich does a fair job of revealing the situation of the working poor and making it clear that something must be done to relieve this "state of emergency" (Ehrenreich 214).

Ehrenreich presents her argument that it is very difficult to "live   2
on the wages available to the unskilled," as "many people earn far

less than they need to live on," through excellent uses of supporting evidence (Ehrenreich 1, 213). Furthermore, to persuade her readers that her claim is important, Ehrenreich shows the wage rise over the years, saying "wages at the bottom are going up, [but] they're not going up very briskly," and "they have not been sufficient to bring low-wage workers up to the amounts they were earning twenty-seven years ago, in 1973" (Ehrenreich 203). The author clearly presents her position and argument through effective diction and by revealing the seriousness of the issue, which should not be ignored, as the experiences of low-wage workers "are not part of a sustainable lifestyle, even a lifestyle of chronic deprivation and relentless low-level punishment" (Ehrenreich 214).

By doing firsthand field research to add to her extensive library   3
and Internet research, the author makes an especially convincing argument. Describing the daily lives of low-wage workers makes her evidence authoritative. For example, in the second chapter, Ehrenreich shares the experience she went through working two jobs: a weekend position as a dietary aide at a nursing home ($7 an hour) and a forty-hour-per-week maid position ($6.65). Even when working two jobs and being thrifty, she reveals the difficulty of managing to pay for rent and food. In terms of rent, she explains that "when the rich and the poor compete for housing on the open market, the poor don't stand a chance" and that essentially "the poor have been forced into housing that is more expensive, more dilapidated, or more distant from their places of work" (Ehrenreich 199). Furthermore, to increase the effectiveness of her argument that wages must be higher, the author reveals that even when the low-wage worker receives aid, it is difficult to get it. When she tried to obtain food from food pantries and emergency aid, it took her seventy minutes of calling and driving to get around seven dollars worth of food, with limited choices (Ehrenreich 103).

In addition to her personal experience, Ehrenreich uses other   4
authoritative sources to enhance her reliability, integrating statistical sources within her text and citing those sources in footnotes. For example, to explain why wages don't rise, Ehrenreich refers to a report by Louis Uchitelle in the *New York Times* on how "many employers will offer almost anything—free meals, subsidized transportation, store discounts—rather than raise wages" (Ehrenreich 204).

Without Ehrenreich's investigative reporting, it would be hard   5
for people outside of the low-wage working class to grasp the reality

of the problem. Through firsthand experience, Ehrenreich effectively reveals the dark world of the daily life of the low-wage worker. She acknowledges that some readers could argue that she didn't truly experience "poverty," as she went in with some advantages: a car (her own) or a rental vehicle (paid with credit card instead of earned wages), the cushion of relying on her credit card if she ever thought she wouldn't have food the next day, and knowing she could end the project at the particular location if she ran out of money for rent (Ehrenreich 5–6). Ehrenreich concedes this objection to her experiment, explaining that "there was no way [she] was going to 'experience poverty' or find out how it 'really feels' to be a long-term low-wage worker" (Ehrenreich 6). Furthermore, she makes it clear that there are people who endure much worse conditions than she does during her experiment: "this is in fact the best-case scenario: a person with every advantage that ethnicity and education, health and motivation can confer attempting, in a time of exuberant prosperity, to survive in the economy's lower depths" (Ehrenreich 10). Ehrenreich lets readers know through such comments that she is not portraying herself as having experienced exactly what the impoverished face every day.

Another kind of objection Ehrenreich anticipates is that she should not speak for others but let them speak for themselves. Although she concedes it would be better if they did speak and act for themselves, Ehrenreich provides some information to support her speaking out on behalf of the low-wage workers. She makes the point that workers are often hesitant to form unions for fear of getting fired because "the poorer they are, the more constrained their mobility usually is." She also notes that "help-wanted signs and want ads coyly refrain from mentioning numbers" so workers can't compare wages, and of course their employers may "make it hard to air [their] grievances to peers or to enlist other workers in a group effort to bring about change" (Ehrenreich 205, 206, 209). Ehrenreich effectively argues that low-wage workers do not have many opportunities to safely speak for themselves, so she is justified in attempting to speak for them.

Overall, Ehrenreich's *Nickel and Dimed* is well written and effectively enlightens readers on a situation facing members of their own community. The author's use of personal experience and authoritative resources gives her argument strength and believability. Her inclusion of personal ethical indignation combined with effective rhetoric gives her argument an intensity that has the potential to move readers to action. She may not provide solutions to the problem she so vividly presents, but Ehrenreich achieves her goal of opening readers' eyes to the hardship of those who make the lives of others more comfortable at the expense of their own well-being.

WORK CITED

Ehrenreich, Barbara. *Nickel and Dimed*. Metropolitan Books, 2001.

Satellite Radio

Julie Plucinski

Triton College
River Grove, Illinois

Julie Plucinski offers an evaluation from a consumer's viewpoint; she explains the benefits of satellite radio, considers potential concerns, and provides readers with details that allow them to make an informed decision. She begins by telling her audience about the merits the company boasts on its Web site, then provides reasons and support for her positive judgment of the service based on her personal experience. This essay can, at times, read like a professional advertisement. As the reader, does this form of consumer enthusiasm attract you to a potential product or service, or are you wary of what might come across as a sales pitch? What other methods does Plucinski employ to justify her evaluation?

It's 4:23 in the afternoon, and I am stuck in bumper-to-bumper traf- 1
fic on the way home from work. Flipping through the local radio stations to ease my tension yields little release from the aggravation. Commercials hawking the new blockbuster movie or cell phone sale with a local wireless company blare through my speakers. Is it too much to ask for some actual music? Satellite radio to the rescue!

"It's like nothing you've ever heard before" boasts the SiriusXM 2
Web site. That statement couldn't be any more accurate. A subscription to SiriusXM satellite radio grants a consumer immediate access to over 130 channels, including 71 commercial-free music broadcasts. If you aren't in the mood for music, you can always turn to one of the many comedy, sports, kid-friendly, weather, or news channels offered for your listening pleasure. Content on SiriusXM radio is static-free (due to its transmission via satellite) and uncensored (Guttenberg and Moskovciak). Additionally, the listener is able to view a song's title and artist on the face of the radio, which can be

171

noted for future downloads to your iPod. A vast array of static-free, clearly displayed channels that are uncensored, and all of the songs played in their original format. What's not to love?

Prior to purchasing a subscription, you must obtain a car radio capable of receiving satellite radio. (Lucky for us, most foreign and domestic vehicles produced over the past few model years are technologically advanced and automatically equipped with satellite capable radio systems as standard.) If your existing vehicle does not come equipped with a receiver capable of obtaining satellite radio, one may be purchased at a cost ranging anywhere from $90 to $249.   3

Some may wish to forgo satellite radio in exchange for a "cheaper" option, such as an iPod adapter wire or wireless transmitter. These devices would allow an individual with an iPod to stream previously downloaded music through their car stereo. However, there would be a cost involved in purchasing an iPod and additional hardware required to stream music that had previously been downloaded for $0.99 on iTunes. If a consumer downloaded 500 songs on their $200 iPod, the total cost would add up to almost $700! Any perceived savings are eliminated and, actually, far exceed the cost of a satellite receiver and subscription to SiriusXM satellite radio. I had personally tested both the wired and wireless music streaming devices. The wired option works well but has one major flaw. If the driver does not want to hear a song that begins to play, the user would need to physically pick up the iPod and navigate the various tiny display screens in search of another tune. All of this manual activity would be highly difficult to do while driving and could lead to an accident. The wireless adapter does not work at all, as reception is fuzzy and wanes in and out in search of a signal. Leave the iPod for the office or gym, and avoid the risk of having a collision. Get a SiriusXM receiver and subscription!   4

Once you have made the decision to purchase a SiriusXM radio subscription, I strongly urge you to write down your satellite radio number. This information will be required to activate your subscription. I purchased a car in 2009 that came with a free six-month trial subscription. When it came time for me to purchase a SiriusXM subscription package I encountered quite a bit of difficulty finding the radio number. In fact, finding the radio number was the most difficult part of the entire process.   5

I would recommend purchasing a subscription via the Web site. The site is very easy to navigate and provides the user with channel information, pricing details, and user testimonials. Once a user has   6 decided on the desired package content, he or she can simply click on the "Subscriptions" tab at the top of the page. The screens walk the future satellite-radio listener through the steps of entering billing data and the radio number, choosing a term length, and activating the subscription. Activating the account does take a few minutes, as SiriusXM must transmit a signal from a satellite to the radio, but the wait is well worth it.

For those who may be initially overwhelmed by the wide variety of content, a channel guide will be mailed to you once you have subscribed and will be an invaluable resource when programming all your preset channels. When in doubt, you can always visit the SiriusXM Web site for up-to-date information on channel content and live concert events. These resources are capable of introducing the listener to a whole new genre of music, providing years of future enjoyment.   **7**

The question you are surely asking yourself is, Why would I pay for radio that I can get for free through my local channels? My number one response to that inquiry would be that satellite radio is commercial-free! There is virtually no need to change the channel to find worthwhile listening content. Yes, you must purchase a plan, which will be automatically renewed until the time in which you cancel your subscription. If you wish to cancel your subscription, you must contact SiriusXM within three business days to incur no additional charges. I spend a considerable amount of time in my car and gladly pay around $15 per month to avoid commercials. Many other consumers appear to be following this trend, as SiriusXM recently raised its projected revenue outlook for 2012 from $3.3 billion to approximately $3.4 billion (SiriusXM). Almost 1.6 million vehicular and Internet sub-scribers can't be wrong.   **8**

Another key feature I like about satellite radio is that the channels are broken down by genre. One day I may need a quick cure for the morning doldrums and blare the eighties channel on the way to the office. On my way home, I may want to be transported back to my high school years and yearn for some grunge rock. Yes, some local radio stations do provide commercial-free radio. However, the channels are few and far between and do not offer the extensive variety SiriusXM satellite radio provides. Occasionally, SiriusXM will even offer specialty stations premiering the work of one specific artist for an entire month. Some friends and family may think that I am a little too old, but a pack of wild horses couldn't tear me away from the Metallica channel in March 2009. I have not yet found a local commercial-free   **9** channel with this advantage. You can always find a genre or an artist channel to suit your mood on SiriusXM satellite radio.

Want to take your favorite channels with you on a road trip? Satellite radio offers coast-to-coast coverage spanning over 3,717,792 square miles (SiriusXM). The days of driving over the Illinois border and losing a radio signal are long gone! SiriusXM satellite streaming ensures that you will be discoing all the way to California. An article from *Travel and Leisure* magazine contradicts my view on this topic. In this review, the author feels that the local music heard over regular radio frequencies connects him to the state or area in which he travels; he cites radio as "one way the world around you gets into the cocoon of your car" (Torkells). Some individuals may prefer listening to country music while coasting through Texas or Bluegrass while driving through Louisiana. I am not one of those people.

SiriusXM satellite radio continually improves its service by launching new satellites into space. However, the listener can expect one minor drawback. Your SiriusXM radio signal will wane a bit when passing through enclosed spaces, such as a viaduct, bridge, or heavily wooded area. The signal from the satellite cannot pass through these types of enclosures. These outages are usually very brief, lasting no more than a few seconds.

Another item that die-hard morning show fans may miss is important or trending local news updates. You can listen to a Chicago-based news station on satellite but will likely be put to sleep by the broadcaster's monotone, sociology lecture, teacher-from-hell simulcast. Sleeping and operating heavy machinery is never a good combination! A few of the pop music channels do offer some of the morning show banter you may have come to love from your local channels, but the listener is constantly reminded of the fact that the broadcast is produced in a New York–based studio. So long as you do not come to expect reports on Illinois politics or happenings in the Chicagoland area, your longing for a locally based morning show crew will be short lived.

Consumers are no longer forced to listen to countless hours of commercials while waiting to hear the latest pop music hit song. Advancements in technology have given us the gift of an alternate means for obtaining entertainment on the road. While SiriusXM satellite radio is not without some minor flaws, the aforementioned nuances are a small price to pay for the sheer variety of listening entertainment offered and commercial-free convenience.

WORKS CITED

Guttenberg, Steve, and Matthew Moskovciak. "CNET's Quick Guide to Satellite Radio." *CNET*, 1 Mar. 2005, www.cnet.com/quick-guide /satellite-radio.

"SiriusXM raises full-year subscriber forecast." *CNBC*, 9 July 2012, www .cnbc.com/id/100156451

SiriusXM. www.siriusxm.com. Accessed July 2015.

Torkells, Erik. "XM and Sirius Satellite Radio." *Travel and Leisure*, 1 May 2009, www.travelandleisure.com/articles/all-everything-all-the-time.

9 *Arguing for Causes or Effects*

Beginning your day, you wonder why your car is increasingly hard to start. Driving to campus, you puzzle over why you seem unable to make better use of your study and homework time. Circling the parking lot looking for a space, you fret about what could be holding up ground breaking for the promised multistory parking structure. This kind of thinking is so natural that your brain does it for you, without any urging or pushing. You couldn't really stop yourself from thinking about the whys and hows of things—even if you wanted to.

But fretful and even obsessive as this kind of thinking may be sometimes, you wouldn't want to shut it off because it could save you time if it inspires you to remove some obstacle; it could make you wiser if it leads to new understanding about yourself, other people, or the world at large; it could make you happier if it results in reaching a long-sought goal. Nevertheless, this daily causal thinking—about how something you notice came to be the way it is, or why something happened or continues to happen—is idle and unsystematic.

Yet this is the basis for a more demanding, sustained kind of causal thinking, the kind you will find in the essays that make up this chapter—essays that present structured arguments for the possible causes or effects of certain phenomena or trends. (A *phenomenon* is something noticeable that occurs or happens; a *trend* is something that has changed or is changing over time.) The student essay writers in this chapter examine causes or effects for these phenomena: What could motivate a person to lie? Why would someone in distress not ask for help? Why are more people right-handed than left-handed? Why would an immigrant to the United States choose not to learn English? These phenomena are the students' subjects, which are well defined and described in the essays. But that's usually the easy part.

The hard part is arguing for the causes and effects of these phenomena. Instead of idle speculation, you are trying to convince readers that your proposed causes or effects are plausible or likely. As you read the essays in this chapter, note the basic features of the genre used to influence readers: a well-presented subject; a well-supported cause-effect analysis; an effective response to objections and alternative causes or effects; and a clear, logical organization. The causes and effects you propose may come from your own experience, from research, or both. The writing engages you in sustained, systematic thinking to answer a significant social, cultural, or political question—sustained because it's going to take you awhile; systematic because you will need to select the most likely of many possible causes and effects, sequence them logically, and support them so that they seem plausible, all with the aim of convincing particular readers to take your argument seriously.

The rewards are great. Along with the other kinds of argument writing in this book, arguing for causes or effects enables you to become the kind of person who confidently inquires deeply into events, who expects that there is probably more to know than first appears. Adopting this stance, you join a new culture of debate, reflection, initiative, and knowledge seeking. Gaining confidence, you shake off old constraints and limits.

Use the guidelines in the Peer Review Guide that follows to practice peer review using the essays in this chapter.

A Peer Review Guide

A WELL-PRESENTED SUBJECT

How effectively does the writer present the subject?

Summarize: Tell the writer what you understand the subject to be and why he or she thinks it is important and worth analyzing.

Praise: Give an example of something in the draft that you think will especially interest the intended readers and help them understand the subject.

Critique: Tell the writer if you have any confusion or uncertainty about the subject. What further explanation, examples, or statistics do you need to understand it better? If you can think of a more interesting way to present the subject, share your ideas with the writer.

A WELL-SUPPORTED CAUSE-EFFECT ANALYSIS

How plausible are the proposed causes or effects, and how well does the writer support the cause-effect analysis?

Summary: Identify the possible causes or effects the writer argues are the most plausible and interesting.

Praise: Tell the writer which cause or effect seems most convincing. Point to any support (such as a particular example, a statistic, a research study, or a graph) that you think is especially strong.

Critique: Tell the writer if any of the causes or effects seem too obvious or minor, and if you think an important cause or effect has been left out. Where the support seems lacking or unconvincing, explain what is missing or seems wrong. If the reasoning seems flawed, what makes you think so?

AN EFFECTIVE RESPONSE TO OBJECTIONS AND ALTERNATIVE CAUSES OR EFFECTS

How effectively does the writer respond to readers' objections and alternative causes or effects?

Summary: Identify the objections or alternative causes or effects to which the writer responds.

Praise: Point out any response you think is especially effective, and tell the writer what makes you think so. For example, indicate where the support is especially credible and convincing.

Critique: Point to any objections or alternative causes or effects that the writer could have responded to more effectively, and suggest how the response could be improved. Also indicate if the writer has overlooked any serious objections.

A CLEAR, LOGICAL ORGANIZATION

How clear and logical is the cause-effect analysis?

Summary: Underline the thesis statement and topic sentences.

Praise: Give an example of where the essay succeeds in being especially clear and easy to follow—for example, in its overall organization, its use of key terms and transitions, or its use of visuals.

Critique: Point to any passages where the writing could be clearer, where topic sentences or transitions could be added, or where key terms could be repeated to make the essay easier to follow. Try suggesting a better beginning or a more effective ending.

The Truth about Lying

Michele Cox

University of California, Riverside
Riverside, California

In one way or another, we have all had experience with lying, whether we lied to others or were told lies by friends, family members, or colleagues. In most cases, lying can be very difficult and make us feel guilty, regretful, or betrayed. So why do people lie? In the following essay, student Michele Cox investigates the motivations for lying, backing up her assertions with findings from psychologists and other observers. By citing these experts, Cox establishes her argument's authority and reviews a variety of motivations for lying, from the desire to get ahead in life to fear and worries about one's self-image. As you read, reflect on times when you have lied or been lied to, and consider the reasons for your or your friend's dishonesty. Do the reasons that Cox offers seem plausible?

Although many people believe that lying is morally wrong and discourage the practice, almost everyone lies at one time or another, from the neglectful student who claims that the dog ate his homework to politicians who stretch the truth. Some of us do it every day, whether or not we fully realize it. But why do people lie? Because each individual is different, there are many possible answers to this question. Usually, however, people lie in an attempt to control some aspect of their lives.

One of the most obvious causes of lying is the drive to do whatever it takes to get ahead in life. For example, some people falsify information on their résumés to get a job that requires a skill that they do not really possess, thus stealing the position from a more deserving candidate. Other people may falsely claim expertise in a particular area to impress their boss or to improve their chances of getting a promotion. People may also lie in the form of committing fraud. CBS News reported that in 2010, $17 billion in fraudulent unemployment benefits were paid out to people who were never eligible for them and to formerly unemployed Americans who had gone back to work ("Unemployment").

Another cause of lying is fear—the fear of being blamed or punished for a wrongdoing. When people do something that they know is wrong, they may not be able to come to terms with it, or they may be afraid of being condemned for it. Therefore, they may lie to get themselves out of the situation, often transferring the blame to someone else or altogether denying their involvement in the misdeed. A desire to avoid negative consequences of misbehavior causes people to start lying at an early age. Beginning at about age three, children will lie to avoid getting into trouble or to try to get out of it (Jesperson). By age five, most kids are expert liars when it comes to dodging punishment, and they do not grow out of this habit (Jesperson). 3

People also lie to improve their own image. A study carried out by psychologist Robert Feldman at the University of Massachusetts revealed that most subjects lie in everyday conversation to appear more competent and more likable to people whom they are trying to impress. Feldman found that 60 percent of subjects lied at least once during a ten-minute conversation and told an average of two to three lies (Jesperson). After the conversation was over, participants were asked to view a tape of it and to identify anything they had said that was not entirely accurate (Lloyd). Initially, according to Feldman, subjects said that they thought they were entirely accurate, but after watching themselves on video, they were surprised to discover that they had said something inaccurate about themselves. The lies ranged from pretending to like someone they really disliked to falsely claiming to be the star of a rock band (Lloyd). Feldman claimed that people tell lies like these almost reflexively (Lloyd). Given our desire to look good to others and to protect our self-worth, such behavior makes sense. As social animals, we want to be liked and respected, and if we cannot achieve admiration through honest means, we may resort to lying. 4

Another subgroup is made up of compulsive liars, who seem compelled to lie even though it does them no apparent good or the truth would lead to a better result for them. For example, they may say that they bought an item from one store when they really got it from another. What can possibly be their reason for lying? Paul Ekman, professor of psychiatry at the University of California, 5

San Francisco, believes that people tell such lies not to get out of trouble but for fun ("Why"). For them, lying is like a drug that provides an adrenalin rush and the feeling of being able to control the person that they are lying to ("Why"). Some individuals seem to lie automatically without meaning to deceive, however. Jerald Jellison, professor of psychology at the University of Southern California, suggests that this phenomenon may have something to do with momentum. If a person gets away with an initial lie, he or she may be inclined to continue lying until it becomes a sort of habit ("Why").

Although people lie to benefit themselves, they may also lie to 6 try to protect someone else. A study by Bella DePaulo, a professor in social psychology, and other researchers reveals that although participants in their research told far more lies to benefit themselves in some way, close to one out of every four lies was told to benefit other people (DePaulo et al.). Even the most well-intentioned person may be guilty of telling at least one of these so-called white lies. For example, when friends ask us for an opinion on something, and we have a feeling that our true opinion might hurt their feelings, we may tell them what we believe they want to hear instead of being honest. Even as children, we are taught to lie to others. Our parents tell us to say that we like presents that we have been given even when we do not, all for the sake of being polite. And people who say that they want an "honest opinion" about something are usually lying. Most are really looking for confirmation that the choice they have made is good. Although it may be considered wrong to tell people what they want to hear when it could end up doing them harm, we do so anyway to preserve our relationship with them and to keep them happy.

Even though lying can be seen as breaking a bond of trust, a sort of 7 unspoken agreement to treat others as we would like to be treated, the bottom line is that almost everyone lies. Whether lies come from selfish or unselfish motivations, it seems to be in our nature to tell them.

WORKS CITED

DePaulo, Bella, et al. "Lying in Everyday Life." *Journal of Personality and Social Psychology*, vol. 70, no. 5, 1996, pp. 979–95, doi:10.1.1.597.8906.

Jesperson, Kathy. "Why Do People Lie? The Truth about Motivations for Lying." *Psychology@Suite101*, 21 Dec. 2009, kathy-j.suite101.com/why-do-people -lie-a181829#ixzz1bzLP2U2I.

Lloyd, Robin. "Studies: People Generally Lie to Preserve Self-Esteem." Fox News, 15 May 2006, www.foxnews.com/story/2006/05/15/studies -people-generally-lie-to-preserve-self-esteem.html.

"Unemployment Payments Fraud Worth $17B per Year." CBS News, 3 July 2011, www.cbsnews.com/news/unemployment-payments-fraud -worth-17b-per-year.

"Why People Lie." h2g2, 1 Sept. 2011, h2g2.com/edited_entry/A996942.

Mayday! Mayday!
Victoria Radford
Texas Woman's University
Denton, Texas

In most essays speculating about causes, conclusions must be tentative. However, don't let this scare you away from discussing phenomena that might not have obvious causes or that might even have multiple causes. Victoria Radford approaches a topic—why people don't ask for help—that seems to have different explanations and systematically examines potential causes in experimental studies, news stories, and statistics she uncovered in her research. Near the end of her essay, she also puts forth a few solutions by examining the tactics of musician Amanda Palmer and author M. Nora Klaver that may help people overcome their reluctance to seek assistance. As you read, notice how visibly Radford signals her move from one cause to the next as her argument progresses.

"Mayday! Mayday!" We recognize this as the cry for help from pilots whose planes are falling or captains whose ships are sinking. And in these situations, it seems perfectly normal and even wise to cry for help. But when is it appropriate for the rest of us to ask for help?

It would be nice to say that when we have a problem, we ask for help. But in reality, many of us feel uncomfortable asking for help, and more often than not, this discomfort is enough to keep us from asking at all. According to one survey, seven out of ten people admit they could have used help in the last week but did not ask for it (Klaver x).

One person who doesn't have a problem asking is singer and songwriter Amanda Palmer. Although she is now a successful rock musician who travels the world on tour, like many artists she initially struggled to make enough money to produce her music. Then one day, Palmer decided to use a strategy she calls "the art of asking." Instead of figuring out how to get people to pay for her music, she would find out how to *let* people pay for her music by asking them to donate directly to her project through the Web site Kickstarter.

This new means of crowdsourcing has received large amounts of criticism from those who do not view it as a legitimate means of income. "It's kind of counterintuitive for a lot of artists," Palmer explains. "They don't want to ask for things. . . . It's not easy to ask. . . . Asking makes you vulnerable" (Palmer). We can all identify with this feeling. Whether asking for directions, for help with a math problem, or for something off the top shelf, we have all felt this sense of apprehension when we need help. In many cases, this is enough to keep us from asking at all. So what causes this aversion to asking for help? What makes the experience so painful for so many people? 4

One reason people may avoid seeking assistance is their inability to find someone they trust to help them. Indeed, Americans increasingly find themselves less trusting of strangers and friends alike. In a 2010 study, researchers Thomas Sander and Robert Putnam reported that less than a third of Americans trust strangers today, as opposed to over half of Americans in the 1960s. About 25 percent of those polled admitted they had no one in whom they could confide, and nearly 50 percent reported they had only one person in whom they could confide (Sander and Putnam 9–10). As Americans become more distrustful of strangers, and close friendships become rarer, people in the United States may struggle more and more to ask others for help. 5

Another psychological cause for this reluctance might be our own misconceptions about other people and their willingness to help. Researchers Francis Flynn and Vanessa Lake had participants at Stanford University ask people on campus for a favor. Before leaving, the participants were asked to make a guess at how many people would oblige and offer assistance. The favors ranged from asking to use a stranger's cell phone to filling out a survey or guiding them to the campus gym (Flynn and Lake 129). What Flynn and Lake found was that the participants *extremely* underestimated the amount of people who helped — by as much as 50 percent (130). 6

Flynn and Lake followed up with another experiment to determine whether or not the type of favor would alter the participants' predictions. Participants were split into two groups: a group asking to use a stranger's cell phone to make a call, and a group asking a stranger for guided directions to the campus gym (Flynn and Lake 132). Participants in the cell phone group, on average, predicted they 7 would need to ask 10.1 people, when in reality they only needed to ask an average of 6.2 people. Similarly, those in the escort group estimated they would need to ask 7.2 people, but only needed to ask 2.3 people (Flynn and Lake 132). This reinforced Flynn and Lake's initial findings: People tend to vastly underestimate others' willingness to help when asked, regardless of the favor. This ingrained misperception may also keep us from asking for help. If we believe most people won't help, it would make sense that we are reluctant to ask in the first place.

So if people underestimate others' willingness to help them, how does this compare to people who are in positions to give help? Vanessa Bohns and Francis Flynn of Columbia University conducted a series of experiments on "helpers" in relation to "help seekers." They asked professors and teachers' assistants to make a prediction about how many students would come to them for help over the course of a semester and to rate their students' requests on a scale of discomfort (Bohns and Flynn 402). Bohns and Flynn found that not only did the "helpers" overestimate the number of students who would come to them, but they also underestimated how uncomfortable their students actually felt in asking for help (407). Bohns and Flynn extrapolate that the attitude of "just ask" does not succeed in getting students to ask for help because it does not address the real reason students have trouble asking for help—that is, the discomfort they feel in doing so (407).

A third reason we may not ask for help is our belief that we can do it more easily on our own. As the old saying goes, "If you want something done right, do it yourself." According to this logic, asking for help would seem counterintuitive and more time-consuming. Why get assistance if helpers would only damage your work or take longer to get it done? While this maxim may work well for some tasks, this method fails when we encounter things we *cannot* do by ourselves. We cannot drive ourselves home after a root canal. We (or at least most of us) cannot move a refrigerator up the stairs by ourselves. And yet oftentimes instead of asking directly, we resort to bargaining. As *New York Times* journalist Alina Tugend explains: "Asking someone else to come to your aid can shift a relationship's power balance. Most of us prefer that the situation be reciprocal: I will help you on this report; you help me with this client. I will pick up your child from school; can you have mine over for a play date next week?" (Tugend). When we are put in a position where asking for help is a necessity, we want the situation to be reciprocal so that we do not feel indebted. Negotiating the terms of assistance may make us feel like we do not owe anyone anything.

However, perhaps the problem is one of perspective: Instead of seeing a request for help as a debt, some, like Palmer, see it as an exchange. Before Palmer was a successful musician, she was a street performer. She stood on city streets, and when strangers placed money in her tin can, she would bow, make eye contact, and hand them a flower. Occasionally, people would drive by in their cars and shout, "Get a job!" (Palmer). This exchange, a dollar for "intense eye contact" and a flower, prepared Palmer for her musical career. Palmer remembered this in response to criticism she received for asking people to pay for her music: 10

> This hurt in a really familiar way. . . . People saying, "You're not allowed anymore to ask for that kind of help," really reminded me of the people in their cars yelling, "Get a job." Because they weren't with us on the sidewalk, and they couldn't see the exchange that was happening between me and my crowd, an exchange that was very fair to us but alien to them. (Palmer)

So when Palmer asks for help funding her musical career, she views this as an exchange: money for music, entertainment, and an experience.

Similarly, in her anti-self-help book, *Mayday! Asking for Help in Times of Need,* author M. Nora Klaver relates an experience where accepting help turned into a connection. While boarding a plane, Klaver had trouble collapsing the handle of her luggage and getting it into the overhead bin. A stranger offered his assistance, but Klaver passed: "Not even taking time to look this kind man in the eye, I shook my head and replied brusquely that I could take care of it myself. After a few more attempts, I finally slammed the handle home, viciously catching my thumb" (Klaver xi). Klaver was unable to lift the bag above her head, and the stranger finally took the bag and easily placed it in the overhead compartment: "As I offered my thanks, I straightened up and finally looked him in the face. I noticed that he was smiling. In fact, his smile transformed me. At that moment I felt connected to this gentleman—not in a romantic, stranger-on-the-plane way, but simply as one person to another" (Klaver xi). Like Palmer, Klaver's experience is indicative of how help can be seen not as a debt to be repaid later but as an exchange and mutual connection between human beings. 11

Klaver and Palmer's enlightened perspectives aside, the research   12
clearly shows a myriad of causes for most people's reluctance to seek
assistance. Whether our discomfort comes from a lack of trust, a
misperception of strangers, or a confident belief that we can handle
ourselves, there is an abundance of psychological evidence to support
the idea that people do in fact feel uncomfortable asking for help.
While we can take heart that others are just as uncomfortable as we
are to ask for aid, this attitude is also worrisome, as this reluctance
may cause most of us to not reach out for help, which can be disas-
trous for our own success and our communities overall. After all, if
we cry "Mayday!" only when the ship is sinking, it does not give us a
chance to keep the ship afloat.

WORKS CITED

Bohns, Vanessa K., and Francis J. Flynn. "'Why Didn't You Just Ask?' Under-
estimating the Discomfort of Help Seeking." *Journal of Experimental Social Psychology,* vol. 46, no. 2, 2010, pp. 402–09, doi:10.1016/
j.jesp.2009.12.015.

Flynn, Francis J., and Vanessa K. B. Lake. "If You Need Help, Just Ask:
Understanding Compliance with Requests for Help." *Journal of
Personality and Social Psychology,* vol. 95, no. 1, 2008, pp. 128–43,
doi:10.1037/0022-3514.95.1.128.

Klaver, M. Nora. *Mayday! Asking for Help in Times of Need.* Better-Koehler,
2007.

Palmer, Amanda. "The Art of Asking." TED Talks, Feb. 2013, www.ted
.com/talks/amanda_palmer_the_art_of_asking.

Sander, Thomas H., and Robert D. Putnam. "Still Bowling Alone? The
Post 9/11 Split." *Journal of Democracy,* vol. 21, no. 1, 2010, pp. 9–16,
doi:10.1353/jod.0.0153.

Tugend, Alina. "Why Is Asking for Help So Difficult?" *The New York Times,*
7 July 2007, www.nytimes.com/2007/07/07/business/07shortcuts
.html.

Left Out

Virginia Gagliardi

Lebanon Valley College
Annville, Pennsylvania

As you begin to conduct research for your essay, you may discover that an issue doesn't always have one clear cause. When this happens, how do you ensure that your discussion of the topic is strong? For Virginia Gagliardi, the biggest challenge was incorporating the various causes she had discovered. She solved this problem by organizing them into three main subject areas: genetics and physiology, general influences, and local influences. As you read, you'll notice that Gagliardi relies on research for both her proposed causes and her support of those causes. Altogether, she makes good use of six different sources for this short essay. Instead of merely patching the sources together, she imposes her own plan and selectively paraphrases and quotes the sources only as they are relevant to the three main causes she addresses.

Behavioral differences that cause one limb or sense organ to be preferred for certain activities, despite the apparently insignificant differences in their morphology, constitute a problem that . . . has fascinated scientists and laymen for centuries. (Coren 2)

Opening a can, drawing a straight line, and writing a sentence are three basic activities that display our *handedness,* or the "differential or preferred use of one hand in situations where only one can be used" (Coren 2). Handedness presents itself in two well-known categories: right- and left-handedness. But what causes each of us to be either right- or left-handed? Why are there so fewer left-handed people than right-handed people? For years, scientists thought handedness was genetic; however, no genetic theory accounts for the ratio of right- to left-handers, and the exact contribution of factors to

188

predisposition to one side remains unknown. Genetic models propose many different ideas about the roles of genes in handedness, but
as McManus writes in *Right Hand, Left Hand: The Origins of Asymmetry in Brains, Bodies, Atoms and Cultures,* "what they cannot do is
tell us exactly what it is that makes us right- or left-handed" (163).
A combination of factors in physiology, history, and society explains
why genetics plays only a minor role in a Western bias toward one
side—the right side—of the body.

Perhaps the most basic explanation of handedness is the initial   2
genetic theory, which states that genetics determines handedness
through a specific gene inherited from parents. If both parents have
the right-handed gene, the children will all become right-handed; in
contrast, if both parents have the left-handed gene, the children will
all become left-handed. Since there are fewer lefties in the world than
right-handed people, the model appears to fulfill conceptions for why
handedness occurs and why left-handedness occurs less often than
right-handedness. In the book *Left Brain, Right Brain,* however,
Sally P. Springer and Georg Deutsch elaborate on the extensive bio-
logical studies of this genetic model. The biologists who conducted
these studies quickly discovered that in comparison with obtained
data about handedness, "this [genetic] model cannot account for
the fact that 54 percent of the offspring of two left-handed parents
are right-handed" (108). So how does this possible cause fail? If the
genetic model were accurate, reported data would show that two
left-handed parents would have only left-handed children. Therefore,
new studies began in an attempt to repair this theory with a comple-
mentary, yet more complex, model.

After many studies attempting to salvage this basic genetic the-   3
ory, the idea of "variable penetrance" arose. Variable penetrance
means "that all individuals with the same genotype [pattern of genes]
may not express that genotype in the same way" (Springer and
Deutsch 108). Simply put, the statement suggests that although the
genes make the parents left-handed, the combination that passes to
the child may not cause left-handedness in the child. This speculation
provides the explanation for two left-handers having right-handed
children; however, "even with variable penetrance built into the
[allele] model, the [variable penetrance] model's 'goodness of fit' to
actual data is less than satisfactory" (Springer and Deutsch 108). The
probability of left-handedness increases as the number of left-handed
parents increases. However, the real-life data do not coincide with

the theory. According to McManus, the fact that handedness "runs in the family" (156) remains distinguishable, but exactly how remains a mystery.

A third theory suggests that nurture determines handedness, not nature—or genetics—itself. Scientists base the theory on how handedness appears, not on which side it appears. In this case, genetics would determine handedness, just not a particular side to the handedness. Simplified, the design suggests, "If your mother and father are strongly handed [very reliant on one side], although we can't predict on the basis of their handedness whether you will be right- or left-handed, we can predict that you will be strongly handed. It is the strength . . . that is genetically variable" (Coren 91). Of all the theories, this idea proves the most plausible.

While genetics undoubtedly participates in determination of handedness, the suggestion that nurture more likely decides the side of handedness continues as the most logical "genetic" explanation. As McManus explains, "there are many things that run in families that are not inherited through genes" (157), such as parents' influence on their children in the development of handedness. The explanation lies in the fact that parents "convey basic pattern[s] of behavior to children" (Porac and Coren 108). Probably the most fundamental behavior learned is in the use of utensils. Parents "teach them [children] to use their first tools, such as spoons, knives, and pencils" (Porac and Coren 108), so if the child's predisposition favors left-handedness but he continually learns right-handed motions, he will essentially develop into a right-handed child. This situation provides yet another example of the formation of handedness and how right-handedness forces itself into culture. The most easily defined reason for handedness presents itself every day in society: Many people adopt right-handedness for ease of life and teach their children to do the same. This thought about the influence of nurture extends into the fact that handedness incorporates history into its origins.

Religion, which tends to be derived from nurture, is one of the most controversial historical justifications for handedness in Western culture. This idea is obviously seen in biblical illustrations. Followers of many Christian religions resort to right-handedness as a result of beliefs or traditions. The notion that left-handedness engages the devil explicates this fact. Passages from the Bible further reinforce these principles, such as the verses found in Matthew 25:34–41 in the New Testament:

Then shall the King say unto them on His right hand, "Come ye blessed of my Father, inherit the kingdom prepared for you from the foundation of the world." . . . Then shall He say also unto them on the left hand, "Depart from Me, ye cursed, into everlasting fire, prepared for the devil and his angels." . . . And these shall go away into everlasting punishment; but the righteous into life eternal. (qtd. in Springer and Deutsch 105)

The Creator's association with the right hand strongly biases Christians toward the right hand, or the right side in general. Thus, this preference flows into other aspects of Christian culture. The most prominent example is in the sign of the cross, performed only with the right hand; using the left hand is sacrilegious. Another example appears during Communion, when the communicant receives the wafer in the left hand so that the clean right hand can transfer the wafer to the mouth (Fincher 32).

The bias, though, does not limit itself to the church; it also   7
extends into portraits concerning religion. Why, then, is there a "marked tendency in classical renderings of the Madonna and child" (Fincher 30) to illustrate Mary holding Jesus on her left side? Analysts propose several reasons. According to Fincher, some analysts of the portraits suggest that the cause lies in the idea of freeing the "right hand for other, better things" (30). On the contrary, Fincher himself distinguishes the motive as something else: "Putting the child on Mary's left puts Him on the viewer's — and the art work's — right, clearly the place of honor" (31). Essentially, religion provides incentive for left-handers to become right-handers; however, religion remains just one aspect of history that influences this partiality for one side of the body.

For those people who lack a religious affiliation, the simple act of   8
speaking holds an effect equivalent to the effect of religion on handedness because language places a stigma on left-handedness. Consistently, favorable connotations referring to right-handedness emerge in several languages. Fincher illustrates this idea from the word "riht, Anglo-Saxon for straight, erect, or just" (37). He also uses the "French word for right, droit, [which] also means 'correct' and 'law'" (37), to further demonstrate the point of language as a root of favoritism in handedness. Springer and Deutsch point out that "the French word for 'left,' *gauche,* also means 'clumsy'" and that "*mancino* is Italian for 'left' as well as for 'deceitful'" (104). They also explain that the Spanish phrase "no ser zurdo," which means

"to be clever," translates directly as "to not be left-handed" (104). As terrible as those definitions appear, most Western languages have them—including the English language.

In English, the term "left-handed" has derogatory connotations. 9 For example, *Webster's Third International Dictionary* lists several definitions of the adjective "left-handed," including the following:

> a: marked by clumsiness or ineptitude: awkward; b: exhibiting devi-
> ousness or indirection: oblique, unintended; c: obs.: given to malevo-
> lent scheming or contriving: sinister, underhand. (qtd. in Springer and
> Deutsch 104)

Similarly, analysis of the English language reveals common phrases filled with bias. "For instance, a *left-handed compliment* is actually an insult. A *left-handed marriage* is no marriage at all. To be about *left-handed business* is to be engaged in something unlawful or unsa-vory" (Coren 2). On the contrary, "to be someone's *right-hand man* means to be important and useful to that person" (Coren 2). Over time, this tainting of a certain handedness carries over into every-day life and remains one of several reasons why left-handers may try to become right-handers or at least ambidextrous. Other motives to switch revolve around the impressions and pressures of social traditions.

One of the largest-scale examples lies in written language. The 10 system of the written English language solely supports right-handed people because "[written] alphabetic languages . . . were designed for right-handers" (Ornstein 83). Coren explains the differences in the mechanics of left- and right-handed writing as follows:

> Our left-to-right writing pattern is set up for a right-handed writer. The
> most comfortable and controlled hand movement is a pull across the
> body. For the right-hander it is a left-to-right movement, and for
> the left-hander it is reversed. (230)

Due to the way a left-hander pulls across his body, his hand will rub over words he has already written, whereas a right-hander always moves his hand away from the words he has already written. This problem forces left-handers into unnatural hand positions during writing; most primary school teachers attempt to persuade left-handed children into writing right-handed. In fact, the "Victorians even invented a vicious leather device with a belt and buckles for strapping the left hand firmly behind the back" (McManus 268).

Writing, although the most obvious of problems, remains just one of many issues for a left-hander in a right-handed society.

Every day, left-handers encounter issues with common tools that right-handers take for granted. A simple household item, such as a can opener, can become the most complex of items for a leftie. Because a can opener "is designed to be held with the left hand while the cutting gear is operated by rotating a handle with the right hand" (Coren 223), using the instrument left-handed "forces the left-hander into a set of ungainly contortions" (Coren 223). Another example surfaces in the use of knives, typically beveled on only one side—the right side. Having the knife designed as such aids the "right-hander by producing a force which holds the blade upright" (Coren 227), causing the slice to peel outward from the material, rather than toward it.

More problems affecting left-handers reside in locations such as school and work. The simple process of using a ruler becomes a difficult task for a left-handed individual. The ruler, designed with right-handers in mind, presents numbers in a left-to-right fashion, much like the written English language. "This [style] makes sense for the right-hander because the motion of drawing the line usually begins at the 'zero inch' location on the far left and continues . . . until it reaches the mark indicating the desired length, somewhere to the right" (Coren 231). For a leftie, however, this system poses several problems:

> [This process] requires the left-hander to cover the numbers while drawing the line with a pulling motion across the body from right to left. The left-hander also covers the end of the ruler . . . causing a tendency for the pen to suddenly drop off the end of the ruler if the line is drawn too quickly and the unseen "zero inch" point is reached before the pen is stopped. (Coren 231)

Saws create problems by exposing body parts dangerously close to the blade. "When the right hand is used, the arm and elbow flare out to the side, safely away from the saw blade" (Coren 237), protecting a right-handed person from injury. Yet "if a left-hander wants to use this equipment, he must either use his right hand to hold the work . . . or cross his body with his left hand which places his arm directly in line with the saw blade" (Coren 237). This design forces a left-hander to resort to right-handedness temporarily or even permanently in many factory and workshop settings. However, these mechanical influences cannot solely explain the phenomena of left-handedness.

The combination of these factors forms a basis for handedness in the world. Right- and left-handedness appear as common expressions in everyday life, but the existence of both presents a misconception. Due to factors in physiology, history, and society, handedness appears in two forms, but not in right- and left-handedness. Rather, handedness categorizes into right-handedness and ambidextrous handedness for the sole reason that "to survive in this right-sided world, left-handers soon learn to do with the right hand many things that the right-hander could never and will never do with the left. The end result is a degree of ambidexterity" (Porac and Coren 95). Perhaps only one form of handedness exists, since, according to Porac and Coren, essentially "the left-hander must become more right-handed" (95). This idea reinforces the reason why right-handedness appears more often than left-handedness. Therefore, even though the exact cause of handedness remains unknown, the residue of known facts points not toward a right- and left-handed world but in the direction of a world that completely relies on one-sided handedness. 13

WORKS CITED

Coren, Stanley. *The Left-Hander Syndrome: The Causes and Consequences of Left-Handedness.* Macmillan, 1992.

Fincher, Jack. *Lefties: The Origins and Consequences of Being Left-Handed.* Barnes and Noble, 1993.

McManus, Chris. *Right Hand, Left Hand: The Origins of Asymmetry in Brains, Bodies, Atoms and Cultures.* Harvard UP, 2002.

Ornstein, Robert. *The Right Mind.* Harcourt Brace, 1997.

Porac, Clare, and Stanley Coren. *Lateral Preferences and Human Behavior.* Springer-Verlag, 1981.

Springer, Sally P., and Georg Deutsch. *Left Brain, Right Brain.* W. H. Freeman, 1981.

Hispanic Pride vs. American Assimilation

Stephanie Cox

Metropolitan Community College
Omaha, Nebraska

Stephanie Cox takes a stand on a hot-button social and political issue: a growing trend among Hispanic immigrants to choose not to learn English. Many Americans would be unsympathetic to a flat refusal to learn English. Cox too admits some preconceived notions on the matter; however, she keeps an open mind. She wants to know more about the subject before she judges the decision. To engage her readers' interest and provide a concrete example they will identify with, Cox first relates the story of a Spanish-speaking mother who loses her little girl and is unable to communicate. Cox then defines the phenomenon of acculturation and forecasts three causes, or explanations, that she will argue for. Her plan is simple and visible, and because her research is motivated by curiosity rather than preconceived ideas, her essay is effective.

My heart ached for the woman. She was visibly distressed and seemed   1
to grow more agitated by the minute. Tiny beads of perspiration were beginning to form on her brow, and the black purse she carried shook in her trembling grasp. She was desperately trying to tell me something, but I was unable to understand. She spoke Spanish, and I didn't. After many awkward attempts at communication, the woman's ten-year-old English-speaking son was located. His translation revealed her worry over her missing toddler. It seems the child had wandered off while her mother was visiting a pastor of the church I work for. With the woman's son's help, we gathered enough details about her daughter's disappearance to locate the child, who had been playing in an empty classroom.

Even though the situation seemed to have ended happily, I was   2
still troubled by it. If only the woman had known some English. The
church offered several excellent programs to help immigrants learn
about American culture and practice the English language. Had she
taken the help offered by the church, she would have been able to
communicate effectively enough to convey her message and prevent
unnecessary frustration and possibly dangerous delay. When I presented my concerns to one of the church pastors, I was surprised by
his response. This woman was at the church to pick up her son from
an English class. When she had been given the same opportunity,
she quietly refused. While she felt strongly about the importance of
English for her son, she herself was proud of her Mexican heritage
and had no desire to become an English speaker.

I was shocked. Why would immigrants want to make their lives   3
more complicated by having to rely on others to communicate for
them? This woman must surely be an exception, I thought, but to
my surprise, she is among many Hispanic immigrants in the United
States who are acculturating rather than assimilating into American
culture (Grow et al.). Many Americans still view the United States
as an ideal nation, a model for the world, and assume everyone must
surely want to "be like us," but there is a new phenomenon among
many U.S. immigrants: active pride in their home cultures. This cultural pride is especially evident among Hispanic immigrants who
choose to adapt to American culture without losing the traditions
and values of their native countries.

Hispanics are one of the fastest growing and largest minority   4
groups in the United States, and they are developing their own version of the "true" American. Nearly nine out of ten Hispanics have
accepted the importance of adapting to American culture, while
nearly nine out of ten also believe it is extremely important to continue to uphold the values and traditions of Latin America (Artze).
This phenomenon of Hispanic acculturation rather than assimilation
can be witnessed in several cities and towns in the United States.

Perhaps one of the best examples of how Hispanics are striv-   5
ing to maintain their own culture can be seen in Los Angeles. As
early as 1950, Los Angeles contained the largest Hispanic population in the country, and the conflict between assimilation and acculturation was already beginning. Immigrants were forced to choose
between American cultural traditions and the distinctive values of
Latin America. Today, you will find groups of new immigrants along

with second- and third-generation Hispanics all with the same goal
in mind: to successfully thrive in an ethnocentric culture without losing their own identity (Rodriguez).

While there may be quite a few reasons immigrants are reluctant   6
to assimilate, forgetting old traits and adopting new ones, three are
most prominent. First is the strong feeling of pride Hispanics have
for their native countries and cultural values, and the security they
feel when segregated from American society. Second is the close
proximity of Hispanics, especially Mexican Americans, to their native
country. Third, and most startling, is the seeming lack of support
from many Hispanic Americans to help new immigrants assimilate.

With the ever-increasing number of immigrants from Latin   7
America, it is not uncommon to find exclusively Hispanic communities within American towns and cities. These communities help
reinforce cultural traditions and pride, and make it unnecessary for
immigrants to adopt new cultural traits or learn the English language.
Many Hispanic Americans not only feel comforted by their segrega-
tion but also are wary of the negative influences American society
may have on their families (Branigin).

The self-segregation of many Hispanic immigrants in America   8
can be compared to that of Americans who live and work abroad
but remain quite isolated from their host culture. A classmate of
mine described living in Japan while her husband was stationed at a
military base there. Day-to-day life revolved around American customs. Her children attended American schools on the military base;
she shopped at military stores geared toward the wants and needs
of Americans; and her family socialized with a close-knit group of
American friends. On the rare occasions that she and her family left
the military base, she was startled by the numerous stares and suspicious glances she and her family received from Japanese citizens.
While confident that she and her family had done their best to adhere
to Japanese societal norms, the reaction of the Japanese left her with
the acute feeling that she was still very different, and the isolation of
the military base offered her family a feeling of security.

My classmate's experience is mirrored by the experiences of   9
many Hispanics living in the United States. In response to unsub-
stantiated fears of America becoming "Mexicanized," some politicians and government officials are being urged to speak out against
Hispanic immigration. Most notably, border states such as California
and Arizona are openly opposing immigration from Latin America

by developing new anti-immigration bills. California's Proposition 187 and Arizona's Proposition 200 would limit the public benefits received by illegal immigrants, and politicians acting on public support of these bills and hoping to seek reelection are motivated to develop even more anti-immigrant legislation (Judis). While these propositions are much more aggressive than suspicious stares, the message is the same: If you are different, you must be a threat.

In addition to feeling more comfortable within their own communities, many Hispanic immigrants see isolation as a way to hold on to their cultural values. In California, where bilingual education is no longer the norm, children from Hispanic families are immediately submerged into the English language and thus into American culture. Many Hispanics feel that this immersion forces their children to choose between the values taught by their parents—such as the importance of family—and those of their new country (Rifkin). 10

Reluctance to assimilate is strengthened even more when traditional, conservative Hispanic families witness their children adopting negative aspects of American culture. Many Hispanics cite American gang violence when defending their decision to keep their children away from American culture. Alarmingly, Hispanic youth may actually be propelled toward gang life by the attitudes and stereotypes of Americans who mistakenly assume that most Latinos are illegal immigrants (Branigin). A quest for group identity and a sense of belonging can be a strong lure for Hispanic teens trying to find their place in an unsympathetic society. 11

Fear of negative influences affecting traditional cultural values is not the only reason Hispanics have hesitated to adopt American culture. Unlike the majority of immigrants from other locations, Hispanics—especially Mexican Americans—have the privilege of living fairly close to their native country. It is not uncommon for many Hispanics to travel between their native and adopted countries on a regular basis. These frequent visits help reinforce the customs, values, and language of Latin America (Grow et al.). 12

This reinforcement of Hispanic customs and values is evidenced not only by immigrants' attitudes toward American society but also by the many cultural traditions Hispanics bring to the United States. One tradition that is growing in popularity in America is the Quinceañera, the celebration of a Latina girl's fifteenth birthday. Historically rooted in Aztec and Roman Catholic customs, the Quinceañera is a time to celebrate a young girl's entrance into 13 adulthood. While this lavish celebration is primarily a Hispanic one, which begins with a Roman Catholic Mass and ends with a reception in which the girl performs a dance with her father and members of her court, it is also showing signs of adaptation to American society. This can be seen in the celebrations held by Hispanics who are not members of the Roman Catholic Church and who tend to invite friends of different ethnic heritages (Miranda). Once primarily a closed ceremony for family and close friends, the Quinceañera is expanding beyond its Latin American roots and replanting itself into Hispanic American culture.

Another example of a Hispanic cultural tradition celebrated in   14
the United States is Cinco de Mayo. Celebrated on the fifth of May, this holiday commemorates the 1862 Battle of Puebla, one of the most glorious victories in Mexico's military history. When France attempted to take control of Mexico by force, a poorly equipped Mexican army was able to halt the invasion of the French powerhouse despite being outnumbered by thousands. This celebration, with its message of success despite overwhelming obstacles, inspires Hispanics to be proud of their heritage (Vargas).

Finally, many new immigrants to the United States may feel   15
more comfortable within their own cultural group and hesitate to adapt to American culture because of discouragement from their own peers. Mexican Americans born and raised in the United States, called Chicanos, often humiliate new immigrants who are attempting to learn English. One immigrant teen, who despite three years in an English as a second language course still did not speak fluent English, believed the other students were laughing at her when she attempted to speak English (Branigin). This kind of teasing can lead to feelings of insecurity among newly arrived immigrants.

Not only are Hispanic children and teens experiencing discour-   16
agement from Mexican Americans, but so are many new immigrant adults who are seeking jobs in the United States. An immigrant named Antonio experienced this harsh reality when he found himself assigned to do one of the most laborious jobs in a meatpacking plant, while his cultural counterpart, a Chicano, was displaying the title of supervisor and taunting immigrant workers like him. In fact, in this particular meatpacking plant, it was quite common to see new immigrants from Mexico performing arduous tasks while enduring snide comments from their Chicano supervisors, who would make statements such as "Go back to Mexico, wetback!" or "Chicanos

numero uno!" (Campo-Flores). Humiliation like this can cause many immigrants to stay within their own communities, where they feel accepted.

The feelings of isolation felt by the immigrant teen and the feel-   17
ings of frustration felt by the immigrant worker Antonio shed new light on the complexities Latin American immigrants must face every day. Distrust of an unfamiliar culture mixed with strong pride in their own heritage has led to immigrants' longing to maintain the traits of their native country. As I remember the distraught woman who quietly yet proudly refused the pastor's offer to help her learn English, I can now respect her decision. She was quoted as saying, "I was Mexican at birth, I am Mexican today, and I will be Mexican forever."

WORKS CITED

Artze, Isis. "To Be and Not to Be." *Hispanic,* vol. 13, no. 10, Oct. 2000, pp. 32–34. *EBSCOhost,* www.ebscohost.com.
Branigin, William. "Immigrants Shunning Idea of Assimilation." *Washington Post,* 25 May 1998, p. A1+.
Campo-Flores, Arian. "Brown against Brown." *Newsweek,* Sept. 2000, pp. 49–50. *EBSCOhost,* www.ebscohost.com.
Grow, Brian, et al. "Hispanic Nation." *Business Week,* Mar. 2004, pp. 58–70. *EBSCOhost,* www.ebscohost.com.
Judis, John B. "Border War." *New Republic,* 16 Jan. 2006, pp. 15–19.
Miranda, Carolina A. "Fifteen Candles." *Time,* July 2004, p. 83. *EBSCOhost,* www.ebscohost.com.
Rifkin, Jane M. "Locked in Conflict with Mainstream America." *Hispanic Times,* Dec. 1998–Jan. 1999: 40–41. *EBSCOhost,* www.ebscohost.com.
Rodriguez, Gregory. "Don't Mistake the Parts for the Whole in L.A." *Los Angeles Times,* 6 July 2001, p. B15.
Vargas, Roberto. "Cinco de Mayo: An Opportunity to Inspire Courage." *Hispanic,* May 1999, p. 48. *EBSCOhost,* www.ebscohost.com.

Analyzing Stories 10

Analyzing a story requires you to make inferences, something you do in your everyday life when you arrive at insights about people and relationships, whether in real life or in fiction. You make inferences when you gossip with one friend about a mutual friend, or judge the motives of a TV or movie character. Rather than being final verdicts, your judgments in these situations are more likely to be invitations to further discussion. The same goes for story interpretations, which can be logical and even insistent without being final or comprehensive. In a classroom in which every student offers a different interpretation of the same story, no one student need be right; sharing and discussing the interpretations will result in a fuller understanding of the story for everyone.

Using your gossiping and character-judging experience as a starting point, analyzing a short story can lead you someplace different and, to be honest, harder to get to. After all, unlike gossiping or discussing a movie, interpreting a short story is a solitary experience, not a social one. It's textual, not conversational. And it is unbending in its demands on your time because it's usually associated with a deadline and requires that you choose every word, shape every phrase and sentence, and visibly and logically connect every sentence to the one before and after it. Writers who analyze stories generally use the same basic features of the genre: a clear, arguable thesis; a well-supported argument; and a clear, logical organization.

Though it may seem daunting, this kind of writing can bring great satisfaction. It teaches you strategies that enable you to deepen and extend any interpretation you wish to make, whether in real life or in the arts, and to support your insights in ways your readers or listeners will find plausible and enlightening. It gives you more confidence in asserting and supporting your insights about anything at all with different kinds of people in various kinds of situations. Most important to you personally, it helps you decide which of your insights are worth keeping—which insights, added to your store of hard-won personal knowledge, will lead you to a place of greater understanding of yourself and your world. Along with the other kinds of argumentative writing in Chapters 6–9, thesis-centered interpretations—logically organized and well supported—can take you there.

Use the guidelines in the Peer Review Guide that follows to practice peer review using the essays in this chapter.

A PEER REVIEW GUIDE

A CLEAR, ARGUABLE THESIS

How well does the writer present the thesis?

Summarize: Tell the writer what you understand the essay's thesis to be and what its key terms are.

Praise: Tell the writer what seems most interesting to you about his or her main claim about the story, whether you agree with it or not.

Critique: If you cannot find the thesis statement or cannot identify the key terms, let the writer know. Evaluate the thesis statement on the basis of whether it

- makes an interesting and arguable assertion (rather than a statement of fact or an obvious point);
- is clear and precise (neither ambiguous nor vague);
- is appropriately qualified (neither overgeneralized nor exaggerated).

A WELL-SUPPORTED ARGUMENT

How well does the writer develop and support the argument?

Summarize: Underline the thesis statement and the major support for it. (Often, the major support appears in the topic sentences of paragraphs.)

Praise: Give an example in the essay where support for a reason is presented especially effectively—for instance, note where brief quotations (words and short phrases), a longer quotation, or summaries of particular events are introduced and explained in a way that clearly illustrates a particular point that is being argued.

Critique: Tell the writer where the connection between a reason and its support seems vague, where too much plot is being relayed with no apparent point, or where a quotation is left to speak for itself without explanation. Let the writer know if any part of the argument seems to be undeveloped or does not support the thesis.

A CLEAR, LOGICAL ORGANIZATION

Has the writer clearly and logically organized the argument?

Summarize: Underline the sentence(s) in which the writer forecasts supporting reasons, and circle transitions or repeated key words and phrases.

Praise: Give an example of something that makes the essay especially easy to read—where, for example, the key terms introduced in the thesis recur in topic sentences and elsewhere, or where transitions are used logically.

Critique: Tell the writer where readability could be improved. For example, point to places where key terms could be added or where a topic sentence could be made clearer, indicate where the use of transitions might be improved, or note where transitions are lacking and could be added.

"In Love"

Sarah Hawkins

University of California, San Diego
La Jolla, California

By the end of her third paragraph, Sarah Hawkins's interpretation of D. H. Lawrence's "In Love" is clear; in the last paragraph, she repeats it. In between, she focuses on details of the relationship between Hester and Joe, with Henrietta speaking for the predictable social expectations and constraints Hester and Joe must struggle against. Hawkins stays extremely close to the story throughout her essay, following through consistently with what is called a "close reading" to support her interpretation. The story offers only a small cast of characters and a small scene, and only a few hours pass; yet Hawkins has more than enough material to select from to support her interpretation. As you read, notice that rather than merely retelling the story, Hawkins has organized her essay around the stages of the argument supporting her interpretation. The first sentences of her paragraphs—where readers look for cues to the staging or sequence of an argument—keep readers focused and on track. Notice also Hawkins's careful use of words to help readers understand the personal and social conflicts at the center of the story.

For most people, the phrase *in love* brings many rosy pictures to   1
mind: a young man looking into the eyes of the girl he loves, a couple walking along the beach holding hands, two people making sacrifices to be together. These stereotypes about what love is and how lovers should act can be very harmful. In his short story "In Love," D. H. Lawrence uses the three main characters to embody his theme that love is experienced in a unique way by every couple and that there isn't a normal or proper way to be in love.

    Hester; her fiancé, Joe; and her sister, Henrietta, all approach   2
and respond to love in different ways. Hester is unwilling to compromise what she really feels for Joe, but she is pressured by her

own notions of how a young woman in her situation should feel. Joe appears to be the typical young man in love. He seems at ease with the situation, and his moves are so predictable they could have come straight from a movie script. But when he is confronted and badgered by Hester and Henrietta, he admits that he was only putting on an act and feels regret for not being honest with Hester. Henrietta is the mouthpiece for all of society's conceptions of love. She repeatedly asks Hester to be normal and secretly worries that Hester will call off the wedding. Henrietta is like a mother hen, always making sure that Hester is doing the right thing (Henrietta's opinion of the right thing, anyway).

Hester and Joe are, in a sense, playing a game with each other.   3
Both are acting on what they feel is expected of them now that they are engaged, as if how they really feel about each other is unimportant. It is only when Hester and Joe finally talk honestly about their relationship that they realize they have been in love all along in their own unique way.

Hester, ever the practical one, becomes more and more frus-   4
trated with "Joe's love-making" (650). She feels ridiculous, as if she is just a toy, but at the same time she feels she should respond positively to Joe, "because she believed that a nice girl would have been only too delighted to go and sit 'there'" (650). Rather than doing what she wants, enjoying a nice, comfortable relationship with Joe, Hester does what she feels she ought to. She says that she ought to like Joe's lovemaking even though she doesn't really know why. Despite her practical and independent nature, Hester is still troubled by what society would think.

Lawrence seems to be suggesting a universal theme here. If   5
Hester, with such firm ideas about what she wants, is so troubled by what society dictates, then how much more are we, as generally less objective and more tractable people, affected by society's standards? Hester's is a dilemma everyone faces.

At the heart of Hester's confusion is Joe, whose personality   6
was so different before they became engaged that Hester might not have gotten engaged if she had known how Joe would change: "Six months ago, Hester would have enjoyed it [being alone with Joe]. They were so perfectly comfortable together, he and she" (649). But by cuddling and petting, Joe has ruined the comfortable relationship that he and Hester had enjoyed. The most surprising line in the story is Hester's assertion that "[t]he very fact of his being in love with me

proves that he doesn't love me" (652). Here, Hester makes a distinction between really loving someone and just putting on an act of being in love. Hester feels hurt that Joe would treat her as a typical girl rather than as the young woman she really is.

Hester is a reluctant player in the love game until the end of the story, when she confronts Joe and blurts out, "I absolutely can't stand your making love to me, if that is what you call the business" (656–57). Her use of the word *business* is significant because it refers to a chore, something that has to be done. Hester regards Joe's lovemaking as if it were merely a job to be completed. When Joe apologizes, Hester sees his patient, real love for her, and she begins to have the same feelings for him again. When she says, "I don't mind what you do if you love me really" (660), Hester, by compromising, shows the nature of their love for each other.

Lawrence uses Joe to show a typical response to society's pressures. Joe obediently plays the role of the husband-to-be. He exhibits all the preconceived images one may have about a man about to be married. In trying to fit the expectations of others, Joe sacrifices his straightforwardness and the honesty that Hester valued so much in him. Although Joe's actions don't seem to be so bad in and of themselves, in the context of his relationship with Hester, they are completely out of place. His piano playing, for example, inspires Hester to remark that Joe's love games would be impossible to handle after the music he played. The music represents something that is pure and true—in contrast to the new, hypocritical Joe. Joe doesn't seem to be aware of Hester's feelings until she comes forward with them at the end of the story. The humiliation he suffers makes him silent, and he is described several times as wooden, implying stubbornness and solidness. It is out of this woodenness that a changed Joe appears. At first the word suggests his defensiveness for his bruised ego, but then as Joe begins to see Hester's point about being truly in love, his woodenness is linked to his solidness and stability, qualities that represent for Hester the old Joe. Once Joe gets his mind off the love game, the simple intimacy of their relationship is revealed to him, and he desires Hester, not in a fleeting way but in a way that one desires something that was almost lost.

Henrietta serves as the antagonist in this story because it is through her that society's opinions come clear. In almost the first line of text, Henrietta, looking at Hester, states, "If I had such a worried look on my face, when I was going down to spend the weekend with the man I was engaged to—and going to be married to in a month—well! I should either try and change my face or hide my feelings, or something" (647). With little regard for Hester's feelings, Henrietta is more concerned that Hester have the right attitude. Although Henrietta herself is not married, the fact that Hester, who is twenty-five, is soon to be married is a relief to her. Not wanting her sister to be an old maid, Henrietta does all she can to make sure the weekend runs smoothly. She acts as though Hester were her responsibility and even offers to come with Hester to take the "edge off the intimacy" (648). Being young, Henrietta hasn't really formed her own views of life or love yet. As a result, she easily believes the traditional statements society makes about love. When Hester says that she can't stand Joe's being in love with her, Henrietta keeps responding that a man is supposed to be in love with the woman he marries. She doesn't understand the real love that Joe and Hester eventually feel but only the "oughttos" of love imposed by society. It is unclear at the end of the story if Henrietta truly recognizes the new bond between Hester and Joe.

What society and common beliefs dictate about being in love 10 isn't really important. In order to be happy, couples must find their own unique bond of love and not rely on others' opinions or definitions. Joe and Hester come to this realization only after they are hurt and left unfulfilled as a result of the love game they play with each other. Hester knew how she really felt from the beginning, but pressure about what she ought to feel worried her. Joe willingly went along with the game until he realized how important their simple intimacy really was. In the end, Hester and Joe are in love not because of the games they play but because of an intimate friendship that had been growing all along.

WORK CITED

Lawrence, D. H. "In Love." *The Complete Short Stories*, vol. 3, Penguin, 1977, pp. 540–47.

Irony and Intuition in "A Jury of Her Peers"

Margaret Tate

DeKalb College
Decatur, Georgia

Margaret Tate begins by briefly establishing the historical context and setting of "A Jury of Her Peers"—the early years of the twentieth century in the U.S. Midwest. Her key terms are *intuition* and *irony;* her theme, the differences between men's and women's intuitions. She does not leave you waiting for her thesis: You will find it at the end of her first paragraph. As you read, notice how she selectively and repeatedly quotes and paraphrases the story without retelling it. Instead, she uses the details of the story to support each stage of her argument.

Though men and women are now recognized as generally equal in talent and intelligence, when Susan Glaspell wrote "A Jury of Her Peers" in 1917, it was not so. In this turn-of-the-century, rural mid-western setting, women were often barely educated and possessed virtually no political or economic power. And being considered the weaker sex, there was not much they could do about it. Relegated to home and hearth, women found themselves at the mercy of the more powerful men in their lives. Ironically, it is just this type of powerless existence, perhaps, that over the ages developed into a power with which women could baffle and frustrate their male counterparts: a sixth sense—an inborn trait commonly known as women's intuition. In Glaspell's story, ironic situations contrast male and female intuition, illustrating that Minnie Wright is more fairly judged by women than by men. 1

"A Jury of Her Peers" first uses irony to illustrate the contrast between male and female intuition when the men go to the farmhouse looking for clues to the murder of John Wright, but it is the women who find them. In the Wright household, the men are 2 searching for something out of the ordinary, an obvious indication that Minnie has been enraged or provoked into killing her husband. Their intuition does not tell them that their wives, because they are women, can help them gain insight into what has occurred between John and his wife. They bring Mrs. Hale and Mrs. Peters along merely to tend to the practical matters, considering them needlessly preoccupied with trivial things and even too unsophisticated to make a contribution to the investigation, as illustrated by Mr. Hale's derisive question, "Would the women know a clue if they did come upon it?" (289).

Ironically, while the men are looking actively for the smoking 3 gun, the women are confronted with subtler clues in spite of themselves and even try to hide from each other what they intuitively know. But they do not fool each other for long, as Glaspell describes: "Their eyes met—something flashed to life, passed between them; then, as if with an effort, they seemed to pull away from each other" (295). However, they cannot pull away, for they are bound by a power they do not even comprehend: "We all go through the same things—it's all just a different kind of the same thing! . . . why do you and I understand? Why do we know—what we know this minute?" (303). They do not realize that it is the intuition they share that causes them to "[see] into things, [to see] through a thing to something else" (294). Though sympathetic to Minnie Wright, the women cannot deny the damning clues that lead them to the inescapable conclusion of her guilt.

If it is ironic that the women find the clues, it is even more 4 ironic that they find them in the mundane household items to which the men attribute so little significance. "Nothing here but kitchen things," the men mistakenly think (287). Because of their weak intuition, they do not see the household as indicative of John's and Minnie's characters. They do not see beyond the cheerless home to John Wright's grim nature, nor do the dilapidated furnishings provide them with a clue to his penurious habits. Minnie's depression and agitation are not apparent to them in the dismal, half-cleaned kitchen; instead, they consider Minnie an inept, lazy housekeeper. Oddly, for all their "snoopin' round and criticizin'" (290), the three gentlemen literally do not have a clue.

The women, on the other hand, "used to worrying over tri- 5 fles" (287), do attach importance to the "everyday things" (299), and looking around the cheerless kitchen, they see many examples of the miserably hard existence of Minnie Wright. Knowing the pride a woman takes in her home, they see Minnie's kitchen not as dirty but as half-cleaned, and the significance of this is not lost on them. And upon discovering the erratic quilt stitching, they are alarmed. Also, they cannot dismiss the broken birdcage as just a broken birdcage. They instinctively know, as the men do not, that Minnie desperately needed a lively creature to brighten up such a loveless home. Upon finding these clues, ironically hidden in everyday objects, the women piece them together with a thread of intuition and create a blanket of guilt that covers the hapless Minnie Wright.

Though there is irony in the fact that the women, not the men, find the clues, and irony in the fact that they are found in everyday household things, most ironic is the fact that John Wright meets the same fate he has inflicted on the poor bird, illustrating that he is perhaps the least intuitive of all the men in the story. John Wright never sees beyond his own needs to the needs of his wife. He does not understand her need for a pretty creature to fill the void created by her lonely, childless existence. Not content to kill just Minnie's personality ("[s]he was [once] kind of like a bird herself. Real sweet and pretty" [299]), he kills her canary, leaving her with the deafening silence of the lonesome prairie. Minnie has endured many years of misery at the hands of John Wright, but he pushes her too far when he kills the bird. Then, ironically, he gets the "peace and quiet" (283) he values over her happiness.

John Wright lacks the intuition to understand his wife's love of her bird, but the two women do not. They understand that she needed the bird to fill the still air with song and lessen her loneliness. After discovering the dead bird, they do not blame her for killing John. The dead bird reminds Mrs. Peters of a traumatic episode from her childhood:

> "When I was a girl," said Mrs. Peters, under her breath, "my kitten — there was a boy took a hatchet, and before my eyes — before I could get there . . . If they hadn't held me back, I would have . . . hurt him." (301–02)

The women see the reason for Minnie's murderous impulse, but they know that the men lack the insight to ever fully understand her situation or her motivation; therefore, in hiding the bird, by their silence, they acquit Minnie Wright.

Through the ironic situations in "A Jury of Her Peers," Glaspell   8
clearly illustrates a world in which men and women vary greatly in
their perception of things. She shows men as often superficial in
the way they perceive the world, lacking the depth of intuition that
women use as a means of self-preservation to see themselves and the
world more clearly. Without the heightened perspective on life that
this knowledge of human nature gives them, women might not stand
a chance. Against the power and domination of men, they often find
themselves as defenseless and vulnerable as Minnie's poor bird.

WORK CITED

Glaspell, Susan. "A Jury of Her Peers." *Lifted Masks and Other Works,* edited
by Eric S. Rabkin, U of Michigan P, 1993.

The Short, Happy Life of Louise Mallard

Justine Appel

Arizona State University
Tempe, Arizona

Justine Appel arranges her analysis chronologically, guiding her readers through Chopin's story as it unfolds. Her thesis—that repression must be resisted and freedom embraced—is presented in her opening paragraph, giving readers a foundation for understanding her argument as it unfolds. The final paragraph affirms this interpretation and expands on it, speculating on the implications of "The Story of an Hour" in the lives of Chopin's readers. As you read, pay attention to the care Appel takes to highlight the nuance of Chopin's presentation of repression and the balance Appel highlights between the physical and emotional aspects of Louise Mallard's revelations. In this essay, Appel moves beyond a simple surface interpretation to present a complex, nuanced reading of "The Story of an Hour."

"There was something coming to her and she was waiting for it, [1] fearfully. What was it? She did not know; it was too subtle and elusive to name" (par. 9). So writes Kate Chopin about Louise Mallard, the main character in her short story "The Story of an Hour." Set toward the end of the nineteenth century, the story follows Mrs. Mallard's reaction to the news of her husband's death, which develops from grief to a state of suspended emotion to a sense of utter freedom. Chopin's tale delivers a powerful message about the repression that women like Mrs. Mallard suffered under the cultural institution of marriage built on male dominance. What makes this message so powerful is the fact that Louise Mallard's sense of freedom isn't immediate or simple, but once it develops, there's no going back.

When her sister breaks the news that her husband is dead,   2
Mrs. Mallard bursts into a "storm of grief" (3), weeping in her
sister's arms, and then retreats to her room. Ironically, it is here in
her room, in an armchair facing an open window, that Mrs. Mallard
develops her sense of freedom. It starts in the contrast between the
way she sits down, "pressed down by a physical exhaustion that
haunted her body and seemed to reach into her soul" (4), and the
freshness she sees through the window, in which "the tops of trees
. . . were all aquiver with the new spring life" (5). Chopin takes care
that the first signals of Mrs. Mallard's repression come through her
senses, so that readers can learn with Mrs. Mallard just how deeply
she has internalized the effects of marital subjugation.

Like Mrs. Mallard, readers only become aware of the character's   3
newfound sense of freedom gradually. They share her experience as
she stares out the window with eyes that reflect "a suspension of
intelligent thought" (8). This "subtle and elusive" feeling doesn't
come in words or accusations. It comes through her senses, "the
sounds, the scents, the color" (9), showing that her confinement is
so penetrating that it has mapped itself onto her sensory experience
of the world around her.

The fact that readers can't name the feeling Louise Mallard has   4
until she can name it herself effectively conveys how deep her sense of
captivity has been. At last, Mrs. Mallard names how she feels—"free,
free, free!"—and she (and her readers) begin to see more than just
an open window (11). She can envision the freedom that window
represents, the "years to come that would belong to her absolutely"
(13). And Chopin emphasizes Mrs. Mallard's bodily feeling of freedom just as much as her mental understanding: "Now her bosom
rose and fell tumultuously . . . [h]er pulses beat fast, and the coursing
blood warmed and relaxed every inch of her body" (10–11). The fact
that it takes a while to name her freedom, and to recognize the sen-
sations in her body as relief and joy, shows that the kind of repression
Mrs. Mallard felt in her marriage worked on a deep psychological
level.

But this is not the only reason that this kind of confinement is so   5
difficult to identify. By showing readers how Mrs. Mallard grapples
with her husband's death, Chopin shows them not only how much
harm has been caused by lack of self-determination but also that
the harm can coexist with affection, kindness, and even love. The
story makes clear that Mr. Mallard was no monster: His "face . . .

had never looked save with love upon her" (13). Here, Chopin challenges the notion that physical and verbal harm are the only actions that can cause suffering or that oppression has to be inflicted on purpose. Mr. Mallard loved his wife, and she had at times even loved him, but here she is whispering, "Free! Body and soul free!" (16), and readers know that her happiness is not a matter of love (or the lack of it). Her happiness at the end of the story is about life's possibilities and how rich they can feel to a person who can now make decisions for herself: "What could love . . . count for in face of this possession of self-assertion which she suddenly recognized as the strongest impulse of her being!" (15). By leading readers away from the picture of her husband as a cruel tyrant, Chopin helps them understand that relationships not only need to be free of violence but also need to be built on mutual independence.

When Mrs. Mallard is given even an hour-long understanding of what living for herself feels like, she can't survive a return to dependency: Brently Mallard, whose death was misreported, walks in the front door, and his wife collapses, dead. After watching Mrs. Mallard come to understand just what her husband's absence means, readers can now understand what her husband's presence means. The power of this story is in the way it uncovers the complicated relationship between repression and love and the way this understanding is embedded in the subconscious and in the body. Chopin's brilliant story sheds light on the underbelly of marital bliss, but more importantly, it implores her readers to recognize and reject repression—in whatever form it takes on—before it is too late.

WORK CITED

Chopin, Kate. "The Story of an Hour." *The St. Martin's Guide to Writing,* 12th ed., by Rise B. Axelrod and Charles R. Cooper, Bedford/St. Martin's, 2019, pp. 409–10.

A Note on the Copyediting

We all know that the work of professional writers rarely appears in print without first being edited. But what about student writing—especially essays that are presented as models of student writing? Do these get edited too?

While it's easy to draw an analogy with professional writing and simply declare that "all published writing gets edited," there are some important differences between student and professional writing. For one thing, student writing is presented as student writing. That is, it's offered to the reader as an example of the kind of writing students can and do produce in a writing class. And since most students don't have the benefit of a professional editor, their work may not be as polished as the models they see in textbooks.

For another, unlike professional writers, students rarely have the opportunity to participate in the editorial process. Companion readers like this one are compiled while the main text is being revised, at a time when the authors and editors are immersed in the work of the text and don't have time to also supervise twenty-five or more student writers. For this reason, students are usually simply asked to sign a statement transferring to the publisher all rights to their essays, subject to final editing, and don't see their work again until it appears in print. For these reasons, editing student writing is problematic.

But publishing student essays without editing is equally problematic. Every composition teacher knows that even the best papers, the A+ essays, aren't perfect. But readers of published prose, accustomed to the conventions of edited American English, aren't always so generous. The shift in tense that may be seen as a simple lapse in a student narrative becomes a major distraction in a published piece. Rather than preserve that tense shift in the interest of absolute fidelity to the student's work, it is more in keeping with the spirit and purpose of the enterprise to edit the passage. After all, the rest of the evidence indicates that the student is a strong writer and that he or she would likely accede to the change if it were called to his or her attention.

The editing of a student essay is not a violation of the student's work, then, but a courtesy to the writer. True, some essays require more editing than others—perhaps because some students did not have much opportunity to revise—but none in this collection has been altered significantly. In fact, every attempt has been made to respect the students' choices.

To give you an inside look at the editing process, we reproduce here the originally submitted version of Sheila McClain's essay from Chapter 4, "Proxemics: A Study of Space and Relationships," along with the Bedford/St. Martin's editor's changes. You might use this sample as an opportunity to consider the usefulness and necessity of editing. What changes were made, and why? Which of them improved the essay? Were all of them necessary? If you are a writer whose work has undergone editorial revision—perhaps as part of peer review—you might think about how the process felt to you. Did you appreciate your editor's work? Resent it? What did you learn from it? If you're like most of us, you probably realized that it's natural to resist but necessary to accept criticism. In other words, you learned to think like a writer.

Sample Copyediting

Proxemics: A Study of Space and Relationships

by

Sheila McClain

Everyday we interact and communicate, sometimes [#] [^]

without even saying a word. Body language, more

~~correctly~~ **formally** known as "nonverbal communication," speaks

volumes about who we are and how we relate to others.

As ~~noted by~~ **Lester** Sielski, an associate professor at the

University of West Florida **^writes^** "Words are beautiful,

exciting, important, but we have over⌣estimated them

badly $\frac{1}{m}$ since they are not all or even half the

message." He also asserts that "beyond words lies the

bedrock on which human relationships are built $\frac{1}{m}$

nonverbal communication" (Sielski 238). ~~As related by~~

~~author Roger E. Axtell~~ **A group of** psychology students at the

University of Texas recently ~~discovered~~ **demonstrated** just how

217

profound ~~and~~ an effect nonverbal communication can have on people. ~~They~~ The students conducted an experiment to test the unspoken rules of behavior on elevators. Boarding a crowded elevator, the students stood facing and grinning at ~~and facing~~ the other people on board. Understandably, the people became ~~upset and~~ uncomfortable; ~~and~~ one person ~~was~~ even ~~heard~~ suggesting ~~suggested~~ that someone ~~should~~ call 911 (5-6) Axtell. Why all the fuss? ~~Normal~~ Unspoken elevator etiquette dictates that one should turn and face the door in a crowded elevator, being careful not to touch anyone else and honoring the sacred personal space of each individual by staring at the floor indicator instead of looking at anyone else. Although they are not written down, strict rules govern our behavior in public situations. This is especially true when space is limited as on elevators, buses, or ~~the~~ subway trains (Axtell ~~the~~ 5-6).

Patricia Buhler, an expert in business management and associate professor at Goldey-Beacon College, confirms the large role nonverbal communication plays. She asserts that as little as 8 percent of the message we communicate is made up of words. We communicate the rest of our message, a disproportionately large 92 percent, with ~~utilizing~~ body language and other nonverbal forms of communication. ~~According to a professor of~~

~~social work,~~ while researchers have long known that nonverbal cues play a large role in communication, for many years they made no efforts to learn more about **them (Sielski).** ~~this component of language.~~ Amid rising public interest, several scientists pioneered new research in the field of nonverbal communication in the 1950s. Among these experts was anthropologist Edward T. Hall. He **focused** ~~pioneered research~~ on a specific type of nonverbal communication called *proxemics*. Proxemics ~~defined as~~ **is** the study of how people use ~~personal~~ space to communicate nonverbally, plays a major role in our everyday interactions with others, whether we are conscious of it or not, **our use of space.**

A review of some of Hall's main terms will help us ~~Proxemics carries great importance because it~~ appreciate how ~~affects our relationships with others. To~~ better understand ~~the impact~~ proxemics ~~can have on~~ relationships, **For example,** ~~we need to know the meanings of two key~~ **according to** ~~terms used by~~ Hall, **in our everyday interactions, we choose** ~~A professor from University of~~ **to position ourselves to create either** "sociopetal" or "sociofugal" space. ~~St. Thomas summarizes Dr. Hall's terms. The first term~~ "sociopetal space" invites communication; ~~The second term~~ "sociofugal space" is the opposite ~~of the first.~~ It separates people and discourages interaction (Jordan). ~~For example,~~ a student in a school lunchroom may ~~choose to~~ sit alone at an empty table in a corner, away from the other students, **creating** "sociofugal space"),

or ~~he may choose to sit~~ directly across from a person
he would like to befriend (creating "sociopetal space"). ~~As the~~
~~examples show, our use of space could greatly impact~~
~~our social relationships.~~

Hall identifies
~~Falling under both "sociopetal" and "sociofugal~~
~~space,"~~ three ~~main types of space~~ kinds of general spaces with in which we ~~interact~~ can create
either sociofugal or sociopetal space. These ~~are defined by Dr. Hall. These include~~ "fixed-feature
space," "semi-fixed feature space," and "informal
space" (Jordan). Fixed-feature spaces are hard, if
not impossible, for us to control or change. ~~"Fixed~~
For example, because
~~feature" refers to the permanent aspects of the space~~
~~in which we interact. A "fixed feature" problem exists~~
~~in~~ my college English class ~~where the room~~ is too
small for the number of students attending, ~~Consequently~~
positioning ourselves so that   all
we have a hard time ~~finding a place where~~ we can see the
overhead projections. We cannot make the walls of the
classroom bigger or the ceiling higher, and the
overhead screen is likewise "fixed" in place. We must
work within the constraints of these space. A semi-
usually
fixed feature space is ~~somewhat adjustable allowing~~
such as furniture   The
~~for space to be~~ defined by ~~more~~ mobile objects, couches
for example
and chairs in a living room may ~~be oriented to~~ face
only the television, thus discouraging conversation
But we are able to reposition
and relationship building. ~~Reorientation of the couch~~
the furniture   to
~~and chairs, so that they face each other, may~~ create a

more social ~~and conversational~~ environment. Informal space is by far the easiest to manipulate. We each ~~have~~ control ~~of~~ our personal "bubble," and we can set distances between ourselves and others ~~which best suit~~ **that reflect** our relationships with them. **Take, for example, the way that** ~~To illustrate this~~, people ~~may~~ approach their bosses ~~in various ways~~ ~~depending upon how they feel about their boss. If~~ ~~people are~~ **A man who is** afraid of or dislike**s** ~~their~~ **his** boss ~~, they~~ may communicate with ~~them~~ **her** from as far away as possible. ~~They~~ **He** might stand in ~~their~~ **her** doorway ~~and not enter the~~ ~~boss' office~~ to relay a message. Conversely, ~~people~~ **a woman** who ~~have~~ **has** known ~~their~~ **her** boss for many years and ~~are~~ **is** good friends with ~~their bosses~~ **him** might come right in **to his office** and casually sit down in close proximity to ~~their bosses~~ **him**. ~~Thus they show by their use of space that they feel comfortable and have a good relationship with their bosses.~~ Individually, we have a great deal of control over our informal space, and how we use this space can speak volumes about our relationships with others.

~~As one source explains,~~ after observing many interactions, Hall ~~further~~ broke down ~~this~~ informal space ~~by~~ **further,** identifying four ~~separate~~ distances commonly used by people in their interactions with others: "intimate distance," zero to one and a half feet;

"personal distance," one and a half to four feet; "social distance," four to twelve feet; and "public distance," twelve feet and beyond ~~all distinguish zones we use for different interactions~~ (Beebe, Beebe, and Redmond 231). "Intimate distance," as the name suggests, is generally reserved for those people closest to us. Lovemaking, hugging, and holding small children all occur in this zone. The exception to this rule comes when we extend our hand to perfect strangers in greeting, allowing them to briefly enter our intimate space with a handshake. "Personal distance," while not as close as intimate, is still reserved for people we know well and with whom we feel comfortable. This zone ~~is~~ usually occupies an area relatively close to us. It can at times be applied, however, to include objects we see as extensions of ourselves. For instance, [while driving] we may feel ~~that someone is invading~~ our personal space [being invaded] ~~when we are driving a car if the~~ [by a] car (behind us) follow[ing] too closely. We see ~~the~~ [our own] car as an extension of ourselves and extend our "personal bubble" to include it. "Social distance" is often considered a respectful distance and is used in many professional business settings as well as in group interactions. ~~To, illustrate~~ [There is a] "public distance," ~~we might think of the distance used when~~ [between a] lectur[er]ing a and a class, or someone ~~large group or~~ speaking publicly from a podium and his ~~This~~ or her audience. ~~distance can also include speakers who are not physically present, such as watching the President address the nation on television.~~

In positioning ourselves in relation ~~As we have seen, proxemics, or how we use the~~ to others, especially in choosing nearness or distance, we ~~space around us, has some impact on the multitude of~~ communicate respect or intimacy, fear or familiarity. ~~interactions we have with others everyday.~~ We can improve a friendly ~~or damage our social~~ relationships simply by using a "warm, personable" distance, ~~with friends,~~ or ~~we may~~ drive potential friends away by seeming "cold and distant," or getting quite literally "too close for comfort." We can put people at ease or make them uncomfortable just by our proximity to them. The study of nonverbal communication, and specifically proxemics, demonstrates the truth of the old adage, "actions speak louder than words."

Submission Form

We hope that this collection is one of many, and that we'll be able to include more essays from more colleges and universities in the next edition. Please let us see the best essays you've written using *The St. Martin's Guide to Writing*; *The Concise Guide to Writing*; *Reading Critically, Writing Well*; or *Sticks and Stones*. Send them with this submission form to English Editor — Student Essays, Bedford/St. Martin's, One New York Plaza, Suite 4500, New York, NY 10004-1562.

Student's Name _____

Instructor's Name _____

Permanent Address: _____

Phone Number(s): _____

E-mail Address(es): _____

School _____

Department _____

Course Text (circle one)

The St. Martin's Guide to Writing   *The Concise Guide to Writing*

Reading Critically, Writing Well   *Sticks and Stones*

Writing Assignment (circle one)

Remembering an Event   Proposing a Solution

Writing Profiles   Justifying an Evaluation

Explaining a Concept   Arguing for Causes or Effects

Analyzing and Synthesizing Opposing Arguments   Analyzing Stories

Arguing a Position

Other: _____